POISON PEN

POISON PEN

The Unauthorized Biography of Kitty Kelley

George Carpozi Jr.

Barricade Books Inc.
New Jersey

Library of Congress Cataloging-in-Publication Data

Carpozi, George.
    Poison pen : the unauthorized biography of Kitty Kelley / George
    Carpozi, Jr.
       p.   cm.
    Includes index.
    ISBN 0-942637-36-4 : $22.00
    1. Kelley, Kitty. 2. Journalists—United States—Biography.
  I. Title.
  PN4874.K42C3 1991
  070′.92—dc20   91–19326
    [B]   CIP

Barricade Books Inc.
1530 Palisade Avenue
Fort Lee, N.J. 07024

Printed in the United States of America

AUTHOR'S NOTE

On or about May 30, 1985, I received a call at the *Star* magazine in Tarrytown, New York, a village on the Hudson River some ten miles north of the New York City line.

"This is Kitty Kelley," said a coquettish female voice I'd never heard before. "I'm doing a biography on Frank Sinatra. I understand you wrote such a book in 1978 and I wonder if I could borrow a copy. I promise I'll return it . . ."

Perfectly okay, I responded and asked how she was progressing. No complaints, she said. She had gathered most of the material for the book and was at home "working feverishly on my typewriter."

She asked if I got flak for my book *Frank Sinatra: Is This Man Mafia?* after it was published. My answer was no. In fact, I told her, when I was interviewed by talk-show host Bob Grant on New York's WOR Radio, a caller identifying himself as the president of a Frank Sinatra fan club, said he and other Sinatraphiles had read the book and found it to be—despite its provocative title—fair, accurate, and a loving portrait.

As we spoke, Kitty asked what new book I was working on. I told her that John Hinckley, who shot President Reagan and was confined as a mental incompetent at St. Elizabeth Hospital in Washington, D.C., was collaborating with me on his autobiography. I mentioned that he was sending me voluminous notes written on legal-size yellow-lined paper which I was finding revelatory. "It's as though he wants me to enter his brain and see what makes him tick," I said to Kitty.

She asked if I had a publisher. I replied that I hadn't sought any yet, but when I was ready to offer my manuscript to one, I'd locate Andrew Ettinger, who published several of my books when he was Editor-in-Chief at Pinnacle Books. I went on to tell Kitty that I lost touch with Andy after he moved to Los Angeles and became an editor at Harlequin Books, publisher of romance novels.

"But Andy is no longer at Harlequin . . ." Kitty put in. She identified the new publishing house he was with and gave me its phone number. I thanked Kitty for the information and said I would get in touch with Andy whom I considered one of the best editors I'd worked with.

I mention the Andy Ettinger incident because his name comes up in the letter I'm quoting here in its entirety. I don't want the reader to be confused, as so often happens in Kitty Kelley's unauthorized biographies, where names pop out of left field without rhyme or reason.

Kitty's letter was mailed to my home in Melville, Long Island, and was dated July 2, 1985. It read:

Dear George,
Thanks so very much for loaning me this copy of your book, *Frank Sinatra: Is This Man Mafia?* As promised, I'm returning it to you.

Your John Hinckley material is fascinating [I had, at her request, sent her several photostats of the would-be assassin's writings, along with the copy of my Sinatra book] and please let me know what happens to the book proposal. Presenting the workings of this poor man's twisted mind will be a public service, plus provide fascinating reading. Surely, it's the first time a presidential assassin has offered to speak so freely.

Do give my best to Andy Ettinger the next time you talk with him. I'm glad I put you two together—again. Again, my thanks for the book and my best to you always.

Sincerely,
Kitty Kelley

****

Fourteen months later, Lyle Stuart, who published Kitty Kelley's first unauthorized biography, the runaway best-seller *Jackie Oh!*, phoned me at the *Star*—just after Kitty's *His Way: The Unauthorized Biography of Frank Sinatra* had been published.

"Have you read it?" Lyle asked.

"Yep."

"What do you think of it?"

"A bunch of garbage. She rips the guy from pillar to post, disembowels Mia Farrow, desecrates Elizabeth Taylor with an even greater vengeance than she does in her Taylor biography."

"Think any of it is true . . . ?"

"How the hell can I know, Lyle? I never saw any of that before. I'm sure there must be a bit of truth among all that rubbish—but who's gonna bother to weed it out? All I can tell you is that Kitty used lots and lots of other people's copy. She manipulated, changed the way quotes were published originally, and she burrowed into the clips like she's never done before." I laughed. "I'll bet the advance on my next book that she gets arthritis from the workout she gave her fingers and arms from all the cutting and pasting she did to put this one together."

"Did you recognize anything from your book in hers?"

"You can bet I did . . . After all, she had my book for a whole month."

"Well, she didn't need it all that time. She could have Xeroxed it in a day . . . By the way, I don't see any credit for your Sinatra story in her book. Any idea why?"

7

"Yeah. The way I figure her, she's a no good ingrate . . ."

A month or so after this conversation, Lyle Stuart sent out his newsletter *Hot News*, the publishing industry's most informative bulletin. Repeated in clear, unmistakable language was what I'd said to him . . .

****

Next, on or about January 3, 1987, I received a typewritten letter from a person professing to be Linda Chasen with an address in Washington D.C. The writer purports to have been a researcher on the Sinatra book, yet I found no mention of her in the credits Kitty gives in *His Way*.

She hoisted me to the mast and let me hang by my toenails from the tallest spar:

"You betrayed Kitty Kelley by telling such terrible lies to Lyle Stuart . . .

"As her researcher, I know Kitty Kelley is eminently fair and accurate with everything she writes about. You were very wrong to criticize what she said about Sinatra's mother and all the other things you claimed Miss Kelley had misrepresented in her book.

"You were extremely cruel to criticize her as you did to Lyle Stuart. After all, she put you in touch with Andy Ettinger . . ."

Believing this letter came from a legitimate complainant, I wrote a note of response to Linda Chasen. I quote in part:

"I have no idea when you were born but I suspect from the adolescent tone of your letter, that you could be quite young. Therefore, I take this opportunity to inform you that Andy Ettinger and I have known each other for many years.

"I've written five of my 70 books for Andy. I've been in touch with him since he left Pinnacle Books. I find it inconceivable that Kitty Kelly should want to take credit for that relationship."

****

Five days after I sent this message to the writer who claimed

8

to be Linda Chasen, the mailman returned my letter with a red-stamped cancellation:

"Addressee Unknown."

Quite surprisingly—and with considerable disappointment—I learned a partial truth about Linda Chasen. That came after I dialed (202) 555-1212, the information operator in the nation's capital. Could she give me the telephone number of Linda Chasen at 4306 Embassy Park Drive N.W . . . ?

"Sorry, sir, but we don't have a Linda Chasen listed for either that address or any other."

At this juncture, I committed all the correspondence to a folder in my Frank Sinatra files.

Not until June 2, 1988, did it occur to me the letter may have been sent by Kitty Kelley herself. I was made aware of that possibility by Gerri Hirshey, a reporter who'd been on assignment since that February investigating Kitty Kelley's background for a series that appeared in the *Washington Post* the following October. I quote from the reporter's *Washington Post* piece that tells it like it is:

"Shortly after I'd begun my research—and shortly after I'd informed Kelley by mail that I was proceeding with the story, interviews or not—anonymous mail began to arrive. The mail wasn't threatening, just strange. And eerily predictable.

"'Oh, you can expect about 90 days' mayhem by mail,' said an attorney who has worked with Kelley. Four journalists who have written about Kelley had also talked about receiving mysterious mail: untraceable names signed to letters with no return addresses, containing both true and false information about Kitty Kelley, the journalists or their employers. Most often the letters were impassioned defenses of Kelley and her work, and intensely specific. Some were unsigned, with no return addresses. Sometimes the letters were on corporate stationery, from *Time*, *Fortune*, or the *Washington Post*. Some were mildly obscene and vaguely threatening. During and after reporting on Kelley, some journalists have gotten strange phone calls and lots of hang-ups.

"The postal barrages are a joke to some recipients, rankling to others . . ."

Miss Hirshey had the goods on Kitty Kelley because her typewritten correspondence was turned over to Dr. David A. Crown, a forensics expert who had been chief of the CIA Questioned Documents Laboratory for 15 years. His analysis led him to the conclusion that an "arthritic" Underwood and a Smith-Corona typewriter had been used to compose those missives. Although her attorney denied Kelley owned such machines, comparisons with letters that Kitty wrote to the Junior League and to others proved beyond any doubt Kitty was the mystery scrivener. Tell-tale broken serifs and other identifying typeface scars inflicted by long years of usage on those antiquated machines conclusively pointed the finger.

****

Gerri Hirshey got in touch with me because she read the item in Liz Smith's *New York Daily News* column of May 25th that addressed the *Washington Post's* forthcoming series, then also mentioned that "Kitty is reported to be the subject of a book . . . by George Carpozi."

That was fact—and here's how I got involved with the project:

In late February, 1988, at 3 a.m. one morning, I was in bed, watching a re-run of the *Larry King Show* on the Cable News Network. It was an hour before I would shower, dress and depart on my 50-mile drive to the *Star's* offices to begin my 6 a.m. stint as News Department Editor.

King had over the years suffered a spate of embarrassments brought on by Kitty Kelley. He had every reason not to have the hardnosed author on his show. Yet because "her books are *news,*" he continued to bring her on as a guest.

Kelley's appearance that night was occasioned by her just-published "expose" about Judith Campbell Exner's purported role as a go-between for President John F. Kennedy and Chicago mob boss Sam "Momo" Giancana.

I had heard Kitty Kelley asked what her response would be if someone were to write an unauthorized biography about her.

She replied, "Oh, it wouldn't matter to me." Then she added, "What could anyone say about me?"

True to my expectations on this night, one of the callers asked:

"Miss Kelley, what would you do if someone were to look into your closets and write about you? Do you have any skeletons in them that you wouldn't want to let out . . . ?"

Kitty's reaction was very subtle—but it was a reaction nevertheless. I read her body language and it told me the question had gotten under her skin, for I detected these signals:

* A facial twitch, an almost imperceptible one—but a twitch just the same.

* Her big brown eyes that always have a wide-open stare expanded ever so slightly as the eyebrows lifted—ever so slightly, yet ever so slightly just the same.

* Then for an instant, I noticed a tic-like movement of her lips—just for an instant, but a tic-like movement just the same.

*Although I didn't detect any discoloration of Kitty's face—going to PALE, as in terrified, or RED, as in mortified, I did detect a new idea in my own brain: a book about the irreverent biographer of celebrity figures.

Her facial gyrations made me sit upright in bed in breathless anticipation of her answer:

"Oh, I don't think anyone will find anything in my closet to scandalize me . . . I have nothing to hide, no skeletons at all . . ."

1

The sun has long ago set on Ronald Reagan's administration. The President and First Lady are back in California, in retirement after closing out the longest White House residency in more than a quarter-century.

The prospect of spending timeless, carefree days lingering on the coastal cliffs high above the beautiful blue Pacific seemed a blessing for this crusty septuagenarian. There are those who believe he earned a serving of peace and tranquility after more than a half-century in the public eye as a radio sports announcer, movie star and TV host, Governor of California, and President of the United States.

For Nancy Davis Reagan, whose career as a movie actress, wife, mother, and First Lady paralleled that of her husband's career for much of that time, it was a retirement that didn't promise to be as placid.

For what she once expected to be a bright and pleasant future has been darkened by a feisty, determined middle-aged Washington D.C. author who set out in her astute, acrid, and relentless style to unearth all the not-so-nice things the public has never known about Nancy Reagan and turn them into yet another one of her notorious poison-pen biographies.

The book Kitty Kelley has written about the one-time actress and former First Lady most certainly won't be added to the

Reagan Presidential Library. This diminutive 49-year-old Spokane-born lawyer's daughter who looks like a steel magnolia from Savannah, doesn't write books about people like Mother Teresa. Yet if the bucks are plentiful enough, she will—as she has made plain more than once—bang out a racy bio "even on Donald Duck."

Kelley, who savaged Jacqueline Kennedy Onassis, Elizabeth Taylor, and Frank Sinatra in her earlier unauthorized biographies, scorches Mrs. Reagan in much the same fact-mixed-with-fiction style. She zeros in on the former Nancy Davis like the "meat-seeking missile of celebrity literature" she is.

That characterization of Kelley was coined by English writer Dermot Purgavie, who also reflected on what the controversy-seeking author aims to accomplish when she hones in on a target:

"Her mission is the demystification of carefully-crafted public lives, and no sin or secret is safe from her tenacious questioning. She will dig out a deceit or an infidelity however deeply buried in the damp humus of the past, and over the last ten years, as if she were avenging all the excesses of the gilded class, she has established herself as the curse of the flawed folk hero."

With a voice reminiscent of Jackie O's breathless whisper and a miniature Dolly Parton bust overhanging a somewhat stumpy hourglass figure, the tiny blonde-haired, hazel-eyed self-proclaimed "Queen of Sleaze" is a woman possessed when she immerses herself in a biographical project.

What makes Kitty tick?

While researching background on the widowed former First Lady for her first unauthorized bio, *Jackie Oh!*, Kitty not only talked in hushed tones but went on shopping sprees—although much more modest than the extravagant outings Jackie is known to take.

When she began literally digging in garbage cans for dirt for her next book, *Elizabeth Taylor: The Last Star*, Kitty started eating more than usual—at the same time that Taylor herself was gaining pounds.

When she was interviewed in her then newly-purchased

palatial home in the prestigious Georgetown suburb of the nation's capital after *His Way: The Unauthorized Biography of Frank Sinatra* was published, Kitty Kelley was asked by *Washington Post* reporter Stephanie Mansfield what bewitchment possessed her while digging for skeletons in Ol' Blue Eyes' closets and garbage.

"That's easy," laughed the 5-foot, 3-inch elfin-faced wicked word scrivener. "I started kicking ass . . ."

****

Kitty Kelley started her career of kicking ass a short time after the last of several meetings with Lyle Stuart, who was characterized by the *New York Times* as the Peck's Bad Boy of Publishing. In his forty years as a book publisher, Stuart specialized in publishing the controversy-packed books that other publishers wouldn't dare touch, from *The Washington Pay-Off*, which listed lobbyists and the congressmen they bribed, to ex-CIA agent Philip Agee's *Dirty Work*, which identified 3,000 CIA agents in Western Europe.

It was in late 1975 that Stuart discovered Kitty Kelley. The publisher was working with Dr. Robert Linn on a book to be titled *The Last Chance Diet*. It offered a regimen featuring a protein-sparing fast. The book went on to sell more than three-million copies in all editions, and Stuart had another winner on his hands.

But to backtrack.

Linn showed Stuart a folder of newspaper and magazine articles about his program of liquid fasting which had run in various publications, and would be the basis of his book. One piece caught the publisher's attention. It contained far better writing than the others. It was from a Washington, D.C. publication. He looked at the byline Kitty Kelley and filed it away in his mind.

While the book was in progress, Linn phoned Stuart. "Would you do me a favor?" the doctor asked. "Remember that girl Kitty Kelley whose article you particularly liked? Well, she wants to write another one. Since you told me not to cooperate on any more stories until the book was published, I don't know what to do."

The book was far from finished. Linn was telling his story to his collaborator Sandra Lee Stuart, a reporter with the *Trenton Times*, who also happened to be Stuart's daughter.

Stuart's response to Linn was, "Just say no."

"I can't. Would you do it for me?" the doctor pleaded.

Stuart agreed. He phoned Kitty in Washington, identified himself, and said, "Miss Kelley, I wonder if you'd do me a favor? Doctor Linn says you want to write another article on his protein-sparing fast. We'd prefer not to have any stories right now. Could you hold off?"

"Why?" Kitty asked.

"Because he's writing a book for us."

A moment of silence on the other end. Then in a voice bristling with anger, she asked, "What . . . kind of . . . a . . . book?"

"On the diet, of course. He's writing the book with my daughter . . ."

"That son of a bitch!" Kelley exploded "He promised that if he ever did a book, he'd do it with *me!*"

"This is the first I heard of that," countered Stuart. "He never mentioned you." The publisher went on to explain to the disappointed writer the circumstances that led to Sandra Lee's participation in the project with the doctor. After she heard the chronology, Kitty came back with "You know I make a living writing articles. Why should I give up the potential income on this one?"

"Listen," Stuart said. "I was impressed by that piece you wrote about Doctor Linn. Do this for me [not write a second article on the diet] and one of these days we'll do a book together. We'll both make a lot of money with it . . ."

Kitty later reported that when she hung up the phone she turned to her then-boyfriend, Mike Edgley, whom she would later marry, and said, "Listen to this bullshit . . ." She then related what the publisher had told her.

"You listen," Edgley responded, "I know this guy's reputation. His word is good. Do it! Go with him."

****

Stuart didn't know or care about Kitty's background at the time. She had come off a series of unrewarding jobs after graduating from college, including a brief but unhappy fling as a teacher in Seattle after she received her degree from the University of Washington. Then she proceeded to follow the reverse of the route recommended by Horace Greeley; she went east, taking a job for the final year of the 1964-65 New York World's Fair. When the Fair was over, she bundled herself off to Washington, D.C. and toiled in the press section of Senator Eugene McCarthy's Capitol Hill offices. More recently she'd been terminated from a researcher-secretarial job at the *Washington Post*.

Her only salvation from the throes of a minimum-wage lifestyle was free-lance writing. So the prospective loss of an opportunity to write and sell a follow-up on her successful first article , on Linn's protein-sparing diet distressed Kitty.

Nevertheless, she phoned Stuart and told him she wouldn't write the article. This paved the way for an every-few-months social encounter between Kelley and Edgely and Stuart and his future wife Carole Livingston, who was then a senior executive at the publishing house. The get-togethers took place in New York during 1976. On occasion, Lyle and Carole took Kitty and Mike to lunch. Other times they all met just for drinks. Each time she planned to come up to New York from Washington, Kitty phoned ahead to ask whether Stuart could see her.

Meanwhile, Robert Linn and Sandra Lee Stuart completed *The Last Chance Diet*. Success was assured when the authors hit the jackpot after Bantam Books' Editor-in-Chief Marc Jaffe, against the judgment of his colleagues, bought the mass-market paperback rights for a $350,000 advance. The cloth edition went on to become an immediate national bestseller. Disconsolate, Kitty Kelley kept abreast of the book's developments.

Edgley, who by this time had married Kitty, tried to placate her with reassuring words: "You heard what Lyle told you . . . Have patience."

***

The day finally came in late 1976 when Stuart phoned Kitty in Washington. "I've got the book subject for you!" he told her. "I want you to write a biography of Jackie Onassis . . ."

"But I don't even know her," Kitty exclaimed.

"Good! That's why I want you to write the book."

"But people won't talk to me . . ."

"Listen carefully. They will talk to you because you'll use a novel approach. You'll say something like, 'you're a friend of Jackie Onassis. So much garbage has been written about her that it's time for an honest and accurate portrait'."

"Do you think that would work?"

"Sure! Because her friends will want to counter all the applesauce that's been printed about her."

Kitty agreed to do it. And just as she plunged into what she expected was to be a monumental research project, she got lucky . . .

****

At the tabloid *New York Daily News*, nationally syndicated gossip columnist Liz Smith was the curator of a huge pile of Jacqueline Kennedy Onassis files. Literally, boxes upon boxes of them. For some ten years, she had collected clippings from newspapers and magazines—as well as most of the books that had been written about Jackie. She intended to write a biography but never found the free time. In that treasure trove were two of the first books ever written about the former First Lady: *The Hidden Side of Jacqueline Kennedy*, published in 1967, and *Jackie & Ari: For Love Or Money?* in 1968. I wrote both of them.

Many seasons had come and gone since Liz Smith arrived in New York, a young woman writer from Texas. Her first New

York newspaper job was on the *Journal-American* ghosting a column for Igor Cassini. Igor's brother is the internationally-famed designer Oleg Cassini. Igor was the Hearst newspaper chain's society reporter whose gossip column appeared under the byline of Cholly Knickerbocker.

Liz Smith left the *Journal-American* to write for women's magazines that included *Cosmopolitan*, *Vogue*, and *The Ladies Home Journal*.

In 1976, Smith launched a new career when she was given the assignment to write a column for the *Daily News*. It became an instant hit. Whipped cream on the cake came when Liz was hired as gossip correspondent for the local NBC-TV evening news show *Live At Five*.

In her travels, after leaving the *Journal-American*, Liz met Kitty Kelley and the two became friends. But it wasn't until 1976—when she began to write her *Daily News* gossip column—that her special accord with Kitty Kelly turned into a professional relationship as well.

"Kitty began providing me with items that I was able to use in my columns," Liz Smith told me.

Liz offered an explanation of the events that led her to give the valued Jackie Onassis files to Kitty Kelley. It began with a phone call . . .

"Guess what?"

"What, Kitty?"

"I've been given a contract by Lyle Stuart to write a biography of Jackie Onassis. How about that!"

"Marvelous . . . but don't write a word before you come and see me."

"Why?

"Because I've got a surprise for you! I'm going to give you something that will make your work infinitely easier . . ."

Kitty, who'd come up from Washington to sign the contract with Stuart, made her way to the columnist's Manhattan apartment.

"These are all yours!" Liz Smith announced to Kitty, pointing to the pile of cartons of Jackie Kennedy data she'd compiled over the decade. "I intended to write a book myself, but it didn't happen, so they're all yours."

"Oh, God," Kitty exalted. "There is so much there. I'll have to ask Mike to drive up here with the car."

The following day, Edgley dutifully drove the 280 miles to Manhattan, loaded the car and hauled the cartons home.

For the more than ten years that followed, Kelley's friendship with Smith continued on an even keel—until the Spring of 1988. Then on May 25th of that year Liz ran the following item in her column and the peaceful concord of almost twenty years was abruptly terminated:

INDIANS HAVE a proverb: "If you sit by the river long enough, eventually you'll see all your enemies float by." Jacqueline Onassis, Elizabeth Taylor and Frank Sinatra have been sitting for some time waiting for one particular person to bob along, going downstream, preferably without a life jacket. Of course I mean Kitty Kelley, the Washington-based author of *Jackie Oh!*, *Elizabeth Taylor: The Last Star*, and *Frank Sinatra: His Way*.

As you may know, Kitty is reportedly the subject of a book herself, by George Carpozi, with the ostensible rather silly title: *Bimbo: The Kitty Kelley Story*. (Somehow I don't believe this proposed work is a reality. Maybe it is, but it seems it might be more of an annoyance, mounted by publisher Lyle Stuart who has been at odds with Kelley since problems over the Onassis book.)

But now comes a real threat to Kitty's peace of mind. There will soon be an in-depth profile of the writer, coming in the *Washington Post* magazine. A very fine reporter is said to have been assigned at the suggestion of Sally Quinn, wife of the *Post* titan Ben Bradlee. Kitty has chosen not to cooperate with this. It will presumably delve into "Kitty's personal life" whatever that means. (It was always my impression, knowing Kitty for many years, that she lived in a quiet, unassuming and nonspectacular manner.) She and her longtime husband are now reported divorcing.

Well, anyway, if they are so inclined, I suppose Jackie, Miz Liz and Ol' Blue Eyes can pack a picnic lunch to the riverside.

****

No sooner had this item appeared in the *Daily News* than Liz Smith received a note in the mail, postmarked Washington but lacking a return address. The writer excoriated Liz for "betraying" her long-time friend. The missive stated flatly that Kitty, because of her "compassionate feelings" towards the columnist, did not chronicle in *His Way* disparaging allusions to Liz that Sinatra had mouthed.

The note taking her to task for "betraying" Kitty Kelley with that column left Liz nonplussed. The untraceable missive ended "Disgustedly" and was signed Barbara Regenstein.

"I suspected that Kitty or someone close to her might be involved," said Smith. "So I sent her the letter and said this woman must be a friend of yours. She denied knowing the woman, wrote me a very curt note on the letter and sent it back. It was one of the rudest things I've ever received in the mail."

After Kitty and the columnist parted ways, a dialogue began between Smith and Gerri Hirshey, the *Washington Post* reporter assigned to do the expository biographical series on Kelley. Miss Hirshey, assigned to the *Sunday Magazine* staff, was put on Kitty's case in February, 1988, and went through what she says were "the most horrendous eight months" of her journalistic career.

Before it was over, Liz Smith convinced Gerri that the falling-out between Smith and Kelley was real. The reporter had strong doubts at first about the columnist's sincerity since she had come to suspect everyone and everything connected with Kelley. Gerri Hirshey had been hounded by so many "Doppelgangers," as she calls the wraith-like clones who pursued, harassed, shadowed, phoned and wrote her anonymously, pulling every trick under the sun to find out what dirt Gerri was vacuuming from under Kitty's carpets.

After the schism, Liz Smith's column returned to straight-forwardness when dealing with the subject of Kitty Kelley. Liz broke the highlights of the *Washington Post* three-parter on the Friday before the *Sunday Magazine* launched the series on October 30, 1988.

Smith reported some of Gerri Hirshey's more significant and spectacular unearthings which showed Kitty:

* Had an alcoholic mother.

* Pilfered a manuscript from a noted author and sold it to a magazine.

* Sent vitriolic notes to reviewers who gave her books bad notices, and inundated other "enemies" with similar correspondence.

* Composed the notes on her own typewriter. [This was proven by the ex-CIA forensic expert (already identified) who examined the documents.]

Liz Smith closed the piece with the comment, "Fascinating stuff."

Kitty Kelley is characterized by many people who know her as a highly neurotic lady who claims to be one of the more interesting story tellers of our time. And, indeed, she is that . . .

These days, Kitty rakes in the advances and royalties from her writings and cries all the way to the bank. The big bucks began to roll in for her in the mid-80s and in 1987 it was reported she had earned $3.5 million, which placed her in sixth place on *Washingtonian* magazine's top one-hundred wage earners in the nation's capital.

2

Bosomy, auburn-haired, green-eyed, ebullient Virginia "Sugar" Hill was eleven years younger than underworld overlord Benjamin "Bugsy" Siegel, but she was in full bloom as a sin-wise sister. And she had much in common with the Bug for, like him, she had come up the hard way, from sordid, obscure beginnings.

Ginny was born in the Alabama hamlet of Lipscomb, one of ten children of a hard-drinking mule trader and tombstone polisher. After an extensive orientation in the art of promiscuity during her teenage years, she became the Cinderella girl of the underworld.

Virginia met Bugsy Siegel in 1941 at the very moment he was being exposed in the *Los Angeles Examiner* as a vicious and unsavory character. For the next six years, Ginny and Bugsy were indispensable partners—although their relationship was volcanic, pocked with frequent shouting matches and brawls.

Bugsy had made many enemies along the way to his rise in the Bugs-Meyer gang as a top underworld chieftain. Yet he lived a charmed life until the night of June 20, 1947, when his luck ran out.

Bugsy by then had become just vulnerable enough to accept Ginny's invitation to move out of his mansion into her spacious Moorish castle in Beverly Hills. Ginny had an uneasy feeling about Bugsy because he'd just had a serious falling out with his mobster partners in Las Vegas' Flamingo Hotel-Casino. They accused him of skimming profits from the gambling tables. Ginny was conveniently absent from her home that evening when Siegel was dispatched with three well-placed bullets in his head while reading the *Los Angeles Times* on Virginia Hill's living room couch . . .

"Hello, I'm Kitty Kelley . . . may I come in?"

The beautiful auburn-haired, green-eyed woman who answered the ring at the front door looked with surprise at the girl with the waist-long blonde braids and high-heeled shoes she'd borrowed from her mother's closet.

Ginny Hill had taken residence in the house at S3905 Skyview Drive in Spokane as a refuge after her uncomfortable experience in Washington, D. C., where she'd been a witness before the U.S. Senate Crime Committee. The committee was chaired by Tennessee's Senator Estes Kefauver who led a widely-publicized inquiry into organized crime. Ginny took the stand and denied knowing who killed Bugsy Siegel. In the telling, she startled the Committee members with her salty language. She snapped at the Senators, slugged reporters who wrote about her, and generally was a one-woman cyclone of epithets and uppercuts.

"Why have you come to see me, little girl?" Virginia Hill asked on that mid-summer's day of 1951. This was a year after she'd gone to Sun Valley, met a handsome Austrian ski instructor named Hans Hauser, promptly made husband No. 4 of him, and settled into what she hoped would be a peaceful life in Spokane.

Looking at the little girl for the first time, Ginny Hill couldn't know that getting dressed up and calling on people was something Kitty Kelley had done since she was two.

Recalling her curious meanderings as a child over the immaculately clean sidewalks of the neighborhood known as South Hill, Kitty described the scenario in a 1987 interview:

24

". . . a lot of old family friends [remember] about my calling on neighbors when I was a little girl. I'd put on my mother's high heels and walk down the drive with an evening bag over one arm and nothing on but diapers. Then I'd knock on people's doors to say hello."

Kitty was still wearing her mother's high-heeled shoes but now, at the age of nine, was out of diapers. So when Ginny Hill encountered the smiling visitor at her door, she found a well-groomed young lady in an orange organza knee-length dress.

"I heard about you . . ." little Kitty Kelley smiled bashfully in reply to why she was at the Hausers' front door. "I came here to welcome you to our neighborhood . . ."

Ginny Hill, who'd just given birth to her first child, took the little visitor by the hand and led her into the foyer. The young girl's friendly face and greeting were a welcome change from the cold shoulder and Arctic stares Ginny and Hans had been getting from the community, which made no secret of its disapproval of the notorious newcomer in their midst.

Kitty hadn't read about Virginia Hill in any newspaper or magazine nor caught a newscast on radio or TV. She got the details by listening to the grownups in her South Hill neighborhood gossiping about the couple who'd moved into a house just two blocks from the Kelleys' imposing red brick home at E310 High Drive.

"She's that gangster's moll . . . you know, the one shot to death in her house down in Los Angeles . . ."

"Oh, you remember her . . . you saw her on TV during the Kefauver Hearings . . . They called her 'Mafia Rose' . . ."

"I hope they don't stay long . . . What I'm afraid of is that they'll send gangsters here to rub her out and some of us will be hit by the stray bullets . . ."

It was talk like this which prompted the precocious nine-year-old eavesdropper to make up her mind that the newly-arrived and much-maligned family needed a welcome-wagon at their home. So Kitty Kelley appointed herself a Committee of One to drop in on the chestnut-haired beauty who left the Hearings in Washington shouting to reporters:

"I hope the atom bomb falls on every one of you!"

****

"Would you like to see my little baby?" Virginia invited, leading the way for her little visitor to the nursery.

"I love babies," Kitty said, ogling the tiny infant in its crib. "My mommy has three at home and I'm their big sister . . . I take care of them . . ."

****

That was fact. And it would continue to be the truth, the whole truth, and nothing but the truth through the birth of three more little Kelleys to round out a family of seven siblings. And throughout her adolescence and far into her teens, young Kitty Kelley would continue to be her mother's faithful little helper in caring for her sisters, Mary Cary, Ellen, Margaret, Adele Monica, and Madeleine Sophie, and brother, John.

It's difficult to assess so many years later just what turn the family's fortunes might have taken had it not been for Kitty's constant watchfulness over those youngsters. In that year, 1951, their 33-year-old mother Adele was too often withdrawn from reality because of her addiction to alcohol, almost always too bombed to provide proper care.

Their father, William Vincent Kelley, a prominent lawyer in Spokane—he served as president of the city's bar association—was eternally grateful that his first-born (on April 4, 1942) became a grown-up so quickly.

Attorney Kelley couldn't look after his brood personally. His frenetic schedule committed him to his law practice for the better part of a 12-hour day.

How fortunate that Kitty became a loving and solicitous sister to the other children and helped to direct their upbringing.

"The main thing you learn about living in a big family," Kitty professed years later, "is that the first one up in the morning is the best dressed."

Kitty sometimes reminisces wistfully about the early years when she was, for a brief time, an only child. She remembers

26

tales about the priest who baptized her and of the way he overruled her father, who proclaimed when he first laid eyes on his first-born:

"Her name will be Kitty."

And there's a yellowed newspaper clipping in her family album that proclaims, "Pretty Kitty Kelley is born."

But at her Roman Catholic christening, the priest made it clear there was no Saint Kitty. Thus the name had to be Katherine Ann. Yet the name on the little girl's birth certificate, which pre-dated the baptismal document, is Kitty. And she's been Kitty ever since.

****

Despite the hardships she faced at home, young Kitty Kelley experienced rewarding and happy times away from her family. But on the whole it seemed her childhood and adolescent years were tormented.

Talk with people who remember Kitty as a young woman growing up in Spokane and you come away with the feeling that you're up against a person who existed with a biformity.

Over a cup of coffee and a toasted buttered muffin in one neighbor's house, you're told:

"Kitty was a charming child. She had a sweetness about her that made her one of the most pleasant kids on our block. She was friendly . . ."

Yet another neighbor's view was a contradiction.

"Kitty was stiff and stilted. She had some sort of a built-in defense mechanism that prevented you from ever getting close to her. She was tough . . . thick-skinned.

"I was afraid of her then—and still am. Not because she was or is physically stronger, but I've always felt she possessed a certain kind of drive for power that I knew I couldn't cope with. She always had this inner strength that dominated you . . . I guess I feel the same way about her today. Am I wrong? Look at the way she defeated Frank Sinatra when he challenged her on her book . . ."

The consensus among those who've known Kitty Kelley best

27

is that her childhood years were more on the unhappy side than the cheerful. Even if she seemed to radiate serenity on the outside, her insides may have been aboil because of the rough times constantly prevailing in the household.

"Kitty didn't get along with her mother," said Marcia Gallucci, the author's closest friend of those childhood years—right up until she spoke with the *Washington Post's* Gerri Hirshey.

The reporter from the nation's capital got to Gallucci early on in her search for Kitty litter. Kitty had heard that Marcia entertained the journalist in the family living room—and spilled many of the Kelley family secrets that others in Spokane were reluctant to talk about—unless promised anonymity. Now Mrs. Gallucci is on Kitty's "Drop Dead" list.

Hirshey had extracted only dribs and drabs of Kitty intelligencia from old neighbors who knew her. Most were close-mouthed. Those who spoke did so with reluctance—and only after assurances that they wouldn't be identified in the story.

"Go see Marcia Gallucci," Gerri was told. Not once but many times.

"They said that Marcia knew 'everything,' but they didn't think she'd say much," Gerri told me later.

It was Gallucci who first made public the news of Kitty's mother's alcoholism. And Gallucci who first described to an outsider the split nature of Kelley's personality—warm and generous on the outside, hungry and anguished on the inside. Gallucci also provided the first information on some of Kitty's other foibles, from dressing up in Mom's clothes, to lying. Gallucci, in other words, showed the rest of us where the Kitty Kelley trail begins.

For more than ten years, Kitty talked about moving from her modest but cramped Washington apartment to toney Georgetown. But just any ordinary house wouldn't do. It had to be a sumptuous, historic dwelling, such as the imposing Georgian manor being vacated by now retired U.S. Supreme Court Justice William J. Brennan at 3037 Dumbarton Avenue, N.W. This residence was on a hill—precisely what Kitty wanted because her parents' home was attractively so situated on Spokane's prestigious South Hill.

"She had to have a house that would show her mother up," observed an acquaintance from Kitty's teen years in Spokane. "She hated her mother with such a passion that she had to show her up . . ."

The fact that her mother was dead by the time Kitty bought the Georgetown mansion didn't alter the view of the neighbor. "Kitty knows that wherever her mother is today, she can see what's happening down here—so she undoubtedly has gotten a vicarious thrill moving into the house, thumbing her nose up at the sky, and murmuring: 'There, you miserable old bitch, what do you think of this? You didn't believe I'd amount to anything, eh . . . ? Well, old drunkie, look at what I have now. More than you ever had . . . !'"

But the house wasn't bought until after the royalties poured in from her first successful book, *Jackie Oh!* Only then did Kitty have the money to fulfill her dream by crossing the muddy waters of the Potomac River and Rock Creek, to live in that beautiful community two-and-one-half miles from Capitol Hill.

****

Georgetown merged into the District of Columbia in 1871, and was annexed to the city of Washington in 1878—just at the time Kitty's great grandfather, John F. Kelley, was homesteading in the state of Washington, fifty miles south of Spokane Falls, as it was originally known.

Soon after its incorporation as a village in 1881, John Kelley moved to Spokane Falls and increased its population by one to 351. Kitty's great grandfather never abandoned the land he had settled in Whitman County. To this day the Kelley family still owns barley and wheat fields in that part of the state.

John Kelley married before his homesteading days and was blessed with the birth of a son, William, who would not live long enough to see his own three sons grow up and marry.

One of those sons was Kitty's father William Vincent, born in

1904. Young Bill and his brothers attended the same Spokane grammar and high schools and—before graduation and departure for college—they showed themselves to be chips off their old grandpa's block. Clearly, it seemed they had inherited his love of nature and his delight of outdoor life. The brothers went at it with a passion: swimming, exploring caves, climbing the craggy foothills of the Selkirk and Rocky Mountains, and sailing on the Spokane River. Because of their deep commitment to life in the open air, the three brothers became Eagle Scouts.

They all went to Cornell University, all were members of Beta Theta Pi fraternity, all became lawyers, and all returned to Spokane where they hung out their shingles. Kitty's father was to attain the quickest success and affluence in the legal profession.

William Vincent Kelley, who also was a member of the honorary law society Phi Delta Phi, made great legal strides after he joined the law firm of Witherspoon & Witherspoon. Soon he was made a partner and the corporate title was changed to Witherspoon, Witherspoon & Kelley—which to this day remains one of Spokane's most illustrious legal partnerships, although the firm has undergone one more re-naming, to Witherspoon, Kelley, Davenport & O'Toole.

And William Vincent Kelley, now eighty-eight, still manages after all these years to make his way on steady legs from his home high on South Hill to the city and put in part of a day's work at his office.

Nearly sixty years ago, when his law career was just under way, the importance of high social standing didn't elude Bill Kelley. He was bitten by the "joiner" bug and he went for memberships in the city's most prestigious organizations: the Spokane City Club, the Gonzaga University Club, the Officer and Civilian Club, and the Fifty-Fifty Club, whose membership was restricted to bachelors—and from whose rolls he was destined soon to be dropped.

****

A time came in the late 1930's when William Kelley met a

30

pretty, tiny young woman, not yet all of twenty-one, named Adele Overton Martin. He was into his thirties at the time. This four-foot-eleven-inch, ninety-pound beauty—affectionately nicknamed Delie—lived clear across the state in Seattle.

She was in Spokane that Summer of 1939 because her good friend, Frances Waldson, had invited her to spend part of her vacation from the University of Washington at the Waldson family home.

One warm August night, Delie went to a dance with Frannie and found herself attracted to a tall, distinguished-looking man who had approached her group to chat. Delie was "properly" introduced to him and, after a while, he asked her to dance.

This was the peak of the swing era. The music played by the local band would have featured Glenn Miller, Benny Goodman, or Tommy Dorsey scores. *In The Mood, Sing Sing Sing, Marie,* and other jumping and jitterbug music populated the top of the charts in that frenetic period of the big bands—music not intended to bring couple's bodies together for any length of time on the dance floor.

Not until the band segued into *The Missouri Waltz* did Bill Kelley have an opportunity to do some serious cheek-to-cheek dancing with his tiny partner. And then the chemistry co-alesced, almost as if by magic.

"Why, I think that's a wonderful idea," Delie smiled into the twinkling eyes of the handsome man introduced to her not more than half-an-hour before. "I'd love to go to the movies with you . . ."

But their first night out as a twosome—to the Fox Theater—was to be their last date of 1939. Summer was nearly over and Delie had to return to Seattle for her senior year at the University of Washington.

"We'll see each other when I come back to vacation at Frannie's." Delie smiled at Bill. "But we'll write to each other."

They kept in touch by mail and soon it was the Summer of 1940 and Delie Martin was back in Spokane, proud possessor of a Bachelor of Arts degree that she could gratifyingly exhibit alongside the diplomas she'd received earlier from the Convent of the Sacred Heart in Vancouver, B. C., and Forest Ridge Junior College in Seattle.

During the Fall and Spring semesters, Delie's love for Bill Kelley seemed to increase with each visit from the mailman bearing her lover's romantic epistles.

All through that time, Delie resisted her parents' objections to Bill—primarily because he was fourteen years older than their little daughter.

Delie had the greatest difficulty selling Bill to her father, Samuel A. Martin, a clothing store owner in Seattle. She had finally broken her mother's resistance and won partial approval—but she just couldn't budge her father from his position that Kelley, at thirty-six was too old and that Delie should find a boy to love closer to her twenty-two years.

But a time soon came when Delie and Bill's romance flamed to such heights that a parental nod no longer mattered . . .

****

The Summer of 1940 changed everything for Delie and Bill. She arrived at Frances Waldson's for another visit and this layover lasted much longer than all her other stays in Spokane. Delie was now caught up in a meaningful relationship with Bill.

Together, they spent the Summer cavorting as sweethearts. They fueled their love with cuddlesome necking dates in the balcony of the Fox Theater, cheek-to-cheek dancing to swing and jazz tunes at Spokane's better nightclubs, concerts under the stars at the municipal stadium and, most frequent of all, exciting romantic picnics in the high grass of South Hill overlooking the pastoral panorama of Hangman Valley below.

Finally, in late August, badgered by her parents' repeated calls to come home, Delie packed her bags, kissed Bill goodbye, and was off on a two-hundred-and-eighty mile journey, clear across the state to the shores of Puget Sound. As she arrived home, her adrenal glands were pumping at an all time high—as were Bill's back in Spokane.

In the last days before she left for home, Bill proposed marriage to Delie—and she accepted. They agreed to tie the knot just as soon as Delie convinced her stubborn father that the family had to accept the inevitable: Bill was the only man in her life, there'd never be another!

On the afternoon of October 17, 1940, the phone rang in the offices of Witherspoon, Witherspoon & Kelley. A frail, thin voice asked to speak to Mr. William Kelley.

"Bill! . . . Bill! It's . . . done! My mother . . . and father have . . . given us their . . . blessings . . . !"

Delie's words were gasped between the tears. Bill Kelley waved his secretary out of the office and once the door was closed, spoke endearingly to his fiance.

"I knew it would all work out," he sighed softly. "It's going to be a great marriage, Delie . . . you just wait and see . . ."

Two days later, Delie returned to town, was met at the railroad station by Frannie Waldson and soon after was in the arms of her beloved Bill. This was Saturday, October 19, 1940.

"Mama has agreed to make the announcement of our marriage a week from next Tuesday," Delie trilled. "We're going to be married in St. Joseph's . . ."

Breathlessly, she spelled out all the details of the wedding—and of the reception that would follow the hymnals. Then the next day, Delie Martin kissed Bill Kelley adieu and went back to Seattle. A busy schedule lay ahead for the bride-to-be: fittings for the bridal gown, ordering flowers, all the other arrangements for a wedding that was not too far off. In fact, when Delie's mother announced the date for the wedding, relatives and friends wondered why everything had to happen this quickly.

Mrs. Martin made the announcement in Seattle on the evening of November 5th. She killed two birds with one stone. She proclaimed the couple's engagement—and immediately set the date for the nuptials, a mere twenty-four days hence.

Why was so little time allotted between the betrothal and the marriage?

No one in Spokane seems to know.

The wonderment was echoed in the second paragraph of the city's newspaper after the first paragraph proclaimed the happy tidings from Mrs. Martin in Seattle:

"It [the wedding announcement] comes as a complete surprise in Spokane. Miss Martin has visited here a number of times, and was the house guest of Miss Frances Waldson, the week-end of October 19."

Whatever reason or reasons for winging it into such a rush-rush wedding, the incontrovertible evidence is that Adele Overton Martin and William Vincent Kelley did go that route.

And on the Saturday morning of November 29, Delie and Bill stood before the altar of God and, with the bride's twin sister Alice serving as maid of honor and the groom's brother John his best man, the couple was pronounced man and wife. Sitting in the first pew were the bride's parents, the Martins; her brother Samuel Martin Jr., and alongside them sat the groom's widowed mother, who had accompanied her two sons to Seattle and met the bride's parents for the first time on the morning of the wedding.

****

For the better part of a year the bride and groom found it cozy living in Kelley's bachelor pad. But then on an August day, Delie Kelley returned from a visit to a doctor and whispered in her husband's ear.

He kissed her as tears welled in her eyes. Just before Christmas, he drove Delie up to South Hill. It was the site of the tall grass where Bill and Delie picnicked and had romantic interludes in the past.

Pointing to a familiar plot of ground just a short distance from the start of Hangman Valley's gentle slopes, Bill Kelley turned to Delie and said:

"I'm going to build your house right here. It will have everything and anything you ever wanted, darling . . ."

"Will it have a nursery?" Delie smiled at Bill.

"Yes, yes, yes," he assured her, gently tapping his wife's bulging stomach. Delie was carrying Kitty Kelley in her womb, now nearing the sixth month of her pregnancy.

Two months later, on April 4th in 1942, Kitty was born. Her parents took her to their newly-finished home and settled her in a white crib, just one of the many pure-white installations Delie Kelley had ordered for the Tudor-style house that itself was perfectly layered with white exterior and interior paint and corresponding spartan decor.

"My mother was an absolute fanatic about white," Kitty said many years later. "She simply wanted everything—inside and outside of the house—to be in white. And she had her way because daddy let her have it. He didn't mind what colors she chose for the house. He only wanted to please mama and have her feel comfortable living in it."

Not long after they moved into the house, Delie Kelly became pregnant with her second baby. Not more than a year-and-a-half after daughter No. 2 was born, Delie had her third child. And by the time she was in her mid-thirties, she had given birth to six daughters and a son.

Child-rearing and household chores were not to be the bane of Delie Kelley's existence as a wife and mother. Bill Kelley saw to it that his family enjoyed a life of entitlement which the substantial income from his law practice enabled him to provide.

Therefore, the Kelleys were privileged to have full-time live-in household help who prepared the breakfast, lunch, and dinner—as well as the many sit-down dinners at which Bill and Delie entertained friends and business associates. The live-in help also did the housecleaning and laundry. But the day-to-day supervision of the growing family was largely in Kitty's hands.

Because by this time Delie Kelley had become a hopeless drunk.

3

Because of her mother's heavy drinking, Kitty became "little mother" to her five younger sisters and brother.

"Her mother was constantly in the study," remembers Sally O'Brien, who grew up with Kitty and knew of Delie's incapacitating bouts with the bottle.

"Delie gave strict orders that she was not to be disturbed and wanted to hear no noise. She was adamant about her period of quietude . . ."

Afternoons were the time for Kitty's mother to convalesce from her alcoholic binges. Delie had to have that private time to come out of her ninety-four-proof stupor before it came time to sit at the dinner table with the family.

Recalling Kitty's duties as a substitute mother for the other children, O'Brien described how their big sister performed that function:

"She had a lot of authority over the children and she used it. Kitty would address her sisters and brother with direct questions or commands such as 'Pick up your things' . . . 'Have you done your homework . . . ?' 'Did you brush your teeth . . . ?' 'Go in and take your bath, right now!' She was the typical oldest child in an Irish family—and loved to boss the others around."

While their existence at home was tormented by Delie Kelley's abuse of alcohol, the Kelleys still were able to enjoy a life of affluence. They vacationed in Europe and spent Summers at Hayden Lake, just across the state line in western Idaho. There Bill Kelley taught his children the same attitudes about outdoor activity that he'd learned from his pioneer grandfather.

But Delie set the ground rules for the time they spent in the Spud State—just as she had invoked certain iron-handed rules at home. In Idaho, there was none of the crowding in one rustic cottage for the Kelleys. Their wealth enabled them to have two lakeside dwellings—one for the parents, the other for the children. And if the youngsters were to have any truck with the parents at their cottage, it was by invitation only. Otherwise the kids slept, ate, and passed away the hours they weren't outdoors in their own lodging.

Her mother ruled with the same strong will at home. Marcia Gallucci recalls vividly:

"Delie roamed the house with a set of keys dangling from her waist. One was for the lock on the refrigerator door. No one could snack between the day's three main meals. No food was accessible to the kids that wasn't served at the dinner table. Delie, who was as thin as a rail and kept her figure by a semi-starvation regimen, felt it to be absolutely disgusting for anyone in her family to be heavy."

Both Gallucci and O'Brien agreed that the most probable reason for the friction between Kitty and her mother was sparked by Kitty's tendency to be plump. That, informants say, grated terribly on her mother's psyche.

"She was obsessed by anyone who gained weight," said one of Kitty's Spokane neighbors. "She was so totally intolerant of fat people. She constantly nagged Kitty about becoming heavy. She was critical of Kitty's fat legs. She was on her back all the time, nagging."

Her mother, in Marcia Gallucci's view, was the catalyst that turned Kitty into the "bitter bitch" she became.

The low grades Delie Kelley scored as a mother extended to her relationship with people outside the home. While she could count Marcia Gallucci's mother as a friend, there were few others. The joke was that if anyone had held a testimonial for Delie, it could have been held in a telephone booth.

"My mother considered her a good and loyal friend," Gallucci conceded. "But she frequently had to defend her to those who didn't like her. Delie could really get after you. She had the reputation of being vicious. So it's fair to say that Kitty learned from a master . . ."

Others who concurred with this view also offered a conclusion about why the much-maligned little girl grew up to be so full of the need to assassinate reputations. One of those who knew Delie well and attended social functions with her at the country club said:

"That's a reaction to all those years of trying with all her might to please her mother, to be a perfect young lady, yet not being able to make a dent with this inflexible and pitifully hopeless alcoholic."

Kitty Kelley's mother wasn't just a closet drunk. She was often a nasty public drunk. One particularly vivid scene was witnessed by a gathering at the Spokane Club when Bill Kelley tried to shush his wife.

"Delie and Bill had an unbelievable shouting match," said a member of the club who recalled other public donnybrooks between Kitty's parents over Delie's drinking.

But the worst scenes were at home, when Kitty's father returned from the office and found his wife spaced out. He'd lecture her about her drinking, plead with her to put herself in the hands of a doctor. In return Delie heaped abuse on her husband and said she didn't need any help, she was managing quite well, thank you . . .

Few of her most intimate friends in Spokane were aware of how Kitty Kelley managed to find deliverance from her mother's unbearable oppressiveness and the interminable friction between her mother and father. Kitty had her own retreat. She sought solace by reading. She'd accumulated books since she was old enough to recognize the written word and they filled a floor-to-ceiling library in the study. Just before Delie entered the room and closed the door for her period of convalescence, Kitty—sensing that the time was rapidly approaching for her mother's siesta—would select several books, and go to the study for an hour or two of escape.

But no one—neither close friends nor family was aware of the one therapeutic mechanism that helped Kitty cope with her miserable home life. Not until *Denver Post* writer Alison Teal made this revelation in the February, 1987, *New Woman* was anyone aware of Kitty Kelly's curative secret. Growing up in a Roman Catholic household and receiving her elementary and secondary education at Catholic schools, Kitty was, nevertheless, indebted for comfort to a piece of statuary that has been ascribed to a mystical and ascetic religious faith founded in India six-hundred years before the advent of Christ.

"The Buddha-like god on the bookshelf has been smiling on me ever since I was a child," Kelley told the interviewer, pointing to her icon tenanting a highly-visible place in the library of her dazzling Georgetown home.

The Buddha was one of the few possessions, other than books, that Kitty carried with her from childhood. "He came from my parents' house. He's supposed to be the god of happiness." she said of the Buddha.

****

After graduating from St. Augustine's Elementary School, Kitty attended Holy Names Academy, a private prep school. At school, Kitty meticulously abided by the rules of dress. Every day she was flawlessly attired in the school's forest-green jumper, stiffly starched Peter Pan collar on her white blouse, and freshly-polished saddle shoes she wore with white cotton anklets.

Kitty's father, who quickly remarried after his wife's death in 1978, has said that his eldest daughter's grades weren't as high as he wanted them to be.

But Sister Edwardine Mary, the Holy Names Academy's archivist since the school was closed, cites records that show

Kitty's academic achievements were surpassed many times over by her "perfection" in every other category as a student.

"On paper," said Sister Edwardine, "this young lady was extremely blessed. Her grades may not have been exceptional but her social life was. She was the school's Lilac Princess who dressed in a long gown, elbow-length white gloves, wore a crown on her blonde hair, and rode the Chamber of Commerce float in our city's annual Lilac Festival . . ."

If there's any aspect of her childhood that Kitty Kelley would like to have emphasized and given full treatment, it is that Lilac Princess contest . . .

The genesis of this story hinges on the afternoon of April 6, 1959, when Kitty Kelley raced into the house screaming hysterically. She'd heard from a classmate that the *Spokane Chronicle* had a story about her. She then rushed to the stationery store near the school, put down a nickel for the paper, opened it to the story, read it, jumped for joy, and sprinted home to break the news to her mother. The story was headlined:

4th Princess
Is Nominated

The article read:

"Kitty Kelley, daughter of Mr. and Mrs. William V. Kelley, E310 High Drive, was chosen today as the fourth member of Spokane's eight-member 1959 Lilac Festival Court.

"The 17-year-old princess was selected by Holy Names Academy . . ."

The item went on to say that four members of the court had not been named yet, but soon would be.

"Kitty," the story continued, "is a 5-foot-2-inch strawberry blonde with hazel brown eyes. She is a cheerleader for Gonzaga Prep, is the academy's Red Cross president, and has taken part in dramatics. Her favorite sports are swimming and skating . . ."

Despite the thrill of reading about this signal honor bestowed on her, Kitty Kelley realized she was still up against tough competition from the other candidates—or "princesses" as they were also called—from seven other schools. Kitty went to bed that night and before she turned out the light studied the competition she faced from a brochure distributed by the Lilac Festival Court.

She looked over the list of candidates from the Spokane area high schools and found herself facing the challenge of seven formidable teenaged high school rivals. Kitty ran over the names:

Roberta Beck of Rogers High; Martha Corkery of Lewis and Clark High; Donna Jeanne Goodell of Mead High; Virginia Jones of West Valley; Sandy Earlene Mithaug of Central Valley, Linda Poulin of North Central, and Linda Rozzini of Marycliff High.

It was well past eleven o'clock that night of Monday, April 6, when Kitty called out:

"Mommy! . . . Come here!"

Mrs. Kelley hurried to Kitty's bedroom.

"Mommy . . . Mommy!" Kitty squealed. "I'm going to win the contest . . . I'm going to be selected the Lilac Princess. . . ."

Kitty gave her mother no reason for her belief that she'd win. Yet the following Tuesday night in Spokane's Coliseum, before a gathering of several thousand, Kitty Kelley was indeed selected over all the other pretty competitors to be the Lilac Queen and crowned in a spectacular coronation pageant that launched the city's traditional eight-day festival.

"No one worked harder at being a good girl, a perfect girl, than Kitty did," Sister Edwardine Mary stressed. "She was always immaculately groomed and for that accomplishment she was awarded the coveted Gold Stripe insignia that she stitched on her Holy Names jumper."

When Holy Names was closed, it folded the books on an illustrious era with one significant record of achievement belonging exclusively to Kitty Kelley. She was the only student in the history of the school to have been elected "Friendliest Girl" for four years running!

In Spokane there was a boys' Catholic high school called Gonzaga, which was run by the Jesuit Brothers of Gonzaga University, Bing Crosby's alma mater.

Because Gonzaga High was an all-boys school, they had an arrangement with all-girls' Holy Names to provide cheerleaders for the basketball and football games. And since Kitty was pretty and shapely, she became a Gonzaga cheerleader. She wore the cute forest-green uniform of the school with a snarling bulldog on her already-ample chest and shook her crepe-paper pompons to attract the handsomest guy in school—Tom Shine.

Nearly thirty years later, Shine has vivid recall of his dates with Kitty during her senior year at Holy Names.

"I was sweet on Kitty from the time we met in second grade," said Shine, now an architect in Spokane who's been married twenty-one years and has four daughters. "I probably dated her more than anyone else [in high school]. Kitty and I were a very popular couple. We were elected king and queen of the dances, that type of thing."

But a time came when the couple went their separate ways. Kitty had a falling out with her mother who accused her of "playing with herself" and then banished her from the house. Delie sentenced her daughter to board during her junior year at the academy, which was like having her enlist in the military.

"We thought boarding at Holy Names was nothing less than being in a prison," said Anne Driscoll Begesaa about the school. "We were in little cubicles, like the army or something. We had to get up at five of six, go off to Mass."

Even as the students got their marching orders and adhered to the drumbeat of the Catholic school's strict directives, there were other rules to live by. It was lights-out-at-nine—and no dating.

Kitty was infuriated with her mother for imposing such a prohibition against her. But she bravely stuck out her chin and tolerated the ban against dating until the end of her confinement to the "brig," as Kitty put it.

Delie Kelley's action was taken after Kitty carried her dates with Tom Shine a bit too far. She'd return home at midnight or later, and wake up one of her sisters.

"Come on, come on, rise and shine!" Kitty would command. "Get dressed and get downstairs for breakfast . . . And hurry or you'll miss the school bus . . ."

The poor kids would go down, have their cereal, not aware of the hour—then sit on the front steps waiting for the bus. At one o'clock in the morning!

****

Kitty's period of imprisonment in Holy Names came to an end after her junior year. Her mother told Kitty that if she behaved over the Summer, she could return to the academy in the Fall for her senior year and be allowed to reside at home.

"Despite the restrictions laid down by the sisters," remembered her father, "Kitty had a pretty gay time while she was at the academy."

Kitty's dates with Tom Shine became more numerous in the last months of their senior year. But even as they went to those final senior dances, Shine sensed a break growing between them. He detected a steel determination about the future she envisioned for herself. Shine soon told himself his relationship with Kitty wasn't fated to last.

In September, following their respective June graduations, it was over.

"It ended for us because Kitty wanted out of Spokane," observed Shine with uncanny perception. "She wanted no part of the prospect of living here the quiet, middle-class life a grocer's son had to offer. She was privileged, and I was not. She went off to college, and I went off to work. I felt Kitty was desperate to achieve some recognition. She yearned to prove herself."

Kitty said goodbye to Tom before she headed south to the University of Arizona in Tucson.

She registered for courses intended to lead to a B.A. degree in English. But her quest for higher learning was destined to

44

become entwined in a web of mystery that eventually forced Kitty to make a sudden departure from the Tucson campus. That was followed by an even stranger eight-month hiatus in a place or places unknown to any of her friends and acquaintances in Spokane. Only after that "exile" did Kitty surface. She turned up at the University of Washington, enrolled as a junior . . .

4

A Niño de su osita rubia—siempre

This message in Spanish is the dedication in Kitty's unauthorized biography, *Elizabeth Taylor: The Last Star*. Trans-
lated literally it means:

*A Child from his little female bear blonde and fair—ever at
all times.*

Conventional dedications traditionally inscribe tributes to
family, friends, associates, or others in appreciation of their
fidelity, fealty, or for any reason that merits the honor. Thus it
seemed strange that Kitty Kelley chose this to send a message to
an unidentified person.

In her unauthorized biography of Jacqueline Kennedy Onassis, *Jackie Oh!*, Kitty's dedication reads:

To my husband and my parents.

Her inscription for *His Way: The Unauthorized Biography of
Frank Sinatra* is penned with a glowing tribute to the *Time-Life*
cameraman who criss-crossed the country as her inseparable
companion in search of information. He used his press pass to
get through celebrities' doors for interviews that she otherwise
might not have obtained. Thus this tribute:

*To Stanley Tretick, whose tireless efforts on behalf of this
book disprove his theory that photographers are a shiftless lot.*

But what can we make of Kitty Kelley's dedication in the Liz Taylor book? Word-for-word, line-for-line? Does it appear to suggest that the author is talking about the birth of a baby . . . ?

"A Niño de su . . ."

"A child . . ."

What child? Who's child?

Kitty doesn't say.

". . . osita . . ."

". . . little female bear . . ."

Who is the female bear Kelley refers to? What's its connection to Kitty Kelley? Is it a real bear—or is it merely an allusion to another member of the animal kingdom, possibly a human being—who went into hibernation for, say, the mysterious missing eight months of Kitty Kelley's disappearance from the University of Arizona?

Not even former best friend Marcia Gallucci knows anything about that period of Kitty's life which began in May, 1962, when she abruptly withdrew from the University of Arizona. As *Washington Post* reporter Gerri Hirshey points out, this was done "with no major declared and no intention to transfer indicated."

"Yes, I called it a *gap* in her life," said Gallucci formerly Marcia Black, confirming the word she was quoted as using in Hirshey's story, which then went on to report:

"She [Gallucci] says that she and other friends of Kitty's did not know for sure where Kelley was [during the eight months] or what she was doing until she entered the University of Washington in Seattle in January of '63."

". . . rubio . . ."

". . . blonde and fair . . ."

Who was "blonde and fair"—not only in May, 1962, when Kitty Kelley inexplicably vanished from the face of the earth, but who was still blonde and fair when she resurfaced upon that campus in the Pacific Northwest early the following year—and has remained blonde and fair to this very day?

Any meaning there? Any significance?

"—siempre."

. . . ever at all times."

What does that mean? Why has Kitty Kelley uttered this postscript in closing the arcane message in her puzzling dedication?

Why has she chosen to write it in Spanish?

To whom is she referring when she states, "A child from *his* little female bear blonde and fair . . ." And why such warmth and sincerity in her closing, ". . . ever at all times . . . ?

Most importantly, what bearing does this tribute have on that eight-month period of her mysterious disappearance?

Has it any correlation with her failure to respond to the first of some fifty questions this author asked Kitty Kelley? [See appendix]

"Why didn't you complete your undergraduate studies at the University of Arizona? I have school yearbooks for 1960 to 1962 with your picture as a member of Delta Gamma sorority. I have contacted your sorority sisters for information on that eight-month gap in your life from the spring of 1962 until you surfaced again in January, 1963, at the University of Washington. I urge you to tell me whether or not you boarded for any part of those eight months in a home for unwed mothers."

An easy query to respond to, but Kitty Kelley didn't.

Then there were other unanswered questions . . .

"Does the saying in Spanish at the beginning of *Elizabeth Taylor: The Last Star*, have anything to do with those eight months that I am having difficulty tracing?"

And:

"Did you actually burst into tears when your then-agent, Lucianne Goldberg, asked you the meaning of those words?"

Rumors abound concerning thefts committed upon Delta Gamma sorority sisters when Kitty Kelley was a resident of Yuma Hall.

"The records are not open to public scrutiny," a security official told the author. Gerri Hirshey received a similar brush-off.

Gerri Hirshey was asked why she didn't dwell more on that

"gap" in Kitty's life instead of dusting it off with one paragraph, which began:

"On her way, there was a stumble, and some mystery . . ."

"The lawyers," Hirshey said with disgust. "They blue-pencilled all the good stuff. They were afraid of it. They are aware of how litigious Kitty Kelley is. She sues at the drop of a cliche . . ."

Seeking information from alternate sources seemed futile because, as a spokesman said, "This matter was handled on the campus and was resolved right here. No report was made to anyone off university grounds."

The clearest explanation of what all the secrecy was about came from Patricia L. Coates of the University of Arizona Library's Special Collections section, who furnished me with photocopies of the 1960, 1961, and 1962 yearbooks which carried Kitty Kelley's photos and blurbs about her activities as a member of Delta Gamma sorority.

"The university library has only public records on students, such as yearbooks, commencement programs, and the like," Ms. Coates explained. "Should you wish to pursue the other questions you posed," she said, "you should contact the pertinent offices on campus, such as the Registrar's Office. However, they will not release any personal information such as grades without the student's permission. This is governed by the Family Education Rights and Privacy Act, and is not negotiable."

During this investigation into her background at the University of Arizona, a rumor surfaced that Kitty Kelley had suffered a "nervous breakdown" because of "mind-boggling pressures" at the school. I also was told that after her parents refused to accept her return, she sought solace by taking refuge in her maternal grandparents' home in Seattle. One report also had the university dropout confined to a wheelchair for part of that period of "hibernation."

****

A mermaid is a fabled marine creature depicted by the head

50

and torso of a lovely woman whose configuration abruptly changes shape below her legless hips into the scaled body and tail of a fish.

Destiny had apparently decreed that Kitty Kelley should play this sea-nymph's role as a member of Delta Gamma sorority in her sophomore year at the University of Arizona.

But Katherine A. Kelley—that's the name she gave the registrar during enrollment week—had never before experienced a class act comparable to Delta Gamma. It was perfectly logical to have such a water spirit performing for this woman's organization since the decorations on their float prepared for Homecoming Day required a nautical theme. However, all eyes were not on Kitty Kelley alone when the 50-foot-long, flower-bedecked pageant display was carted onto the football field on that sunny Saturday afternoon in the early fall of 1961 before the Arizona Wildcats took to the gridiron. Unlike those nine days back home when she reigned as the center of attention following her crowning at the spectacular Coronation Pageant, Kitty had to share the spotlight with four other mermaids beautifying the float: Lynda Gray, Gretchen Dickey, Linda Long, and Annalee Ferguson.

Nevertheless, Kitty received high grades for this outing and her participation in the activity, however minuscule, merited a brief mention in the 1961 edition of the university yearbook *Desert* and the placement of her photo, with those of 79 other sorority sisters, on page 313 of that volume.

A year earlier, in 1960, Kitty had received attention even as a freshman in a group picture on page 270 of a commemorative edition of the *Desert*, for the university's seventy-fifth anniversary. Kelley is shown with a gaggle of other girls standing in front of the colonnaded entrance to Yuma Hall, one of the most popular women's dorms on the UA campus.

Kitty was still the perky, outgoing girl she was back home. However, she no longer collected glossies of her sugary-faced idol, Debbie Reynolds, whom she once was convinced she resembled. She also gave up her earlier dream of one day becoming a movie star.

Her sister Ellen deserves credit for pricking that bubble.

"One actor is all this family can take," is how Kitty put it as she watched her sister's acting career develop in New York. Ellen had studied for several years under Alice Garvin Windsor, regarded as Spokane's leading teacher of acting at the time, then went East to make her mark in the theater as a character actress and comedienne. Ellen participated with the New York Shakespeare Festival and performed in *A Midsummer Night's Dream* in Lincoln Center—many years before Kitty Kelley achieved her place in the sun.

Acting wasn't the only field in which sister Ellen was an achiever—a factor that added to the color green (as in envy) that Kitty was seeing insofar as Ellen was concerned. For, after graduation from college, Ellen taught elementary school classes in Bedford Village, an upper-crust community north of New York City.

That lofty perch in pedagogy didn't sit well with Kitty who found her own experience unrewarding when she tried teaching in one of Seattle's most deprived neighborhoods.

"I was very unhappy in my work," Kitty remarked about her brief fling as a teacher. "I didn't like that environment . . ."

For contrast, listen to Ellen:

"I loved teaching—it is really like being an actress. You have to sell a subject and relate to an audience."

Ellen immersed herself in teaching to such a depth that during Summer recess she took graduate courses at her father's alma mater, Cornell University, and at New York University as well.

But when acting became all-important to her and Ellen headed for the Great White Way and made notable progress—until she discovered three casting directors had given another Ellen Kelley some coveted parts because of an identity error. So Ellen made her last name her first, took her mother's maiden name as her last—and it's been Kelley Martin on billboards and theater programs ever since.

****

Kitty's grades weren't exceptional but her social life was. Although she eventually got her act together after that eight-month "gap" in her life and walked off the University of Washington campus in 1964 with a degree, she was always second to Ellen in educational and career accomplishments. That is, until she became a celebrated name with the publication of *Jackie Oh!*

A set of baffling occurrences drove the security forces up the trellises outside of Yuma Hall at the University of Arizona to catch a thief they were convinced was one of the dormitory's residents.

While all those social affairs—open houses, Christmas and Spring parties, and senior breakfasts—were happening downstairs, someone upstairs was systematically stealing articles from the dorm's occupants' belongings. The loot consisted of such items as costume and real jewelry, trinkets, perfumes, toiletries, articles of clothing and, here and there small amounts of cash that too trustingly were left in dresser or night table drawers.

Because it has a policy of not giving out information on security matters, the university wouldn't reveal when the thievery ended.

My research of her University of Arizona years left me with one final mystery. It concerns Kitty Kelley's membership in Delta Gamma. It is lodged in the sorority's national headquarters in Columbus, Ohio. The sorority's executive director, Mrs. W. Hale Watkins, authorized a search of the records for clues about Katherine A. Kelley's progress in Delta Gamma after her departure from UA and that untraceable eight-month period that followed.

"I'm afraid I cannot be of much help to you if you're looking for a record of Miss Kelley beyond 1962," I was told by Mrs. Beverly Brown who handles the Delta Gamma membership rolls. "I find that she was initiated into the sorority in 1960 and she was a member for the next two years."

There is no further mention of either a Katherine A. Kelley or of a Kitty Kelley in all the subsequent years on Delta Gamma's rosters. The clerk explained that the written records kept on members and their whereabouts were transferred to a computer file some years ago.

And what does the computer readout on Kitty Kelley's record show?

"It simply says 'lost,'" the clerk replied. "We have no further record of her after 1962."

"Could it be that Kitty Kelley was a dropout?"

"That may be fair to say," came the reply.

"And to say anymore may not be fair?"

"That sounds fair enough . . ."

****

Before we pick up on Kitty's trail eight months hence, when she moved on to the University of Washington, let's peek at a curious paragraph in *New Woman* magazine's profile of Kitty Kelley written by Alison Teal, former columnist for the *Denver Post*, who is quoting "an old friend":

"She [Kitty] has always fought a weight problem, and at the University of Arizona she was losing the battle for a while. But it never got her down. She was just funny about it . . ."

We know that in later years whenever weight was a problem, Kitty could take it off by going to health spas. But we have no idea how she lost the pounds she put on in Tucson that the friend alluded to. All we know as a matter of certainty is that after dropping out of view for eight months, she turned up at the University of Washington looking pretty much like the streamlined mermaid who rode the Homecoming Day float at the University of Arizona on that fall day of 1961.

5

When Kitty Kelley stepped onto the University of Washington campus in January 1963, she was fulfilling her mother's wish. "More than anything, I would like to see you going to my college" Adele Kelley would say. But Kitty's mind was fixed on the university in Tucson. Years later, in an interview, Kitty let it be known she could have done better than to attend such plebeian universities as Arizona and Washington.

"I was supposed to go to Vassar," she told *Washington Post* feature writer Stephanie Mansfield for a piece that appeared in *Us* magazine in 1987.

When Kitty emerged as the newly-materialized Katherine A. Kelley at the university in Seattle, she matriculated there with a far more reserved profile than in Tucson. No more pageants or homecomings. Nor did she go all out for the camaraderie and high good times she sought at Arizona. She was a serious, nose-to-the-grindstone student. C-grades were a thing of the past. Now she was petitioning for a place on the dean's list. Her grades were B-pluses, even some A's.

Although her Delta Gamma sorority career seems to be something of a mystery, Kitty Kelley's photo shows up in the 1964 University of Washington yearbook section devoted to Delta Gamma activities.

"How is it you haven't listed Kitty Kelley in your archives as a

Delta Gamma member at the University of Washington?" I asked Mrs. Brown.

"The only explanation I can offer is that the Delta Gamma branch at the University of Washington just didn't report her membership to our headquarters in Columbus [Ohio]. Why, I cannot say . . . It's conceivable that she may not have been a member of the University of Washington sorority and was alluding to her membership in Delta Gamma at the University of Arizona. I have no other possible explanation for it."

Kitty's other extra-curricular activity at the university in Seattle was membership in the Junior League, which she retained for many years after graduating *cum laude* in March of 1964 with a Bachelor of Arts degree in English and a teaching certificate.

What the yearbook didn't mention was that Kitty had a rollicking association with one Norman D. Dicks. While Norm's middle initial is D. as in Donald, his colleagues dubbed him "Dizzy."

"Dizzy Dicks" was so named because of his performance on the gridiron with the University of Washington football team.

A heavy-duty defensive back, Dizzy Dicks performed Herculean service for the Huskies. He had the distinction of being on two of the Huskies' teams that won back-to-back Pac 10 titles and were victorious twice in a row in the Rose Bowl, defeating Big 10 champions Wisconsin, 44-8, in 1960, and Minnesota, 17-7, in 1961. Dicks was a class act on the football field.

He didn't do badly off the gridiron either—he scored touchdowns with a number of coeds, but most prominently and enduringly with one named Kitty Kelley.

Dicks was a senior, Kitty a junior when the friendship started. After Dizzy graduated he didn't let his cleats take him on a course followed by an earlier grad, Thomas A. Foley, who—after his matriculation at the University of Washington in 1951—went on to obtain a law degree at his alma mater in 1957, then on to Washington as a Congressman in 1964.

Dicks chose instead, after receiving his bachelor's to pursue studies for a doctor of jurisprudence degree, which he received five years later, in 1968.

After that he was off to Washington, D.C. to toil in the offices of Washington State's U.S. Senator Warren G. Magnuson. Dicks was taken on as legislative assistant, a post he held for the next five years before winning a Congressional seat for himself.

Although the timetable is clouded, the recollection of people near to Dizzy and Kitty recall that there was an almost-instant resumption of rapport in the nation's capital between the two University of Washington grads.

Kitty's teaching career in Seattle was short-lived so she returned home to Spokane and took a few months to get herself together. She then set out to seek her fortune in the East. She knew quickly enough that teaching wasn't her bag—at least not in the elementary school where she held class.

"That didn't last," she would say about the experience, "because I was teaching in what they call a culturally deprived area, a ghetto. I decided I wasn't ready for that yet."

In New York City Kitty struck paydirt almost at once. The 1964-65 New York World's Fair was opening for its second year and General Electric was recruiting young women to serve as VIP hostesses for its Progressland Pavilion.

Had Kitty Kelley spent five years getting a college education only to wear a colorful uniform so she could usher celebrity visitors around a World's Fair exhibit? Was the oversized beret she was given to wear at a jaunty angle on the back of her head emblematic of a new station in life after she had discarded the mortar board and tassel from her graduation? Kitty harbored higher ambitions.

"Powerful people fascinate me," Kitty admitted not long ago to London *Daily Mail* reporter Mary Fletcher. She was relating the reason she was drawn to Washington and to a job on Capitol Hill—less than a year after her tour began at the Fair.

Among the young women who started the second season at GE's Progressland were Myra Waters, a precocious 20-year-old with theatrical ambitions who went into her job with the conviction that it would not be the meek who shall inherit the earth.

"I'll be frank with you," she told *New York Post* reporter

Leonard Katz. "My engagement at the Fair was an opportunity to display my talent."

She confessed: "If I see the visitor is a big producer or someone who might be able to help me, I just kind of shoulder the other girls aside."

In the short time she'd been hostessing, Myra said, she impressed a famous Hollywood actor, who sent her a metal statuette, and was signed by a record company after someone heard her singing during a show, which almost got her fired.

What did Kitty Kelley do to make an impression?

"Kitty Kelley as VIP hostess at the General Electric Progressland at the New York World's Fair greets many a celebrity," wrote columnist OJ Parsons in the *Spokane Chronicle* on September 29, 1965. That was just nineteen days before the Fair closed and Kitty—after a brief detour—headed 280 miles down the pike to Washington, D.C. and a job on Capitol Hill.

By then Kitty had "shouldered" her way to a visitor who, as Myra Waters put it, "might be able to help me."

While hostessing, she found actress Julie Andrews "charming," and enjoyed showing the former President's daughter Margaret Truman (Mrs. Clifton Daniel) through Progressland.

"It is a role in which they must be well versed in the background of the individual she is entertaining," Parsons' *Chronicle* puff on Kitty continues.

"She remembers, for example, to ask some industrial giant if he had enjoyed his Dartmouth College reunion the day before—that sort of thing.

"But the greatest tribute to the vivacious, friendly Kitty came from the father of a crippled lad.

"His touching letter and a picture of Miss Kelley were published in the *Progressland* magazine.

"The letter to company executives read:

"'Thank you for a wonderful afternoon at the pavilion escorted by Kitty Kelley of Spokane, Wash. My son has been tragically crippled since birth and because of this has had a most difficult time accepting life.

" 'People often stare at him and seem repulsed by his handicap.

" 'Miss Kelley must have done quite a bit of work with the handicapped or else she is truly a genuine person.

" 'She did more for my son today than all his trips to the clinic.

" 'First she appeared to not even notice his handicap. Then she started talking to Jim and for the first time in six months I really heard my son laugh.

" 'This might seem slight to you, but to me it was heavenly! I am deeply appreciative to Kitty Kelley for making my son feel like a human being and for making me try a little harder!' "

That was the end of the story. However, a huge chunk was left out of the Kitty Kelley chronicles as a VIP hostess. Because OJ Parsons didn't tell us anything about the picture that ran with the column and which was captioned:

"Kitty Kelley, daughter of Mr. and Mrs. William V. Kelley, greets Rep. Thomas S. Foley."

The photo shows Kitty, in her hostess' uniform, standing beside Foley, who towers more than a head-and-a-half above the five-foot-three Kelley, who had grown an inch since her high school Lilac Princess days. They're both smiling, looking quite comfortable together.

And well they should have been. For what Parsons hadn't reported was that Kitty Kelley had shouldered her way to Foley, a Democratic Congressman from Spokane, Washington, and plastered her boobs against the legislator's torso for a very telling picture.

This was a fortuitous meeting of the guide and the legislator, and provided a giant step for Kitty's eventual meteoric rise.

Representative Thomas Stephen Foley was thirty-six years old when he met Kitty Kelley on his visit to the GE Pavilion in 1965. He was a first-year Congressman.

Foley felt obligated to give William Kelley's daughter the squarest shake he could. In Spokane, Foley's roots were closely entwined with Kitty's father's. Kelley was a lawyer who not only defended clients against Foley's own father, Ralph E. Foley, when he was a prosecutor, but tried cases before his bench when the elder Foley became a Washington State Superior Court Judge.

When young Foley ran for his congressional seat, he had finished tours as deputy prosecutor of Spokane County and as Assistant State Attorney General for Spokane. He had been projected, through his father's political clout, for appointment as United States Attorney for the Eastern District of Washington. But President John F. Kennedy selected another appointee for the job. Tom Foley then became special counsel to Washington Senator Henry M. Jackson's Senate Interior Committee—until he was persuaded to run for Congress.

One of Tom Foley's ardent backers in the race for the House was Kitty's father, Bill Kelley. It would seem inevitable that a rapport would develop between the lawyer's daughter, looking to make a mark in life, and the Congressman, looking to advance his options as a freshman legislator.

Foley gave Kitty Kelley an open invitation to come to Washington, D. C., promising to help her find a firm footing in the nation's capital. The Congressman let her know he could open doors that could get her "politically connected . . ."

But Kitty didn't take Foley up on his offer—not just yet. Because she had other interests to pursue first—romantic ones. She explained to a co-worker, "There is sex that you do for your career and sex that you do for yourself."

Michael Edgley was one of several bartenders behind the mahogany at the Lion's Head, a popular gathering place for writers. It was in the heart of Greenwich Village, where Kitty Kelley was staying during her six-month tour at the New York World's Fair.

The subway ride on the Interborough Rapid Transit's Flushing line from the World's Fair stop to Times Square took twenty-five minutes. After a change of trains, less than ten minutes more carried Kitty to the Christopher Street-Sheridan Square station of the IRT's Seventh Avenue line.

She made daily round trips on the two subway routes because she was living in a single bedroom studio apartment in the West Village. In this period—from the Fair's opening in May to its closing in October—Kitty was involved with three people who would figure significantly in her life.

One was Foley, thirteen years older than the twenty-three-year-old Kitty. Congressman Foley was single and a very eligible bachelor after his election to the House of Representatives the previous November 3, 1964. Of the three alliances Kitty Kelley forged in New York, the one with Foley has endured the longest—even through his long marriage to his wife Heather. To this day, Kitty is often seen together with the Foleys at social and political gatherings. The friendship endured Foley's meteoric rise to power as House Majority Leader and, in the year 1989, Speaker of the House—after Texas Congressman Jim Wright resigned from that post.

Foley thus became second in line to succeed George Bush, should the President become incapacitated and Vice President Dan Quayle unable to serve.

Second was Kitty Kelley's friendship with Janet Donovan, who also worked as a hostess at the General Electric VIP lounge. This friendship came to a screeching halt in 1988. Of this, more later.

A breakup also occurred with the third person Kitty became acquainted with in New York—bartender Michael Edgley, who later became her husband.

Kitty met Mike in the late Spring of 1965 when she went to the Lion's Head for a cocktail. Kitty hadn't learned the lesson she should have from her alcoholic mother.

"Kitty made an instant hit here," recalls Mike Reardon, one of the bartenders who worked with Edgley—and is still behind the stick at the Lion's Head today. "She and Mike hit it off beautifully. . . ."

So beautifully that, in no time at all, Kitty and Mike were living together.

"Yes, Mike moved in with Kitty," said Wesley Joyce, who together with his wife Judy and the late Mike Sydell founded the popular Village landmark tavern. "Mike needed someone like Kitty to look after him because he had a severe drinking problem . . ."

Edgley's boozing was attributed in part to his frustrated ambition to be a writer.

"He fantasized that he'd be another James Joyce," a knowledgeable source in Washington, D.C., told me on condition of anonymity. "Kitty was also determined to become a writer. Her college classes in English and literature convinced her that was what she most wanted to do."

Edgley had also tried his hand briefly in publicity work at the Fair in a part-time capacity for one of the exhibitors. But this didn't start him on the road to literary success that he'd hoped it would.

Although Mike became Kitty's live-in lover in the World's Fair days, he wasn't the only man making it with her. Friends insist Kitty has never been a one-man woman. Kitty had at least one other well-known "heavy" liaison, with "a very wealthy Jewish businessman" who took her on weekends to his home in the Hamptons.

Literary agent Lucianne Goldberg, who represented Kelley for some two years after she wrote *Jackie Oh!*, told me: "Kitty used to say that she liked Jewish men. She particularly liked wealthy Jewish men. Although I always believed she was as Irish as the Blarney Stone, I heard people say she claimed her mother was Jewish . . ."

As the last days of the Fair drew near, Kitty and Mike decided to continue their co-habitation, but not in New York.

"They had to get out of the Village," my Washington source continued. "They both knew that Mike was drinking too much and couldn't keep working behind the bar and survive. Kitty's weight had begun to soar from her own drinking. She realized it would have to stop. She also blamed the drinking for Mike's lack of sex drive.

"Shortly after the Fair closed, Kitty and Mike packed their bags and drove to Stockbridge, Massachusetts.

"They rented a small house there and Kitty decided to renovate the place. By then, she had gained so much weight from her drinking with Mike that she began to rely heavily on weight-reduction pills. Soon she found herself hooked on a drug that was comparable to *speed*.

"She'd gulp a handful of pills in the morning, become so charged up she'd throw herself into redoing the house. Then she'd pick up the brush and start painting. One room she did and redid and redid until it sagged under six or more coats. She was popping pills so heavily she didn't know what she was doing."

Kitty convinced Mike that he couldn't drink anymore and persuaded him to join Alcoholics Anonymous.

She attended meetings herself. After a time, Mike and she stopped boozing completely. Mike went on the road lecturing at AA meetings. But eventually he went back to drinking—and also became a cocaine user. Not Kitty. She became a Tab-aholic.

"After he was off the sauce," a Lion's Head source said, "a sober Mike Edgley proved [literally] impotent. The 'Wild Irish lover,' as we called him, now was a dud. Moreover, he couldn't write and he knew it."

Kitty recognized Mike's literary limitations, having found that, even when she rewrote his manuscripts, he couldn't sell them to the pulps. His stories, predominantly fiction, relied on "lame love plots without any punch," according to one of the sources familiar with his efforts.

What most distressed Kitty was that Mike wasn't bringing any ardor to their bed. "I do all the work. He never gets off his back," she complained. Kitty looked elsewhere for fulfillment.

"She began taking weekday trips to New York and renewed old romances. She was hellbent to make it with the businessman who lived in the Hamptons. She spent most of her time there when she was away from Mike. But she was seeing others too. With Kitty's need to be liked, often all you had to do was ask.

"Before she'd leave for New York, she'd tell Mike she was staying with a friend who didn't have money enough to install a phone in her place. So there was no way for him to check on

63

her. "But there'd be times when she did leave a phone number where he could reach her. On these occasions, he'd call and either get no answer or be told Kitty had stepped out—when in fact, she'd gone off to make it with her Jewish lover on Long Island. Just how much of this Mike believed, no one seems to know. Yet it's obvious he endured it . . ."

A day came when Kitty Kelley saw no future for herself—or for Mike—holed up in a rustic New England community. She wanted to go where the action was—and decided Washington, D.C., was the place to be. She remembered Congressman Tom Foley's open invitation.

Foley was just a phone call away from Stockbridge. He listened to Kitty's belated acceptance of his offer to "introduce you to people in the proper places" in Washington. Foley told Kitty, "Come on down!"

Kitty Kelley was on her way . . .

6

One of the first people Kitty Kelley met on her arrival in Washington was Robert Gene "Bobby" Baker. It isn't clear whether the introductions took place in his Senate office or the infamous Quorum Club, the Capitol Hill hideaway where Senators and Congressmen discreetly sipped Scotch with their favorite lobbyists—or favorite party girls.

Representative Tom Foley was said to have arranged the meeting between the sweet 23-year-old newcomer from his home state and the 37-year-old former Secretary to the Democratic Majority in the Senate because he felt Baker had more clout than the freshman Congressman for landing Kitty a job.

Bobby Baker was about to switch from parliamentarian to prisoner. Even as Bobby and Kitty exchanged "hellos" the Justice Department prepared to prosecute Baker. A grand jury had indicted him for theft, tax evasion, and conspiracy in a pre-Watergate scandal.

The Bobby Baker saga—written in a town where fame can come swiftly and inexplicably and then vanish suddenly—was a twisted version of the Horatio Alger chronicles. The plot has a greenhorn youngster from the piney woods of South Carolina going to Washington and gravitating from a Senate page at age fourteen to a wheel of inordinate influence in the very highest echelons of government. In the select milieu to which he was elevated and enshrined, Baker was the trusted friend, confidant, and adviser of the men who exercised absolute control of the Senate power structure—just the ticket for Kitty Kelley's admitted lust for power brokers!

John F. Kennedy called Baker "the 101st Senator" and Lyndon B. Johnson confessed that "Bobby is the first person I talk to in the morning and the last one at night."

Even as a newcomer to the capital in 1966, Kitty could not have been unaware of all the scandalous press Bobby Baker had commanded for the preceding three years. He'd been forced to resign his Senate post in October of 1963 after disclosures that he peddled Congressional influence and had taken payoffs said to be in the hundreds of thousands of dollars for selling his political influence.

Bobby's bubble burst earlier that year during one of the FBI's exploratory forays into Congressional hanky-panky. Baker was named as the go-between in the exchange of huge sums of money, most of it purported to be campaign contributions, much of it from savings-and-loan officials sympathetic to the Democrats.

Baker was said to have pocketed substantial amounts for himself, which explained how the man who emigrated from Southern poverty achieved as much wealth as he had power. The scandal that swirled around him was an embarrassment to his surrogate father, Lyndon Johnson, who'd become Kennedy's Vice President two years earlier—and who only a month after Baker's resignation would succeed the assassinated JFK to the presidency.

Even before the ink dried on the big black headlines announcing the first disclosures of the scandal, Bobby Baker was no longer the first person Johnson talked to in the morning. Nor was he the last one that the Vice President chatted with at night. The wheeler-dealer had become *persona non grata* as LBJ distanced himself from Baker.

Yet his banishment from Johnson's good graces didn't crimp Bobby Baker's clout. Though he wasn't any longer in the driver's seat in the Senate, which had been his power base, Bobby still carried plenty of muscle. He continued to pull strings—and continued to pile up personal booty.

In 1972 a book was published that received scant attention from the press or the public. It was called *The Washington Pay-Off* and was written by lobbyist Robert N. Winter-Berger and was his story of corruption at the very top of the United States Government.

Winter-Berger named senators and representatives to whom he'd paid bribes. He described time, place and amount.

None of this was taken seriously by the press. This was preWatergate and few would countenance the thought that the very people running our country were among its most corrupt citizens.

Bobby Baker's role was described in detail in the pages of *The Washington Pay-Off*. But no part was more dramatic than the following exchange. Before publishing this account, Winter-Berger's publisher insisted he take a polygraph (lie-detector) test. He did and came through with flying colors.

Winter-Berger was sitting in the office of House Speaker John McCormack. Suddenly Lyndon Johnson, the President of the United States, strode into the room in great strides. In his agitation, he seemed oblivious of Winter-Berger's presence:

In a loud hysterical voice he said: "John, that son of a bitch is going to ruin me. If that cocksucker talks, I'm gonna land in jail." By the time he had finished these words he had reached the chair at McCormack's desk, sat down, and buried his face in his hands. Then I knew why he had come here, and I realized how desperate the situation must be.

To the best of my recollection at that shocking moment, McCormack said: "Mr. President, things may not be that bad." He got up and went to Johnson and placed a hand on his shoulder.

"Jesus Christ!" Johnson exclaimed. "Things couldn't be worse, and you know it. We've talked about this shit often enough. Why wasn't it killed, John?" When Johnson looked at McCormack I could see he was crying. He buried his face again.

"We tried, Lyndon," McCormack said. "Everybody did."

Johnson said: "I practically raised that motherfucker, and now he's gonna make me the first President of the United States to spend the last days of his life behind bars." He was hysterical.

"You won't," McCormack said helplessly.

"How much money does the greedy bastard have to make?" Johnson said. "For a lousy five thousand bucks, he ruins his life, he ruins my life, and Christ knows who else's. Five thousand bucks, and the son of a bitch has millions."

"We all make mistakes," McCormack said, glancing at me. "How could he have known, Mr. President?"

"He should have *given* him the goddam machines," Johnson said. "He should have known better. Now we're all up shit creek. We're all gonna rot in jail."

"We'll think of something," McCormack said. He rubbed Johnson's shoulder. "Please. Calm down. Control yourself."

In a burst, Johnson said: "It's *me* they're after. It's me they want. Who the fuck is that shit heel? But they'll get him up there in front of an open committee and all the crap will come pouring out and it'll be *my* neck. Jesus Christ, John, my whole *life* is at stake!"

"Listen, Lyndon," McCormack said, "remember the sign Harry had on his desk—THE BUCK STOPS HERE? Maybe we can make this buck stop at Bobby?"

"You *have* to," Johnson cried out. "He's got to take this rap himself. He's the one that made the goddam stupid mistake. Get to him. Find out how much *more* he wants, for crissake. I've got to be kept out of this."

"You will, Lyndon," said McCormack. "You will."

The President moaned. "Oh, I tell you, John, it takes just one prick to ruin a man in this town. Just one person has to rock the boat, and a man's life goes down the drain. And I'm getting fucked by two bastards—Bobby and that [defense attorney Edward Bennett] Williams son of a bitch. All he wants is headlines."

"It'll pass, Lyndon," McCormack said. "This will pass."

Johnson got angry. "Not if we just sit around on our asses and think we can watch it pass. You've got to get to Bobby, John. Tell him I expect him to take the rap for this on his own.

Tell him I'll make it worth his while. Remind him that I always
have."

Even if Kitty hadn't been aware of who Bobby Baker was
when she came to Washington, she certainly couldn't have
remained in the dark for long about Baker's power. For a day
came, barely four months after she exchanged hellos with him,
when he got her a job. It took just one phone call to open the
door of Minnesota Senator Eugene J. McCarthy's office on
Capitol Hill. Ostensibly, the job—"assistant to the Senator's
press representative," as Kitty once described it—was to have
been "on a temporary basis, for six weeks." Yet she remained
there for almost four years.

What prompted her to do that? What attraction did she find
in working with Senator McCarthy?

A possible reason may be gleaned from the statement she
gave to *Spokane Chronicle* columnist Harriet J. O'Connor during a visit home.

"In this office you are not told what to do—you look around
and decide in your own way how you can be most useful. That is
what makes it such a challenge."

In the beginning, according to Kitty, she was content to
"read and clip stories in newspapers and magazines that referred to Senator McCarthy." This she deemed excellent basic
training for the future—when she'd launch her career as an
author and put to full use her experience as a clip-and-paste
virtuoso.

What else did Kitty do while in McCarthy's Senate office?

Unavoidably, she couldn't have just been looking for written
material about the boss because, for a protracted period in late
1966 and early 1967 all the big headlines—especially in the
Washington Post—were generated by the daily diary of Bobby
Baker's criminal trial.

Could Kitty have been astonished or disillusioned—or could
she have experienced any other emotions—about the kingpin of
influence peddlers when she read of his other activities? Surely
she couldn't have missed the stories about the swinging private

parties Bobby tossed for his Senate cronies, usually at the residence of his secretary and paramour Nancy Carole Tyler, a former Tennessee beauty pageant queen, at other times at secluded hideaways that included a suite of private club rooms in a hotel across the street from the Senate Office Building. And always at those parties, the dazzling call girls went with the territory.

Did it shock Kitty to learn that these shenanigans went on at the very time Bobby was living with his wife Dorothy and their five small children in a $125,000 mansion in Spring Valley, a most fashionable and pricey residential neighborhood?

Is it possible that Kitty hadn't heard—or read—about Bobby Baker's relationship with Ellen Rometsch, the German mystery woman who frequented the Quorum Club and was preceded by a reputation for her intimacies with many of the boys on Capitol Hill?

Why, it must be asked here, did Kitty Kelley breathe nary a word about Ellen Rometsch in her *Jackie Oh!* book? Why, also did she fail even to mention Bobby Baker in that unauthorized biography of the former First Lady?

Of all the many women, with identities and without, who Kitty claimed had made it with John Kennedy as a Senator and President, why did she ignore the one woman she could have named—and named in a great big way: Ellen Rometsch?

Of all the key members in Baker's call girl stable, Rometsch had by far the most scandalous credentials possible to qualify for a starring role—certainly more ignominious than those of Judith Imur Campbell Exner, a non-member of Bobby's entourage whom Kitty parlayed into a *cause celebre*. Exner is the self-described former paramour of Chicago mob boss Sam (Momo) Giancana, and who claimed to also have made it with JFK.

Rometsch's significant role in the life of JFK—and by extension his wife Jackie—isn't only ignored totally by Kitty in the text of *Jackie Oh!*, but even in the real world Kelley refuses to discuss that obvious omission.

Of the fifty books listed in the *Jackie Oh!* bibliography, there's no mention of Baker's book, *Wheeling And Dealing*. That tome was co-written by noted author/Broadway playwright Larry S. King, most widely known for his *The Best Little Whorehouse In Texas*.

In an interview in the Spring of 1989, King told me: "Bobby Baker never brought up the name of Kitty Kelley while I was writing the book—and there was certainly no reason that I knew of then to ask about her."

Could Kitty's failure to mention Baker's role in bedding Rometsch with JFK have been a case of reciprocity— a *quid pro quo* that says: you didn't write about me in your book, so I won't dangle your name in mine . . . ?

Consider this:

In the Spring of 1978 the *Washington Post's* Style Section published an interview with Bobby Baker in which he told feature writer Myra MacPherson:

"The Kennedys are all mad at me for saying I fixed up John Kennedy with Ellie Rometsch, and Bobby had her deported."

Right after that, the article expands with a direct quote from Baker's book:

"Ellen Rometsch was a German lady-about-town who sometimes visited the Quorum Club and I introduced her to Jack Kennedy at his request. Bobby Kennedy couldn't get her out of the States fast enough when the newspapers revealed she'd had an affair with a Russian diplomat . . ."

Fraulein Rometsch was booted back to Germany after Attorney General Robert F. Kennedy discovered she had married a U.S. Army sergeant—ostensibly so she could emigrate to the United States and carry on suspected espionage activities in Washington for the Soviet Union.

Bobby, it's safe to conclude, wanted Rometsch out of the country to protect his brother, the President.

Another explanation of why Kelley never picked up on this most significant episode in JFK's sexual escapades may be lodged in the mistiness of a report that crossed my path while I was digging into Kitty's Washington past.

Soon after Tom Foley introduced Kitty Kelley to Bobby Baker—when the early Washington period of association with the Congressman's fellow Spokanite was still in full flower—a relationship developed between the two. In no time at all, Kitty was being squired by Baker and escorted to some of Washington's poshest eateries.

Baker took a deep liking to the diminutive blonde and let it be known that she was one of his special people who would perform "special favors" if he told her to. Thus Kitty rated favored-friend treatment, which many of Baker's other girls weren't receiving—such as being Bobby's companion on hegiras to his sumptuous resort motel in Maryland's Ocean City, The Carousel, a million-dollar enterprise that had fallen on hard times almost immediately after opening its doors. Yet the shaky financial situation didn't deter Baker from escorting his favorite woman of the moment to his Free State retreat.

When at the peak of his power as Secretary to the Democratic Party in the Senate, the entry of girls into the orbit of Bobby Baker's world was inevitable in a town such as Washington—a man's town that isn't run the way politicians' wives would probably prefer to run it. It's also an "action town," as any habitue of Capitol Hill knows. Thus Kitty became one of the "action girls."

The two women who played the most prominent roles in the Bobby Baker saga, both government employees, were his secretary Nancy Carole Tyler and her friend Mary Alice Martin, a former secretary in the office of U.S. Senator George Smathers, a Florida Democrat.

Nancy Carole and Mary Alice caused eyebrows in the capital to scoot skyward after it was disclosed they shared living quarters in a $28,000 townhouse newly-built in 1963, and whose owner of record was Bobby Baker.

The girls took occupancy of the digs sometime soon after Bobby signed the lease for the purchase. Little time passed before neighbors noticed how quickly Nancy Carole and Mary Alice became popular hostesses to a wide variety of visitors.

Reports had the visitors in the capital negotiating big deals, and attending "swinging" parties at the townhouse where, among other services, the guests were treated to such delights as dancers in harem pants and bathing with nude girls in champagne-filled tubs.

But untold numbers of girls were involved with Bobby Baker and his cohorts. Writing in *Look*, a national magazine of the time, at the height of the scandal, Keith Wheeler put in focus the roles girls played with artful precision:

"Washington enjoys the pleasant advantage of being plentifully stockpiled with girls. Flowing into and out of the myriad government offices, young single women outnumber everybody else. In this atmosphere an attractive girl can lead an active social life despite the population imbalance of males either suitable or capturable for wedlock. Just how active depends on the girl. She can confine it to the decorous role of embellishing numerous parties. It can lead her into an irregular but relatively stable liaison with a single admirer. If she's a 'swinger,' as the term is used locally, it may take her on weekends to such glamorous pleasure domes as Bimini, San Juan, Miami Beach, New Orleans, or the bullfights in Mexico City.

"She may find herself practicing part or full-time prostitution. One way or another, young women become more or less legal tender in the ancient and crafty commerce of getting things done. Thus, although the mere mention of it does seem to petrify some Washington sophisticates, it does not appear to surprise them that the rustle of skirts—sometimes in the process of being taken off—echoes as a faint silken obligato to the uproar over Bobby Baker.

"Such girls appear mainly as companions or adjuncts of the art of lobbying. Thus, one way and another, they also appeared in Bobby Baker's political, social and business orbits. Some knew him. Some had been at parties where he was a guest. Some were frequent guests at the Q Club."

But how many of those girls could say, as Kitty Kelley could—if indeed she'd not been to the other exotic locales from Bimini to Mexico City, that they were taken by Bobby Baker to his Carousel in Ocean City . . ?

Or, how many girls could say that Bobby Baker obtained a White House *Pass* for them?

That isn't a White House *Press Pass*, which any ordinary journalistic stiff gainfully employed by a legitimate publication or a radio-TV outlet is entitled to have.

A White House **Press Pass** allows the newsperson only a backdoor entry to the Press Room at 1600 Pennsylvania Avenue. **A White House *Pass*** gives the privileged bearer access to the front door of the Executive Mansion. That admission means the holder of the pass has been accorded an invitation of admittance by the President himself—and ostensibly is anointed with freedom to roam the stately residence from the Oval Office to the Green Room and to the upstairs living quarters and—even to its various bedrooms . . .

Later, we'll hear from former Senator George Smathers about the way his best friend, President John F. Kennedy, entertained women in the Lincoln bedroom and in other of the White House's comfortable and commodious compartments conducive to uninhibited love-making. This, while First Lady Jacqueline Kennedy was away, perhaps stomping over India on an elephant's back or sailing the rippling blue waters of the Mediterranean with a family friend, Greek billionaire shipping magnate Aristotle Onassis.

While he's admitted his part in arranging the affair Kennedy had with spy Ellie Rometsch, Bobby Baker has not described what services he may have performed for Lyndon Baines Johnson's extra-marital fancies after he became President following JFK's assassination.

Nor is it at all clear why Baker got Kitty Kelley into the Johnson White House with that special **White House Pass**.

The author sought some answers from the U.S. Secret Service which, in addition to guarding the President and his family, screens all persons who come into contact with them.

The significant question posed to the Secret Service was what connection Kitty Kelley had with the White House—and was there a record of the number of times she used her White

House *Pass?* The dates would have been useful in determining whether Kitty's visitations came at times when Lady Bird Johnson was off *Keeping America Beautiful.*

The response came in a letter dated June 13, 1988, written by Dana A. Brown, ATSAIC, Freedom of Information & Privacy Acts Officer:

"Reference is made to your Freedom of Information Act request concerning Kitty Kelley, received in this office May 19, 1988.

"A search for documents concerning Kitty Kelley was conducted and no documents were located in Secret Service files. *However, our records do indicate that Kitty Kelley was a White House Pass Holder at one time* [The emphasis is mine], but the records have routinely been destroyed in accordance with standard destruction schedules."

The Ronald Reagan White House press office also conducted a search of Executive Mansion files but turned up no information about Kitty Kelley—other than that she had sent requests for interviews with the President when she was researching her Sinatra biography.

This author spoke to Bobby Baker on several occasions about his association with Kitty Kelley, and found him most reluctant to talk about her. The response Baker offered me after I told him what I had already learned from other sources:

"You did your homework, George . . ."

Finally I said "Bobby, I want specific details of your relationship with Kelley."

"I'm embarrassed by your inquiry. It comes quite unexpectedly. Let me have a little time to mull it over—and I'll get back to you . . ."

Bobby Baker then became inaccessible to me for further interviews.

Precisely when Kitty Kelley and Bobby Baker parted company isn't recorded. But this much is fact:

Baker was indicted for theft, tax evasion, and conspiracy on January 6, 1966—a few weeks before Kitty accepted Tom Foley's invitation and trekked to the capital with Mike Edgley.

Sometime in mid-Summer of 1966, Baker introduced Kitty to Senator McCarthy, who hired her on the spot. Some months later, on January 28, 1967, the jury returned with a guilty verdict that doomed Bobby to serve, after all his appeals were exhausted, a 14-month term in Allenwood, a Federal penitentiary. That confinement ended on June 1, 1972.

If you ask why Foley, the freshman Congressman, hadn't found a spot in his own office for the young woman whose father helped in his election, there's a perfectly logical explanation. Such a move would have greatly displeased Heather Strachan.

Daughter of Mr. and Mrs. D. Alan Strachan and *The Woman* in Tom Foley's future, Heather was a lady of substance. Her father was a veteran senior official of the Agency for International Development who'd seen tours of duty throughout the Mideast and Far East while providing his daughter with the finest education she could want.

Like Foley, Heather had worked in Washington, D.C. for Senator Henry Jackson. Her fondness for the gangling Tom Foley developed after he moved over to the Democratic Central Committee which was organized in 1964 to campaign for the reelection of President Johnson. Heather had also made her way as a campaign worker with the Committee.

That November, LBJ handed Senator Barry Goldwater one of the worst thrashings any Presidential candidate ever received at the polls. On that same Election Day up in Washington State, Tom Foley battered his incumbent Republican rival and snatched away the Congressional seat the loser had held for more than a quarter century.

Even before he settled in Washington, Foley's eccentric streak became apparent. He decorated the blue walls of his office with paintings on loan from national galleries.

The decor was to a great extent the work of his administrative assistant and future wife, Heather Strachan, a plain-looking woman with straight, pulled-back, long brown hair who wore clothes no one would call particularly stylish. She was known to prance about the office in sneakers or thongs when the weather was warm.

Heather Strachan, some staffers began to say after he presence in Foley's office became permanent, "is indifferent to fashion but devoted to sensible shoes."

The woman Foley befriended and invited to live and work in Washington was too flashy to fit into the staid surroundings the future Mrs. Foley was painstakingly fashioning for the Congressman's office. So Kitty Kelley was bounced to Bobby Baker. And Kitty understood why—just as she understood why Bobby couldn't maintain his relationships with all the women he once courted after becoming mired in the preparation of his defense for the upcoming trial.

****

Landing in Senator McCarthy's office was, in Kitty's view, quite a feat. She said as much during a visit to her parents in Spokane.

She laid it on thick for *Spokane Chronicle* columnist O'Connor—barely sixteen months after Kitty had been put on McCarthy's payroll. In this interview, Kelley told the columnist that, although she was listed as a "secretary in the office" of the Senator, her role was "more accurately an assistant to the Senator's press representative."

"What is it like to work in McCarthy's office?" O'Connor asked.

"It is an education every day," Kitty responded.

She said she was amused by the number of people who ask her: "Have you ever seen Senator McCarthy?" She quickly answered the question:

"I see him every single day when he is in Washington."

The columnist poses The $64,000 Question: How did Kitty obtain the job in the Senator's office?

"I heard there was an opening on the staff on a temporary basis for six weeks," Kitty is quoted without so much as a fleeting reference to the roles Foley and Baker exercised on her behalf. "It was probably the only wise decision I have ever made. I thought it would be good experience—so I took the position."

Kitty was quick to point out that the office in which she worked was separate from the "McCarthy For President" headquarters. Only a month earlier, the Senator announced his intention to enter Presidential preference primaries in 1968 to oppose President Johnson's Vietnam War policies that were aimed at intensifying and escalating the conflict.

Kitty would eventually perform in the Minnesotan's campaign—but it wasn't a consummation that either Kitty or McCarthy wish to describe or even discuss today.

This author phoned the former Senator's law offices nine times between late November of 1988 and late February, 1990.

"He is on a trip to the Far East," a woman in his office said at the outset. After he returned from his mission, another response came: "He has your message and will get back to you." Finally, after repeated efforts to reach him, an aide finally phoned and said: "Senator McCarthy doesn't wish to be interviewed about Kitty Kelley . . ."

"McCarthy won't talk about Kitty," I was told by the aide, "because she is like a bad dream to him—in fact a nightmare!"

What exactly did that mean?

"See if you can find his estranged wife and ask her."

My search for Mrs. Abigail McCarthy was unrewarding. She had taken an editor's position with *San Francisco* magazine, but by the time I searched for her, the publication had folded and there was no forwarding address for her. Further efforts to elicit a response from her ex-husband, the one-time novice in a Benedictine monastery-turned college professor and politician, were fruitless.

"Mr. McCarthy will absolutely not talk about Kitty Kelley," the response echoed anew.

While Foley had appeared to have distanced himself from a one-on-one relationship with Kitty after his betrothal to Heather Stracham, no such disentanglement had come between Kitty Kelley and "Dizzy" Dicks once he alighted in the capital as Senator Magnuson's legislative assistant.

Nor was Dicks moved to tone down his close friendship with

Kitty after he had married his wife Suzanne despite her reported displeasure. Word was that Suzy didn't share her husband's
healthy admiration for Kitty Kelley.

In the years since, "Dizzy" Dicks has continued to make
progress in his political career. He rode on Senator Magnuson's
donkey for five years as the powerful Democrat's Legislative
Assistant, then in 1973 was elevated to Administrative Assistant.
He held that post until 1976 when Magnuson cut him loose from
the office to enable Dicks to make a run for a Congressional seat.

This ex-football player, whom we've found in pictures in his
University of Washington yearbook playing a rollicking, laughing Santa Claus handing out gifts to coeds at a campus Christmas
party, himself was handed an early Yule gift from the voters of
the Evergreen State's Sixth Congressional District. Dicks was
easily elected in the heavily-Democratic Kitsap County and has
since been reelected a half-dozen times. His hallmark in the
Lower Chamber has been his ability to demonstrate the aggres-
siveness and political shrewdness that were the hallmarks of
Senator Magnuson's combined staff in their golden days.

Out of the Halls of Congress, "Dizzy" Dicks cut a gay blade's
swath around Capitol Hill's precincts—he was a frequenter of
the same clubs that Bobby Baker attended before he went off to
do his hard time—and exuded much of the former Senate
Secretary's *Joie de vivre*. Yet Dicks, because of his enormous
physical size, was—and still is—looked upon more as the "jock-
type."

Thus, in that well-rounded mold, "Dizzy" served not only as a
legislative bellwether on defense and military subcommittees,
but as a frontrunner in the social whirl. Kitty Kelley was joined
on his calendar by other, even more attractive women.

In researching Kitty Kelley's peripatetic private life over the
years in Washington, it appears that only one other woman I
know of appears to have been more active in the Halls of
Congress—perhaps only because she has chosen to trumpet her
conquests with the written word in a different literary style than
Kitty's. She is Elizabeth Ray, who made screaming headlines in

the 1970s when she was revealed to have been a $150-a-week secretary to Ohio Representative Wayne Hayes, yet in reality was his mistress. The scandal erupted, in part, because Miss Ray admitted she couldn't type. No one could ever accuse Kitty Kelley of that, for during her four-year tenure in Senator Mc-Carthy's office, she pecked on typewriter keys with more than acceptable skill.

Most significant about the services Kelley rendered as a staffer in McCarthy's office was the depth of her dedication to her duties. Various sources revealed Kitty was so imbued with the spirited belief that McCarthy could dramatically change the politics of 1968 with his surprising run for the Democratic Presidential nomination that she plunged wholeheartedly into the campaign as a paid staffer.

She was caught up with the army of volunteers made up largely of professors, suburban housewives, and college students who believed McCarthy was providing a political focus to the widespread dissatisfaction with the bloodshed in Southeast Asia. Listen to Kitty's enthusiastic appraisal of the man she came to admire profoundly:

"He has a marvelous sense of humor—the kind that makes you think. Senator McCarthy doesn't settle for easy answers and he doesn't do things on the spur of the moment. He is a man of the highest principles.

"His staff has more than a political commitment to him—it's a personal commitment. He never asks you to work long hours— you just do it . . ."

How many hours Kitty put in working for McCarthy and his campaign have not been enumerated. But one former aide who didn't wish to be identified said:

"She worked well into the night . . . she was a lot of fun to have around after the sun went down. You could say she brought a lot of experience to the campaign from her greening at the knee of Bobby Baker . . ."

Another source brought her role into even clearer focus:

"Kitty Kelley was one of the most popular gals on the campaign trail. She was a heck of a better companion than some of the 'McCarthy kids,' the beat generation coeds who left their campuses with the guys who shaved their beards and hit the road with the Senator to work for him and give the political scene a fresh look."

How hard did she work?

"Very hard. One of the chores she performed was handing out autographed copies of the latest of McCarthy's four books as gifts . . . The Senator liked that. He thought it was very thoughtful of this young blonde loyalist to do that."

In the course of performing in McCarthy's Senate office and plodding with him in the campaign that nearly upset Vice President Hubert H. Humphrey for the nomination, Kitty found herself rubbing knees with the candidate's wife Abigail, a Phi Beta Kappa, a working theologian, a successful magazine writer, an attentive mother of four—and a tireless campaigner.

"She is one of the most intelligent women I have ever known." Kitty was quoted after the Senator's wife was awarded an honorary doctorate of letters by Trinity College in Washington, D.C., for her outstanding leadership in the ecumenical and liturgical movements in education."

Kitty would also speak highly of Heather Strachan, after she was married to Tom Foley on December 19, 1968—six weeks after former Vice President Richard Nixon defeated the sitting Vice President, Humphrey, for the Presidency.

The wedding took place on the southeast Asian island of Ceylon, in Colombo's St. Mary's Roman Catholic Church. The 29-year-old bride wore a Thai silk ivory-colored knee-length frock and a Spanish mantilla. Foley, ten years older than the woman he took for his wife was resplendent in a black single-breasted business suit but a startling contrast next to Heather— yet even more so aside the traditional temple dancers dressed in scarlet cloth, swathed into voluminous pantaloons and their chests adorned with multicolored beaded breastplates.

The story of the wedding was communicated on the Associated Press wire. It described how, after the ceremony, Foley and his bride drove to a road leading to the Strachan family house, then walked two-hundred yards along the road dappled with shadows from massive overhanging cassia and flame forest trees. As drummers beat a ritual tattoo, the dancers escorted the couple to the front entrance of the residence. Next day the bride and groom motored to the holiday resort of Nuwara Eliya in the mountains of central Ceylon.

Two clippings of the story of the wedding that ran the next day in the afternoon *Spokane Chronicle* and the morning *Spokesman-Review* were sent by Kitty's mother to Washington to enlighten her daughter about an event that she was already aware of, for she'd read one of those AP dispatches in the *Washington Post*.

When the Foleys returned to Washington after the new year, Kitty and Mike Edgley visited the newlyweds. They joined other well-wishers and drank toasts to the couple.

Kitty's friendship with the Foleys endured. And so had her penchant to champion Foley's causes whenever she could. For we find her giving her most enthusiastic endorsement for re-election to his ninth term in 1980.

Perhaps Kitty had in mind the clean bill of health that was given Foley in 1977 after he faced the most embarrassing moment of his long career in Congress. Foley, then Chairman of the House Agriculture Committee, was revealed to be one of three Congressional bigshots to have received contributions from Korean rice dealer Tongsun Park, the wheeler-dealer then at the center of a probe into influence-buying schemes.

Redfaced, Foley admitted he accepted a $500 contribution from Park in 1970—but fell over himself to point out that he subsequently rejected two of Park's requests for favors.

In a letter to the *Spokane Chronicle* published October 15, 1980, Kitty sang Foley's praises with this libretto:

"I have been living in Washington, D. C., for 14 years but I still consider Spokane my home. And since the District of Columbia remains a Federal colony without voting representation, I still consider Tom Foley my congressman.

"As a transplanted Spokanite living in the nation's capital, I admit my constituent claim on Congressman Foley is tenuous but I claim him nonetheless—and with pride!

"Tom Foley is respected for his brilliance, his honesty, and his unwavering commitment to public office. He is one of the few members of the House of Representatives whose effectiveness has not been diminished by scandal."

In 1980, Kitty Kelley could have counted on her fingers all the congressmen who'd been mired in scandal in the decade since Foley himself was shaken to his very foundations by that influence-buying probe. And she'd have had digits left over to take pen in hand and apologize to the *Chronicle's* editor who, without checking facts, gave credence to and published her fallacious letter.

We'll never know how much the endorsement from Kitty Kelley influenced Foley's re-election, which he won easily—and has done so four more times. However, the noted author of the unauthorized biographies—despite the millions of books she's sold in the time since—has not had another word published in the *Letters To The Editor* columns of the *Chronicle*.

It was soon after the election of '88, when Foley was returned to the House to serve his thirteenth term that fate smiled on the Spokane politician. By then he was Majority Leader, but bigger things were in store for him. For with the scandals that rocked Texas Congressman Jim Wright and forced him to resign in the face of threatened impeachment proceedings for violating House ethics rules, Kitty Kelley's favorite politician—the man she owed so much for getting her career launched in the city by the Potomac—was elected by his peers to serve as Speaker of the House.

Foley was sworn into office before a packed gallery. Two hundred on-lookers were guests of the one hundred Representatives comprising House membership. The Congressmen had been allotted two tickets each. Foley's went to his two favorite people.

It surprised no one to see Heather Strachan, now his wife, in one of the seats. His salary jump from $75,100 to $97,100 meant a $22,000 raise.

The guest attending on Foley's second ticket sat next to Heather. She was a bleached blonde wearing excessive makeup who drew some curious glances. She was Kitty Kelley.

No sooner had Foley been elected to the post then he was buffeted by a memorandum issued by the Republican National Committee which urged the Speaker to "come out of the liberal closet." It compared his record to that of Representative Barney Frank, a Massachusetts Democrat and an acknowledged homosexual. All hell broke loose from the opposition party.

The memo's author, Mark Goodin, promptly resigned as the National Committee's Communications director and conceded he had erred in judgment when he composed the letter in such a way as to raise questions about Foley's own sexual orientation.

The *New York Times*, seemingly eager to milk the story for all the mileage it could get, went on to report that "members of Congress, speaking privately with Mr. Foley have been told . . . that he is heterosexual. He has been married for 20 years."

No mention in that story of a report published in Washington newspapers the previous February about a young boys prostitution ring operating in the capital that allegedly involved members of Congress. Foley's name surfaced in that scandal as well, but nothing came of it.

Scores of legislators expressed displeasure and anger about the "dirty pool" the GOP's National Committee had played. In the midst of the bitterness and hostility the memo created, Kitty Kelley's voice remained strangely silent—possibly because she was too busy firing up the barbecue for the Nancy Reagan roast to sit down and dash off a vote of support for Foley to the *Spokane Chronicle* or *Spokesman-Review*.

Nevertheless, Kitty isn't known to have received demerits from Tom Foley for standing voiceless in the attack on him. He is still her good buddy and is likely to hold that place for as long as he inhabits the Washington political arena.

7

Before she took "alternative employment" at the *Washington Post*, Kitty Kelley was soaring on the eager hope that she'd come in for a landing on the White House lawn as a press secretary or some such significant appointment in the Democratic administration of President Eugene J. McCarthy.

In the waning days of winter, 1968, the Minnesota Senator seemed to be on his way to a face-off against former Vice President Richard M. Nixon, to win a four-year residency at 1600 Pennsylvania Avenue. McCarthy had thrown his hat into the ring when he entered the New Hampshire primary—and wrested 20 of the 24 delegates from incumbent President Johnson. A few days later, LBJ announced an end to the bombing of most of Vietnam—and his decision not to seek re-election.

"Kitty was doing cartwheels," I was told by a former McCarthy For President campaigner. "She had visions of attending Cabinet meetings and of taking notes for the President, transcribing them, and having private conferences with him in the Oval Office."

The vision took on a larger glow after McCarthy scored a somewhat diluted triumph over the non-candidate President in the Wisconsin primary. Then, following the assassination of Martin Luther King, McCarthy began flowing through the primaries like a river, handily winning races over minor opponents in Pennsylvania and Massachusetts. He had such smooth sailing because Vice President Hubert H. Humphrey sat on his hands for four weeks, assessing the advisability of running as his boss' replacement on the November ballot following LBJ's stunning refusal to seek a second term.

But by then Robert F. Kennedy, the former Attorney General and at that time a U. S. Senator from New York, leaped into the race and took dead aim at the White House formerly occupied by his brother JFK.

Kitty Kelley was "one of the girls" on the McCarthy campaign train that was roaring through the Midwest and following the sun that dreadful Spring day. She tried to keep a stiff upper lip. RFK had just shocked both the Minnesota Senator and Governor Roger Branigan by winning the Indiana primary.

"To her credit," said a former associate, "Kitty had a wonderful sense of political acumen. She seemed to be a born optimist and claimed to have considerable savvy when it came to forecasting election results."

This informant suggested, however, that Kitty's views on election trends and results often grew out of her "close ties with so many of Gene's inner sanctum."

"Was it pillow talk that gave Kitty such a hang?" I asked.

"Well," was the reply, "she slept on a lot of pillows." He went on: "Kitty didn't think that Bobby could gather enough momentum to win other significant primaries. She went into her assignment with renewed gusto as the campaign train, instead of heading to the preferentials in the District of Columbia, which was RFK's to claim as his own, steered a northwestern course to Nebraska.

"We all believed that Gene would take Oregon hands down, especially Kitty. She was from the neighboring state of Washington. She had the feel of the voters' pulses. She kept saying, 'There's no way I see victory for that carpetbagger [so labelled because RFK moved from Massachusetts to New York to run for the Senate because brother Edward M. Kennedy already occupied a seat in the Upper House from the Bay State].'"

But Primary Day in the Cornhusker State established that Kitty Kelley was no political Nostradamus. While the results didn't exactly demolish her credentials as a political pulse-taker, they did diminish them.

RFK did to McCarthy what the then-Attorney General had done to fraulein Ellen Rometsch after she was exposed as his brother Jack's bed-partner: Bobby sent the rival Senator packing. Unlike Ellen, who headed with her tail between her legs to Germany, McCarthy staggered into Oregon, Washington's sister state, still determined to do battle with the scion of the Kennedy dynasty.

Kitty felt right at home in the Beaver State and her confidence was never higher. "She was telling everyone that Gene couldn't possibly lose there. 'I feel it in my bones . . . I know the people in this part of the country. They can't go for that bum Bobby . . .' "

Kitty went to every rally held for McCarthy—almost always managing to sit in the front row of the spectator section, among his legion of young campaign workers. Photos taken at those rallies were shown to McCarthy campaign workers who uniformly identified her as the pretty blonde with shoulder-length hair, positioned always closest to the dais where McCarthy was orating. In almost all the shots she's seated with legs crossed, hem of her mini-skirt raised thigh high—sometimes higher—her face angled in an expression of intense concentration, her lifted hand cupping her chin as a convenient headrest.

"For most of the campaign, Kitty took the rubberbands out of her tresses. In that way she looked like another of the flower-children who were in the vanguard of Gene's campaign . . ."

Just as Kitty Kelley had predicted, McCarthy zapped Bobby Kennedy with his first election setback by winning the Oregon Presidential Preference Primary with 45 percent of the state's vote to 39 percent for the "carpetbagger."

But McCarthy's—and Kitty's—joy over the victory was to be short-lived.

"Kitty led the singing of *California, Here I Come* as the diesel-driven train clickety-clacked down the Pacific peninsula to the Golden State. She was really turned on. 'After we win this one, we're home free . . . Then it'll be Mrs. O'Leary's cow, the lantern, and the Chicago fire all over again . . .' "

Kelley was referring to the location of the Democratic National Convention in late August—in America's second-largest city on the shores of Lake Michigan. The Republican Party would stage its own quadrennial political gymnastics in Miami Beach—with no doubt whatsoever that Richard M. Nixon would be the party's choice.

A week after winning Oregon, the McCarthy campaign was routed by RFK who won the California primary—only to be gunned down by an assassin just before midnight on June 4th as he headed for a victory celebration.

McCarthy backers viewed Kennedy's death as a plus for their candidate because Kennedy had won primaries in which Humphrey finished poorly. But the Vice President came to the Convention in Chicago with a surprising number of delegates from states without primaries, to give him apparent control over his rivals. McCarthy delegates at the Convention took a hard line against Humphrey and the Administration he represented, giving rise to hopes for McCarthy's chances of ultimate success.

In the end McCarthy was defeated by Humphrey, who went on to lose the election to Nixon.

During the Democratic National Convention that week in late August, the Windy City was swept by an epidemic of protests by an amalgam of peace groups. The city's 11,900-member police force and some 13,000 National Guardsmen and Federal troops came out to greet them. By the time it was over, more than 1,000 demonstrators had been treated for tear gas inhalation and other injuries and 101 had been hospitalized; 192 policemen were injured, 49 hospitalized, and 63 newsmen were attacked by police.

The riots and the defeat of Senator McCarthy were enough for Kitty Kelley. She decided her future didn't lie in politics. She returned to the nation's capital and a job with *Washington Post* Editorial Page Editor Phil Geyelin. Kitty was offering herself for the only opening on the paper at the moment: research assistant on the editorial page.

Kitty was determined to make something of the opportunity at the *Post*. One of the first persons she befriended was Donna Crouch Mackie, a secretary to editor Ben Bradlee for some 20 years.

"Everybody on the paper knew her in those days," said Mackie, "She's easily one of the most outgoing, sparkly, friendly, energetic persons in the world. It's almost theatrical. I'm reminded of Shirley Temple's mama, who would always caution Shirley to sparkle before she went on camera.

"And Kitty has always *sparkled*.

"She constantly talked her head off about how badly she wanted to make it as a writer," said Mackie.

"But she also told me gobs of things—personal things—like about the trouble she was having with Mike Edgley. Kitty talked about how he beat her and abused her verbally. A lot of people know this, so I'm not telling tales out of school . . ."

What Mackie said about Kitty and her relationship with Edgley was repeated by more than a dozen people I interviewed in Washington. It seems that Mike went back to the bottle and hit it as often as the mood moved him—which was often.

"He was also on coke," I was told. "That's why a time would come some years later when Kitty would boot Mike out of the house and send him drifting off to the South Pacific to live the life of a beach bum."

Once Kitty's friendship with Bradlee's secretary, Donna Mackie, was established, she moved off for new conquests.

Kitty was at her "sparkling" best when she set her sights on one of the *Post*'s top male editors . . .

"It began one late afternoon when the editor put on his coat and headed out of the office for home," I was told by an observer at the scene—a columnist whose eye for gossip is still one of the best in the business. "When the editor got into the elevator, Kitty entered behind and, since there were a few other people in there, she found the opportunity to do what she does best. She pushed herself up against the editor so that he got a good feel of Kitty's tits . . ."

That was how it all started—or so the story goes.

"After a few more of Kitty's maneuvers in the elevator and other parts of the *Washington Post* building, the editor melted.

"Of course, as I have it figured, Kitty was playing the game of enticement with the editor not because she had the hots for *him*—but because she was looking to advance herself at the *Post*. If she could make it with him, the editor might consider her for a reporter's niche in the newsroom or in the features department."

In the weeks and months that followed these first encounters, rumors began circulating through the *Post*.

Ben Bradlee was distressed to learn that one of his editors was involved sexually with a low-level employee, whom he knew only as a note-taker at the daily editorial meetings. He felt she had no business carousing in the newsroom when her duties should have confined her to the editorial page section.

"Kitty finally persuaded the editor to drive her home evenings. At the outset he was merely dropping her off at her place, an apartment which she shared with Mike Edgley . . .

"You don't need a roadmap to figure what happened once the editor began tooling Kitty to her destination. Eventually, she invited him upstairs. After he departed and Kitty was alone, she phoned a friend and sighed:

" 'Guess who just left my bed?' "

Kitty identified the editor she claimed to have seduced.

"They set a pattern," I was told. "The editor would tell his wife he had to work on Saturdays. He'd make a brief appearance at the *Post*, then ring Kitty and head for her apartment in Southwest Washington.

"She doted on him. She made him feel powerful and young. She pressed him for a reportorial job. He would promise to 'look into it,' and he did. But to no avail."

Meanwhile the romance steamed up. The editor was so at sea

with his hellion that he found a new port for their maneuvers. The editor boldly steered his playmate to his place—whenever his wife was away, of course.

How long this cozy arrangement lasted hasn't been catalogued. But what's been recorded is the climax to the liaison, which came with stunning suddenness.

The editor's wife returned home one evening and found a pair of panties under the bed.

How the editor talked his way out of that one isn't known. What is certain is that the editor recognized that he was up to his hips in danger so he broke off the relationship. But not before lambasting Kitty.

He told her that he didn't think it very cricket of her to have baited his bedroom with her underwear. He had no doubt the panties were hers—and that the maneuver was designed to harpoon his marriage.

Kitty is said to have been amused that her golden opportunity for advancement came to nothing. "The bastard wasn't even a good fuck," she complained.

Weeks later, to make amends with his wife, the editor booked a flight on an airline to take the forgiving lady on a Bermuda vacation.

Arriving at Washington's National Airport just minutes before flight time, the editor went to the American Airlines reservation counter to pick up the tickets he'd ordered by phone a few days before.

"Oh, sir," the clerk said in a surprised tone, "your reservations were canceled. Your secretary called this morning and said you couldn't make the trip . . ."

The editor suspected who pulled that dirty trick on him, but could never confirm his suspicion.

****

Now that her voyage with the editor had washed up on the shoals of deceit, ambitious Kitty looked elsewhere to advance herself at the *Washington Post*. She did a complete flip-flop about her ex-lover's prowess in bed. While they had the bedsprings performing like pistons, she raved about the editor's virility, sighing with praise such as, "He's my gray headed ol' fucker. He keeps me going all afternoon . . ."

Now she constantly spoke of him with disdain, referring to him as "Old limp-pecker . . ."

Kitty soon found another fall guy at the *Post*—a reporter whose beat was one of Washington's most important centers of government activity.

"This newsman was close to Ben Bradlee because of his extraordinary work on the Pentagon Papers stories. The way I figure it," my source said, "if Kitty had caressed his loins and elevated him to a state of high titillation, he just might have gotten Ben's ear and put in a good word for Kitty."

The *modus operandi* Kitty employed to entice the editor into her lair proved just as effective in snaring the reporter. After Kitty kept brushing against him it was only a matter of time before they became lovers.

"Kitty soon had the reporter in her bedroom as one of her regulars."

This relationship too ended abruptly.

"They were on the Sealy-Posturepedic or Beautyrest—or whatever other recliner Kitty had in her pad at the time. It was around high noon and she was atop him, which happens to be her favorite position.

"All at once as she was pumping him the reporter began experiencing chest pains. Instantly Kitty interrupted the action, jumped out of bed, and helped the reporter dress. Then after draping something on herself, she escorted the poor guy downstairs to his car.

"She helped get him behind the wheel and said, 'Now you just hurry up and drive to the hospital. You must get yourself examined . . .'

"Her concern was to get him the hell out of her pad."

Meanwhile, Kitty hurried back to her apartment and phoned the *Washington Post*.

"I won't be in for a few days, she informed her department. "My sister is ill and I've got to be with her . . ."

Kitty had to allow a decent interval to pass away from the office—in case the reporter checked out.

"She wanted no part of answering questions like, 'What happened, Kitty . . . have you any idea of how he died . . . ?' "

At the hospital, the reporter was examined in the emergency room and his condition was diagnosed as a "myocardial infarction." The poor man *was* having a heart attack—and, instead of summoning an ambulance or driving him to the hospital, his enchantress sent him off alone to get medical attention.

The seriousness of the reporter's condition is catalogued by the hospital's records—and by his own account. He underwent triple by-pass surgery, recovered, returned to his duties as a reporter for the *Post*—but never looked Kitty Kelley in the eye again.

As she had after she broke off with the editor, Kitty once again spoke derisively about the reporter as a lover.

Kitty has that capacity, as I was told by a number of sources: While an affair is under way, the man in her bed is the best in the world sexually. Once she drops him—or he dumps her—she becomes Lady Scornful.

****

Not long after this episode, Editorial Page Editor Philip Geyelin and Editor Ben Bradlee confronted a problem involving Kitty Kelley that they had been aware of for some time. Even today, more than twenty years since she worked there, whenever the people at the *Post* talk about Kitty they laughingly refer to *The Case Of The Missing Notebooks* . . .

While Kitty Kelley "sparkled" aplenty in bedrooms with *Washington Post* biggies she believed could advance her career, her luminosity cast a different light up in the board room where Publisher Katharine Graham presided over the daily editorial conference.

When he hired Kitty, Geyelin assigned her to attend the editorial conferences with pad and pencil. She was told to take notes of discussions among the editors, then type the dialogue in a report and submit it to Geyelin.

After many months of such daily get-togethers, Geyelin and others at the meetings noticed Kitty was taking voluminous notes far in excess of what her daily transcripts offered: summaries of what the editors discussed.

Notes that involved research were her principal responsibility. For example, if Mrs. Graham, the chairperson of the *Washington Post* Company, suggested a profile on a member of Congress who headed a committee investigating some matter, Kelley was then duty-bound to dig up biographical and other material on that legislator—as well as to unearth clippings from the library on the subject under scrutiny—and submit the package to Geyelin right away.

"It became apparent she was taking notes during the editorial conference that had nothing to do with her research assignments," Geyelin said. "That strongly suggested she was collecting string for some other purpose, such as a book about, I guess, Katharine Graham."

What made the editor reach such a conclusion in 1971, when Kitty Kelley was still some two years from writing her first book, *The Glamour Spas?*

"That's all Kitty talked about." Donna Mackie said. "Of how she was going to write books and become a famous author . . ."

Geyelin discussed Kitty's curious exercises with his boss, Ben Bradlee. They decided what she was doing warranted looking into.

"Ask her to give you the notebooks," Bradlee snorted. "That'll tell you if she's pulling anything."

Geyelin went to Kitty.

"Do you have the pads in which you took notes of our meetings?"

"Yes."

"May I see them, please?"

"Oh, Phil, I brought them home . . . for safekeeping, you know . . ."

"Well, bring them to work tomorrow. Ben and I want to check out some things we discussed at the meetings which weren't in your reports . . ."

"Okay, Phil, I'll bring them in tomorrow . . . but I just hope I can find them."

Geyelin smelled something rancid.

Next morning Kitty showed up at the office—empty-handed.

She approached Geyelin, who was prepared for the snow job he knew Kitty would try to give him.

"Oh, Phil, they're not at home . . . I remembered last night . . . it all came back to me . . . I threw them away . . ."

"Why'd you do that, Kitty?"

"Because I didn't think the information in them would be of any further use to the *Post*—and I didn't want them to fall into wrong hands . . ."

Geyelin went to Bradlee's office and reported his conversation.

"Do it now," Bradlee said quietly. "Fire her!"

Although he couldn't have made it clearer to Kitty Kelley that she was fired, a time came 15 years later when we find Phil Geyelin giving Betty Culberti, a *Los Angeles Times* staff writer, a watered-down version of how Kitty left the newspaper. The interview was published on September 26, 1986.

"I asked for her resignation and received it," Geyelin said after explaining that Kitty took notes during editorial conferences "that had nothing to do with her research assignments . . ."

In the same article, Kitty Kelley disputed that version of the way her employment at the *Post* was terminated.

"I do not remember Phil Geyelin asking me to resign at all," Kitty protested. "I did take copious notes, indeed. That was my job.

"What I do remember is a great deal of bad blood between Geyelin and Ben Bradlee. I got into the crossfire between these two."

Kelley claimed her problem began when Bradlee assigned her to research the expository series of articles the newspaper broke on the Pentagon Papers. That work, Kitty insisted, took her away from the editorial staff—and angered Geyelin to the point where he clashed with the boss. Kitty's assertion that there was cannonading between Bradlee and himself, prompted Geyelin to retort:

"I never had any crossfire with Bradlee. The Pentagon Papers didn't have anything to do with my decision."

Bradlee agreed with Geyelin's recollection in only one respect:

"As far as getting caught in a crossfire, that's off the wall."

Bradlee then closed the file by putting into proper perspective how Kitty Kelley's tenure at the *Washington Post* actually ended:

"We canned her!"

8

After her firing from the *Washington Post*, people in the editorial department composed a commemoration for her departure. One version began:

"Before the editors and staff on the *Post* had ever become acquainted with the body of her work, they knew the work of her body . . ."

One staffer described her tenure with the newspaper this way: "She seemed to be on the make for practically any of the big shots she felt could advance her career. But it didn't work at the *Post*."

The staff was wise to her antics and aware of her obsessive drive to get ahead. So they watched in amusement as she dispensed her charms. The way Kitty let men score with her was good for gossip and laughs. She began as a research assistant, and at the time of her departure, she was a research assistant.

But the former "Miss Available" at the *Washington Post* wasn't without her scrapbook of personal press clippings. All during her days with the *Post*, Kitty scratched out copy for the monthly *Junior League Newsletter*. She'd transferred her membership in the organization from the University of Washington. She flashed the news to the *Spokane Chronicle*, which promptly

97

announced in the women's section that Kitty was "a reporter" for the monthly handout.

Kelley wrote with considerable regularity for the *Newsletter* throughout her McCarthy and *Washington Post* years. But writing for house organs offered no promise of recognition as a journalist. Friends like Janet Donovan and Donna Crouch Mackie remember that Kitty was deeply depressed when she couldn't find a publication that would give her employment—or even a free-lance assignment.

Later, after she had broken the ice and sold her first major story to the capital's No. 2 newspaper, the *Washington Star-News,* she described those lean days:

"I'm a writer who barely pays the rent by grinding out articles like 'How to Lose Weight and Seduce A Senator.' "

That piece was a prelude to the even more successful story on the protein-sparing fast, under the guidance of Dr. Robert Linn, a Pennsylvania osteopath who was treating overweight people on a production line. This was the article that attracted the attention of publisher Lyle Stuart. As chronicled earlier, Stuart then dissuaded her from writing a follow-up story.

The year was 1972 and her future wasn't promising. Money and work were scarce. But Kitty would come up with a shortcut to a quick buck. She'd steal and peddle a story someone else had written!

****

The victim of Kelley's machinations, Barbara Howar, needs no introduction to a vast television audience familiar with the *Entertainment Tonight* show, nor to those who've read some of her best-selling books of the last 15 years.

She is a polar opposite of Kitty. A statement Mrs. Howar gave to *People* magazine puts it in clear focus:

"I never have been any good at sleeping around to get what I want. If I'd had the ability to do that, you wouldn't have seen me for my dust. It never crossed my mind to get in bed to further myself."

These words were published in early 1976. It was a rough

time for Barbara Howar. Her first novel, *Making Ends Meet*, was yet to be published. The breakup of her marriage to realtor Ed Howar for whom she bore two children was traumatic.

The marriage self-destructed after Barbara had an extra-marital affair with a White House adviser. Ed Howar and four private detectives made a middle-of-the-night surprise call on Barbara and her inamorato in a love nest in Jamaica, West Indies.

She and Ed Howar reconciled briefly, then divorced in 1967.

Soon afterward she began a three-year affair with editor-writer Willie Morris and was also a sometime companion of Henry Kissinger. Barbara's connection with Washington society began with Lyndon Johnson when she became a volunteer in LBJ's 1964 presidential campaign. Her earliest duties had her performing as Lady Bird's hairdresser, later as fashion adviser and chaperon to the Johnson daughters.

Those links with the White House and First Family gave Barbara the wherewithal to write a juicy autobiography, "a real insider's look at Washington" that would ultimately be entitled *Laughing All The Way* and become the number one best-seller on the *New York Times* list where it had a long tenancy.

But before that, Kitty Kelley—seemingly not cured of her suspected bad habits in Arizona—meandered to a garage sale at Barbara Howar's 31st Street house in Georgetown. Howar, at the time, was in the doldrums. Her syndicated TV interview show, co-starring Joyce Susskind, had been taken off the air.

Barbara faced hard times, something she hadn't encountered before. She'd come to Washington from Raleigh, North Carolina, expecting riches and power. Her mother, along with the editor of the *Raleigh Times*, for whom Barbara had worked for two years, had encouraged her to go.

"But my father had been opposed to the move," Howar wrote, telling me vehemently that Washington was a den of wolves and thieves and that all politicians were whores and crooks. His message proved ultimately to contain much wisdom, but I was not to be deterred from my glamorous date with destiny. I was going to plunk down in the middle of the action—conquer Congress, so to speak. There was never any question in my mind but that I would do all this from a vertical position."

Barbara came, saw, and conquered—for in the next eight years she had not only married and was enthusiastically welcomed at the White House. but also became known as the golden-haired socialite of the Great Society. She was the kinky, trendy, swinging hostess *par excellence* of the nation's capital. Her kooky clothes, her shameless cultivation of power figures, her refreshing candor, her radical-chic camaraderie, and her celebrity-studded parties at her 31st Street Georgetown house gave her a status that few others in Washington ever enjoyed.

Yet, in 1972 she was living less lavishly, if not actually "sitting on an earth floor eating flower seeds," as said in a published interview.

Then in January of 1973 Barbara Howar saw hope on the horizon. She was writing an autobiography that had the promise of big sales. Her agent had negotiated a First Serial Rights sale with the *Ladies Home Journal* and there were other subsidiary income possibilities. There would be syndication to newspapers and, most significantly, a mass-market paperback edition sale.

But until then Barbara was strapped and she decided that one way to raise revenue was to dump some of the artifacts and furniture from her spacious Georgetown house. She planned to move to a smaller, more affordable residence.

So she announced a garage sale. When the doors were opened shortly before noon to admit the crowd, people were ushered into Barbara's first-floor living room. After the sale got under way, Howar cast an eye around and caught sight of a heavily made-up pudgy blonde sitting on a couch. She seemed to be out of place in the crowd largely composed of conservatively attired and coiffeured ladies from the middle and upper echelons of Washington society.

"Who is she?" Barbara asked.

"Kitty Kelley," she was told.

"Who is Kitty Kelley?"

"She worked for the *Washington Post.* Now she's a free-lancer."

"Kitty Kelley," mused Howar. "A cute name . . . I wonder what she's doing here . . . I wonder if she's the blonde who used to drop in at the White House when Lady Bird was . . ." The words drifted off and Miss Howar said nothing more.

But Barbara Howar had a far different view of Kitty Kelley's name a few days later when she heard it again.

"Barbara," the voice on the other end of the phone whispered. "You're getting your book excerpted in the *Washingtonian.*"

"I'm what!"

"You don't know about it?"

"Certainly not. It's going to be condensed in the *Ladies Home Journal.*"

Howar was thunderstruck. How could the small monthly magazine that had only recently begun publishing have gotten her book?

Howar was on the horn at once with *Washingtonian* editor John A. Limpert.

"Yes, I bought it from Kitty Kelley," he answered. "She told me she purchased the manuscript for two dollars from an elderly woman who had bought a small Sheraton table at your garage sale. Kitty said the manuscript was in the drawer and that the woman had no use for it."

Barbara Howar was beside herself with rage.

"That manuscript isn't hers to sell!" the author fairly shouted. "It was stolen from my house! I kept it in my writing studio on the third floor. The upper floors of my house were off limits for the garage sale. People were to stay only on the first floor and bid for the items on sale there. That woman had no business going upstairs. She's a thief! She stole my manuscript, and I tell you right here and now that I'll sue your butt off, and hers as well, if you dare to publish one word of it! *I want that manuscript returned!*"

The *Washingtonian's* lawyers took the issue in hand and, after

a lapse of considerable time spent in examining the legal ram-
ifications, decided the magazine would have no defense against
a damage suit if it so much as published the material. The only
way excerpts from the manuscript could be published was with
the author's or her agent's consent.

Advised by the lawyers that he couldn't run *Laughing All The
Way* because it wasn't Kitty Kelley's property to sell, the editor
notified the literary buccaneer that he couldn't publish the
story. Later he explained publicly why he bought the pirated
manuscript:

"The *Washingtonian* was a very small magazine back then,
with very little going for it. We were just trying to have some
fun and get some attention. We were surprised that Barbara
took it as seriously as she did."

Barbara took it very seriously. In fact, it cost her some
$16,000 in lawyers' fees to extricate the script from Kitty's
clutches. The unpublished writer refused to stop peddling the
plundered story of Howar's life no matter how often Howar
tried to cut her off at the pass.

Even as the *Washingtonian* flap ended, another one rose to
hector Howar . . .

Over at the *Washington Post* there was yet another staffer
whom Kitty Kelley had wooed during her employment at the
paper in the hope that this friendship could engineer a good
word for her advancement. She was society columnist Maxine
Cheshire who, in the very month when Kitty got her hands on
Howar's manuscript, had had a horrendous run-in with Frank
Sinatra.

It happened at a pre-inaugural party in Washington's Fairfax
Hotel for President Nixon's second-term swearing-in ceremony.
When Sinatra arrived at the hotel, he was hot behind the ears.
He'd just left the Kennedy Center where comedian Pat Henry,
who was on the bill with Frank, wasn't allowed on stage because
he hadn't been cleared beforehand by the Secret Service. Sinatra blew his cork and stormed out of the center, leaving entertainer Hugh O'Brian to fill in for him.

Accompanied by the recently-divorced Barbara Marx, ex-wife

of Zeppo Marx and former Las Vegas showgirl who was soon to become his fourth wife, Frank was met in the lobby by a phalanx of reporters and photographers. One of these was Maxine Cheshire, whom Sinatra had encountered with some unpleasantness a few months earlier at a dinner.

"Mr. Sinatra," Cheshire asked back then, "do you think your alleged association with the Mafia will prove to be the same kind of embarrassment to Vice President Agnew as it was to the Kennedy Administration?"

It was a combative question to toss out at a social function, yet the Chairman of the Board answered it with uncharacteristic self-restraint:

"Nah, I don't worry about things like that. I look at people as friends and that's all I worry about . . ."

To say Sinatra hadn't been stewing all those many months would be a gross understatement in light of what ensued when he saw Cheshire making her way to Barbara Marx at the Fairfax. The next Mrs. Sinatra was holding Frank's arm and Cheshire's approach appeared like an attempt to interview her.

Suddenly, Sinatra's face turned beet red and he went into an apoplectic rage.

"Get away from me, you slut!" he roared. "Go home and take a bath. Print that, Miss Cheshire."

Then he wheeled around and addressed the guests standing behind him. "You know Miss Cheshire, don't you?" he started up again slowly. "That stench you smell is coming from her."

Turning back to the columnist once more, he shouted in his loudest voice:

"You're nothing but a two-dollar cunt. C-U-N-T. You know what that means, don't you? You've been laying down for two dollars all your life."

Sinatra then pulled two one-dollar bills from his pocket and stuffed them into the drink Cheshire was holding.

"Here, baby," he goaded, "that's what you charge . . ."

Then Sinatra took Barbara's arm. "Let's get the hell out of here," he said and led her out the door.

Cheshire was able to shake off Sinatra's outburst and go back to her typewriter to continue her gossip society outpourings—and to zero in on Barbara Howar's autobiography that she'd received from Kitty Kelley. She selected choice items from the unpublished script, and they popped up with such recurring frequency in her column that they nearly drove Howar out of her mind. And she was unable to put a stop to them—until her lawyers went after Kitty.

Even then, it was too late to stop Cheshire from giving the autobiography a monumental put-down—months before it was published—in what amounted to a *Washington Post* review.

Editor Limpert also was sour on the book, damning it in his magazine, the *Washingtonian*. "It reads like a reject from *True Confessions*," he wrote.

When the book made it to the bookstores, Cheshire and Limpert ate crow. For it became a major best-seller and remained one for more than six months. Its success paved the way for Barbara Howar's next book and led her to renewed TV stardom on *Entertainment Tonight*.

Kitty Kelley continued to insist that she'd done nothing wrong, that she hadn't pilfered the manuscript but merely "bought it from the elderly woman" at the garage sale.

"For all the furor over the matter," Kitty said in her defense, "you'd think I purchased a copy of Dr. Teller's atomic secrets."

Kitty's first legitimate writing project was a feature for the *Washington Star-News* on fighting flab alongside rich matrons at the Golden Door Spa—a first-person piece that was totally accurate insofar as she describes how ". . . a moose-size masseuse takes me in hand. Appraising my short, squatty body, she says, 'Well, this is bad, but I've seen worse . . .'"

Kitty Kelley had nothing more to say about the manuscript that worked its way from Barbara Howar's third floor to the *Washingtonian* and *Washington Post*, but Barbara Howar had plenty to say at the time, and today. More than eighteen years after the fact, Mrs. Howar still fumes when the incident is mentioned.

"The real crux that explains the weirdness of Kitty Kelley," she said in a recent interview, "is that she believed she owned my manuscript. She felt she was entitled to it, to print excerpts to skim my book buyers, or embarrass me. Even if she had paid ten million dollars for [the typescript] *it wasn't hers!*"

"Darlin'," Howar sighed, "I have gotten down with that dog and come up with fleas . . ."

Barbara went from *Entertainment Tonight* to her own syndicated TV show, *Unauthorized Biography*, and was asked not long ago if Kitty Kelley, might be profiled on one of the upcoming segments.

Howar responded simply:

"I have neither the stomach nor the time for her. When I worked at *Entertainment Tonight*, somebody asked me, 'Do you want to do a piece on Kitty Kelley?' and I said, 'Not unless it's her obituary.' "

After publication of her free-lancer's *Washington Star-News* article making fun of wealthy matrons who participate in "Fat Farm Follies," Kitty made a ten-strike in 1973 when she landed an interview with U.S. Senator Joe Biden, the Democrat from Delaware. People from beyond the outer perimeters of his political bailiwick will recall that Biden made a bid for the 1988 Democratic Presidential nomination in a seven-man race. But Joe had to take his hat out of the ring in embarrassment after he was found to have "plagiarized" speeches from other political figures. Biden employed much of the style of Kitty Kelley: taking someone's text, changing a word or two here, adding another word or three, subtracting still another word or two here and there, then dispersing the manuscript as a personal literary creation.

Biden was fifteen years away from the big race in late 1973, when Kitty Kelley interviewed him. The Senator—then newly elected and the youngest member of the Upper House—was still mourning the death of his wife and small daughter in a highway accident.

Biden had met Neilia at poolside in Nassau. "I said to my friend, 'I get the blond.' So we ended up flipping a coin and I won . . . Neilia and I hit it off immediately . . ." And not long afterward they were married.

105

Neilia helped mastermind his campaign for election to the Wilmington City Council. Two years later, the Bidens decided—brashly—to tackle the U.S. Senate. Joe started running in 1970 for the '72 race. By then he and Neilia had two sons and an infant daughter, nicknamed Caspy because she reminded them of the comic strip character *Casper, The Friendly Ghost.*

No one gave Biden much chance to win the race against the popular two-term Republican incumbent Hale Boggs, the former Governor and Congressman. Yet, as popular as he seemed to be, Boggs lost to Biden—by fewer than 3,000 votes—because he had ignored his rival.

At 29, Joe Biden had it all. A celebration followed his election. Then in December, one month before he would be sworn into office, he went to Washington to interview applicants for staff jobs. Neilia and the children remained behind to prepare for the Christmas holidays just ahead.

Just six weeks after being elected Biden received a call in his new Senate office. While Neilia was driving home after shopping for a Christmas tree their station wagon had been struck by a truck. Neilia and one-year-old Caspy were dead; the two boys, then two and three, were critically injured.

For more than a year following the tragedy, Biden refused to talk to the press. The fact is that he wanted to resign his Senate seat the day he got the phone call. Only the persuasive pleas to stay from Mike Mansfield, then Senate Majority Leader and former Vice President Hubert Humphrey, who sat with Biden in his office, kept him anchored in Washington. He was sworn in at his sons' hospital bedsides.

The period following Neilia's death was one of despair. It was also a time that attached words like "arrogant" and "shallow" to Biden's name. He developed considerable antagonism toward the press, and once told a labor leader waiting to see him to "stick it."

When Kitty Kelley made her pitch for an interview, Biden had been softened by his staff. They told him it was time to talk to a reporter. Kitty had come along just when Joe had finally capitulated to the pleas.

Kelley caught Biden with his media savvy down—the worst position in which to be in the crossfire of an interrogator as tenacious as Kitty.

"Tell me, Senator Biden, about your love life with your lovely wife . . ."

The question totally disarmed the widower and he promptly burst out with confessions about his dates with his future wife—and details about the sex life they shared together.

Kelley looked around the office and saw pictures of his wife and children on the walls. That observation prompted her to question Biden at greater length about his wife and the sex activity they shared.

"She sat there and cried at my desk," Biden recalls with a shudder. "I found myself consoling her, saying. 'Don't worry . . . it's okay. I'm doing fine.' I was such a *sucker*. I opened up and told her the most intimate secrets of my marriage, never expecting her to shaft me the way she did."

In the story she wrote for the *Washingtonian*, Kitty described Biden's office—because of the array of family photos displayed—as "a shrine to Neilia." That provoked the harshest rebuke from Biden, who phoned the magazine to protest this fiction to editor Limpert.

Biden not only rapped Kitty for writing of his photographic display that it was "a monument . . . his wife's tombstone," but also for shading with her own words an anecdote Biden related about a conversation with Missouri Senator Thomas Eagleton that involved a joke with an anti-Semitic punchline, which was off-the-record.

Kitty included it in her story, as she did all the other ammunition she obtained during the interview to shoot down Biden.

Kitty was forced to write a full-fledged retraction in a subsequent issue of the magazine. She was compelled to admit that Biden had told the Eagleton anecdote merely to illustrate anti-Semitism he'd encountered in a certain Delaware county—and that the photo display she had seen on the Senator's wall wasn't his wife's "tombstone," as she wrote in the article.

The "scoop" that Kitty sold to *Washingtonian* for $500 and then had to retract, should have alerted Limpert that Kelley was no triple-threat as a reporter.

Today, Limpert says he doesn't regret having published the Biden piece or almost printing Kitty Kelley's pilfered story on Barbara Howar's life.

But a voice of conscience does speak out in Kitty Kelley's encounter with Senator Biden. It is the voice of Janet Donovan, Kitty's then close friend from their World's Fair days in New York.

"After I read what Kitty had written," Donovan said, "the only thing I wanted to point out was that Kitty did an awful thing to Joe Biden. I called her and told her so. I couldn't imagine anyone turning something so awesomely painful [the family tragedy] to their own advantage. It must have caused him enormous pain."

Indeed it had. Kitty had caused so much pain to Senator Biden that it was *fifteen years* before he granted another interview to any reporter. And when he did, he spoke for the first time to *Washington Post* staff writer Lois Romano, who wrote a 4,000-word feature that spoke about Biden's entry into the Presidential sweeps—yet stressed with thorough candidness the shafting Kitty Kelley gave the Senator.

Despite Kitty's flawed literary endeavor at the *Washingtonian* she got lucky. Her earlier newspaper story on the Golden Door Spa attracted an agent's attention and led to a contract for a paperback book on the subject.

9

"To thoroughly research this book, I decided to spend one week at each spa, participate in every program, follow the diet, do the exercises, talk to the guests, interview the employees and then tell the truth, the whole truth, and nothing but the truth, so help me God . . ."

What Kitty Kelley didn't tell *Spokane Chronicle* society columnist OJ Parsons after her first book, *The Glamour Spas,* was published in 1975 as a paperback original by Pocket Books, was why she undertook the project. She did it to enjoy the facilities of expensive spas without paying for them.

She spared none of the fat farms her poison darts—but zeroed in particularly on La Costa Hotel & Spa in California.

This luxurious eight-thousand-acre resort she described as "the West Coast watering hole for the mob," saying it was built with "Teamster money and Mafia know-how." Then Kelley went on to say La Costa "was a natural meeting place for John Dean, H. R. Haldeman and John Ehrlichman, who went to the resort to plan part of the Watergate cover-up."

She concluded that the meetings took place there because of its close proximity to then-President Richard Nixon's Western White House in San Clemente, less than thirty miles up the California coast. Of course, there never was a word in all the millions of words of Congressional hearings concerning Watergate to support this electrifying claim. As she did so frequently in her subsequent books, Kelley came to a false conclusion based on weak evidence. She was far from the truth about why the three White House bigs were at La Costa in early January of 1973.

When editor Herb Alexander met with Pocket Books' publisher Leon Shimkin and went over a list of proposed books recommended by the editorial staff, they agreed Kitty Kelley's proposal to write a book on the reducing shrines was a good idea.

She was offered a modest $1,500 advance, and jumped at the opportunity to write her first book. Her agent was David Obst, who just barely fitted Kitty into his busy schedule. He was inundated at the time by a cascade of book ideas from Watergate's famous and infamous figures-turned-authors. But Obst had liked the newspaper feature she had done on a fat farm and thought it might be a good idea to expand the article into a book.

"My agent says," Kelley would tell us all later, "the only things that sell are sex, fat, and violence."

Kitty went whole hog, so that by the time the book left the bindery, its cover stressed that this was "the spicy inside story of the fabulous fat farms where Liza Minnelli, Barbra Streisand, Joan Kennedy . . . reduce and relax." Lawyers from Pocket Books' parent company, Simon & Schuster, meticulously went over the finished manuscript to insure that it was libel-free. They insisted that Kelley corroborate claims she attributed to such fat farm devotees as Ava Gardner, Claire Booth Luce, Mamie Eisenhower, Jessica Mitford, Kim Novak, Zsa Zsa Gabor, Dinah Shore, Frank Sinatra, Joshua Logan, Jack Nicklaus, O. J. Simpson, and Buddy Hackett. But the legal eagles were not as scrupulous in checking out the reason Dean, Haldeman, and Ehrlichman were at La Costa. Since all three had already been branded evil masters of the cover-up and would soon be heading to Federal prison, none was likely to sue if Kelley was inaccurate.

Actually, as the FBI already knew, the trio was on the Coast to hammer out a deal with Frank Fitzsimmons, President of the International Brotherhood of Teamsters. Fitzsimmons had one million dollars in cash to pass on to Nixon for three favors: springing the imprisoned Teamster ex-President James R. Hoffa from the Federal penitentiary, ending the Justice Department surveillance of Chicago Mafia chieftain Anthony Accardo and others mixed up in Teamster monkey business (including the financing and building of the La Costa Hotel and Spa), and dropping all other investigations by the Attorney General into the union's activities.

If Kitty had been diligent in her research, she would have learned the true story. It had no bearing on the Watergate coverup.

After the meeting at La Costa, Fitzsimmons boarded Air Force One and flew back to Washington with Nixon. On the flight, Fitzsimmons is reported to have said: "Mr. President, I know you've been in touch with the gentlemen I met earlier today at my hotel [Dean, Haldeman, and Ehrlichman]. I don't believe they told you what we're prepared to pay for the request I put on the table."

Fitzsimmons reportedly went on:

"You'll never have to worry about where the next dollar will come from in any future campaign you're involved in, nor after you leave the White House . . . We're going to give you one million dollars up front, Mr. President . . . and then there'll be more to follow to make certain you are never left wanting."

A few days later, in Las Vegas, White House aide Charles Colson assertedly received a first installment of five-hundred thousand dollars. Two months later, on March 21, 1973—still some five months before Kitty Kelley started on her free-loading tour of thirteen of the nation's fat farms—the FBI concluded that the full million had been paid to Nixon's envoys. For here are the words spoken by the President in an Oval Office taped conversation with John Dean while discussing the Watergate burglars' demands for huge sums of hush money:

"What I mean is you could get a million dollars . . . And you could get it in cash. I know where it could be gotten . . . We could get the money. There is no problem in that . . ."

****

In order to obtain material for her book, Kitty claims she promised anonymity to spa employees and others who did the "tattling," as she put it. Result: Unattributed quotes pour like Niagara Falls in *The Glamour Spas*. In fact, they outnumber identified sources in some chapters in ratios as high as twenty-to-one.

But Kelley didn't spare the public figures from her caustic prose. "People in the public eye have no anonymity, of course," she told columnist OJ Parson during the visit home after the book was published. Months earlier, while gathering material for the manuscript, Kitty stopped in Spokane and let her mother and several friends read what she was writing and listen to tapes of those she'd interviewed.

"I read the book, which is hilarious," Delie Kelley later told Parson. "No, I wouldn't call it pornographic, but I also wouldn't recommend it for Sunday School reading . . ."

What made the book palatable for her mother was the emphasis Kitty placed on her rejection of the casual sex that she stressed was readily available at the spas. Kitty also claimed she turned her nose up at "kookie medical treatments" and other off-the-wall services the spas provided.

Pressing her theme that she was out to "tell the truth, the whole truth, and nothing but the truth . . ." Kitty then wrote:

"I kept wondering what it would be like to go to one of those glamour spas and have cucumber paste spread all over my face, or be covered by warm mud . . .

"Within the limits of libel and literary license, I have done exactly what I intended, although honesty compels me to admit a few deviations from my original plan. I didn't always stick to the eight-hundred-calorie-a-day diet at The Bermuda Inn, and I refused to take the hormone diet shots at Soboba Del Sol, nor did I go for face lifting, fanny tuck and mammoplasty the doctor recommended."

She did however participate in exercise classes, calisthenics, massages, hydrotherapy, and beauty lessons offered by the various spas she visited—and, of course, pigged out on the sometimes delicious but, all too often, dreary food served at those reducing shrines.

"I was massaged, manicured, pedicured, pampered, preened, stretched, steamed, slimmed and pounded in the course of my research, and only when I was home and left to my own devices did I manage to undo every bit of it," she went on.

Kitty said she started her assignment with illusions of grandeur, fully expecting to walk into golden mansions and meet movie stars, models, and all the "beautiful people" who populate the pages of *Women's Wear Daily.*

"Alas," she sighed, "what I expected did not square with what I found. After all the huffing and puffing, I now know there is no such thing as the 'good fairy' of fat."

Certainly there was no such fairy when it came Kelley's turn to tell about her visit to The Greenhouse, the Dallas spa run by the famed Neiman-Marcus department store. This was after President Lyndon Johnson purportedly "noticed his wife and daughters were looking like Texas heifers" and sent them to the spa to lose weight, change their hair styles, learn how to apply make-up and buy flattering clothing."

Kitty described LBJ's wife and children as "plump little corn pones who went through a pudgy-to-pretty transformation" at The Greenhouse Spa.

Kitty's most believable interview, and perhaps the most revealing in the book, was with chef Michel Corrado at The Golden Door Spa. He spoke of the outrageous diets he prepared for some of this fat farm's famous guests—and of how grateful clients rewarded him with physical gratuities. His salty four-letter words to describe those "tips" run endlessly.

"My mother was there at the gathering when Kitty read from the manuscript and played the taped interviews," said Kelley's long-time Spokane friend Marcia Gallucci. "It was really graphic sex stuff. My Mother's eyes were rolling back in her head."

"I told him," Kitty said about her encounter with chef Corrado, "that my editors wouldn't believe the things he was telling me . . . I didn't believe him at first either."

Kitty concluded that the writing in the book "crawled since each chapter had to go to a libel lawyer" because of what she wrote about the spas and their famous guests. It took months before the book was approved for publication.

"It was one great big pain in the ass," editor Herb Alexander said after the book was published. "It just wasn't worth the time and effort to check out all the unsubstantiated material Kitty Kelley had given us. It was an editor's nightmare."

Kitty's serendipity benefit from the book was that she lost fifteen pounds at the thirteen spas. Each of them had let her stay for one week at no charge.

When interviewed by the *Spokane Chronicle*, Kitty claimed she went out to do her number on the spas with a $10,000 advance from Pocket Books. This was a lie. As reported earlier, her contract gave her a $1,500 advance. She received no further money because the book was a commercial flop.

Kitty had to look elsewhere for income.

But income would be a long time in coming.

10

"Kelley is just a pain in the ass as well as a substantial provocateur . . ."
—Former U. S. Senator George Smathers

Question: Why does the Democrat from Florida have this caustic opinion of Kitty Kelley?

Answer: Because our Spokane scalp-hunter did a heavy number on handsome George Smathers.

A close friend of John F. Kennedy's since their days together in the House of Representatives, Smathers was an usher at JFK's wedding to Jacqueline Bouvier in 1953. When Kelley dropped in at the former Senator's Florida law office in 1977, she was poised to strike.

"It seems she'd been my ex-wife's roommate at a fat farm." Smathers later explained. "Oh, I can see those two yakking until the wee hours. She walked in here and announced: 'I know all about when you and Jack went to the Vendome to vacation in the south of France in 1956 . . .' "

Nothing was said by either Kitty Kelley or George Smathers about the "good old days" in Washington—the era when Kitty and George were pals extraordinaire with Congressmen Tom Foley and "Dizzy" Dicks, or about associations with Bobby Baker.

115

Kitty used the approach Lyle Stuart had suggested for her: this book would be an honest portrait of Jackie.

Smathers still bristles today about the way Kitty disarmed him and loosened his tongue by quoting his ex-wife's tales about his escapades with JFK before either was married and the two men shared a Potomac love nest. He talked at great length—and in considerable detail about Jack's sexual dalliances and love-making techniques.

"She giggled at every anecdote," Smathers recalled. He remembers with discomfort telling Kitty about the time, just before the wedding Jack pointed out Jackie's father to him. Smathers told Kitty he learned from Jack that Jackie had a "big father crush" on her good-looking papa, Jack Bouvier, known as "Black Jack" because of his dark, swarthy complexion.

"He pointed out her dad to me at the rehearsal dinner," Smathers recalled to the interviewer. Kelley, who didn't use a tape recorder, is remembered by the Senator as "this squatty little thing with the fat ankles who was writing very vigorously . . ."

Perhaps too vigorously. At least that's what Smathers believed months later when he found his words between the covers of the just-published *Jackie Oh!*—words that zapped him right between the eyes.

"He [Jack] pointed out her [Jackie's] dad to me at the rehearsal dinner," Kitty quotes Smathers on Page 19, allegedly saying, " 'There's Black Jack with the blue balls.' "

Kitty went on with Smathers' recital of what JFK had told him about Jackie's father: "Bouvier had bluish-black skin from some disease he had, but his features were quite handsome. He was very striking, and Jackie was just crazy about him."

****

It was Wednesday, February 22, 1977, when he spoke to Kitty Kelley, Smathers remembers. He needs no yellowing pages in an old calendar to remind of the date. He met with Kitty on the day traditionalists celebrate George Washington's birthday. Smathers may have been emboldened by an urge to tell the truth—perhaps not as our Founding Father had by his purported admission that he chopped down the cherry tree, but by the way George Bernard Shaw put it: "My way of joking is to tell the truth. It's the funniest joke in the world . . ."

What Smathers told Kitty was no joke to JFK's family and friends, who promptly put the former Senator on their "get lost" list after *Jackie Oh!* was published and made him a "do-not-invite" to future Kennedy family get-togethers.

"Kitty took liberties with what I told her, and made the most of it to suit her purposes in bloodying Jackie with the sharpest side of her hatchet," Smathers complained bitterly.

On Page 127, for example, Kelley describes how Kennedy women "swooned over their brothers' good-looking friend. Even his sister-in-law, Lee Radziwill, pursued Smathers, ignoring the fact that both of them [Lee and Jackie] were married at the time."

Then Kitty comes in with the zinger, which Smathers says he meant only as a joke for the pert blonde who was interviewing him.

"A mere oversight on their part," she quotes the Senator, then tells the reader that Kennedy "encouraged Lee, and tried to arrange a session for her with his good friend."

Smathers is still kicking himself in the butt for having given Kitty the fodder to embellish this anecdote with his own words:

"No one was off limits to Jack—not your wife, your mother, your sister. If he wanted a woman, he'd take her. I have no doubt that he gave it a run with Lee, but I don't think it happened. Then again, it wouldn't surprise me if it did. Jack was driven in that regard more than any man I've ever known. Just in terms of the time he spent with a woman, though, he was a lousy lover. He went in more for quantity than quality. I don't know how women tolerated it."

****

One of the most telling tales spoken out of school by Smathers was his account of the time Jack sought his good friend's advice about marrying Jackie.

117

"Jack came to me and said 'Do you think I ought to marry her?' " Kelley has Smathers recalling. "Like a fool I said, 'No, I don't think you should.' I told him he was making a mistake. Then, don't you know, ole Jack gets into bed with Jackie and, just to prove his love, the idiot says, 'I'm going to marry you even though my best friend told me not to.' Naturally, she wheedled out of him exactly what I had said and she has hated me ever since. She threw that up to me for years, even in the White House. Every time I danced with her, she'd say, 'I know you didn't want Jack to marry me. You didn't think I was good enough for him.' I'd say, 'Oh, now, Jackie, where did you ever get that crazy idea?' and she'd zero in on me with one of those looks of hers and I'd know damn well where she'd gotten the idea. Jack admitted to me later that he'd told her, the dumb fool. He absolutely ruined me with her after that. I just thought the world of her but she really had a hard time warming up to me, and understandably so."

Kelley emasculated Smathers with her stiletto by excising many more intimate details about Jack and Jackie. To this day he marvels at how ingenious she was in drawing him out. No one ever went on the record the way pal George did about all the JFK assignations in the Executive Mansion.

"One time I caught him messing around in the Cabinet Room in the White House and asked him how in the hell he thought he was going to get away with that kind of thing. He was convinced Jackie would never find out, but the fact of the matter is that she probably knew everything that was going on. I was always on the defensive with her because she was constantly giving me the needle. She knew about my trips with Jack, but I'd have to deny everything so he wouldn't get caught."

Smathers spilled other irreverent stories about JFK's exploits. Kitty pulled out all the stops when she wrote about this one:

"Jack Kennedy's sexual curiosity frequently led him into orgies at the Carroll Arms Hotel across the street from the Senate Office Building. While his colleagues were on the [Senate] floor voting on various pieces of legislation, Kennedy would amuse himself with a couple of girls. That kind of thing was probably his favorite pastime,' said Smathers, who can barely repress a smile when he thinks of his old friend. Even as President, Kennedy managed to have a few gleeful romps in the White House with two or three women at a time."

"And not all of his women were good-looking," said Smathers. "He had a couple of dogs working for him in the White House nicknamed Fiddle and Faddle who he was always playing around with. I couldn't believe it when I saw them. And if Jackie knew about them, I'm sure she didn't believe it either, because those two girls were the ugliest things I'd ever seen. They were awful . . ."

Kelley struck one of her cruelest blows. She managed to do it through Jack via the deluge of words that poured from unsuspecting Smathers' lips. He was explaining how a White House Press Secretary was picked for Jackie to guard her privacy by giving "minimum information with maximum politeness."

Jackie felt the need for such an aide after she went on CBS-TV and led network correspondent Charles Collingwood on a tour of the White House. Some 45 million viewers watched as the First Lady, looking more like a movie star than a President's wife, strolled through the Presidential Mansion's rooms and described the gifts and the names of the donors who had contributed hundreds of thousands of dollars for her restoration of the interior.

While the show generally received good reviews, including a rave from the *Chicago Daily News* which called it, "Television at its best," Norman Mailer, at his most astringent, wrote that Jackie's performance reminded him of a "voice that one hears on the radio late at night, dropped softly into the ear by girls who sell soft mattresses, depilatories, or creams to brighten the skin."

Kitty Kelley borrowed generously from the acerbic author's piece in *Esquire* magazine to compound her assault on Jackie.

Kelley quotes Mailer: "Jackie Kennedy was more like a starlet who will never learn to act because the extraordinary livid unreality of her life away from the camera has so beclouded her brain and seduced her attention that she is incapable of the

119

simplest and most essential demand, which is to live and breathe easily with the meaning of the words one speaks."

The show, Mailer concluded, was "silly, ill-advised, pointless, empty, dull and obsequious to the most slavish tastes in American life."

That hypercriticism from the noted author stung Jack and Jackie so badly that they agreed the First Lady's privacy must be protected with the prism of a Press Secretary, Kitty concludes on Page 141 of *Jackie Oh!*. She introduces us to the woman of Jackie's choice—one who wouldn't be "some high-charging, tub-thumping fool with previous experience" but "someone like herself . . ."

She was Pamela Turnure who, Kitty tells us—not for the first time by any means—was "the obvious choice" because she "wore the same sleeveless dresses, tripled-stranded chokers and low-heel pumps as the First Lady. She sported the same bouffant hairdo and had the same speaking voice. When asked to describe a tree, the 23-year-old press secretary replied in a breathy whisper, " 'Oh, it's an, oh, some sort of a tree . . .' "

All this colloquy was presented by Kitty as a prelude to her dispatch of another squadron of B-52s to atomize Jackie with yet one more delivery of Smathers' nukes:

"Kennedy himself," Kitty wrote, "suggested Miss Turnure to his wife, saying she would be ideal to handle the kind of tasteful press relations Jackie wanted to establish." Then Kelley uses Smathers to drop the blockbuster on the First Lady.

"Of course he suggested her," the author had George laughing. "That way she'd be right there in the White House close at hand when he wanted her."

But why would Jackie consent to hire a young woman who "had had an intimate involvement with her husband?" Kitty asks. She had already reported that JFK was making it with Pam during the first year of his marriage. Actually, as Kitty reconstructed the affair, Kennedy scored with Turnure even when she was a sweet little thing of twenty who worked as a secretary in his Senate office. That was before he took Jackie as his bride.

"I think it was a smart move on Jackie's part," she quotes

Smathers. "She figured, 'I'm going to make this so obvious and easy for you that you are going to get bored.' She knew what was going on."

Kitty also put the sting in quotes from Smathers about Jackie's profligate spending:

"Kennedy's only complaint about Jackie in all the years I ever knew him was that she spent too much money . . . 'That Jackie,' he'd yell. 'She's unbelievable. She absolutely does not appreciate the value of money. Thinks she can keep on spending it forever. God, she's driving me crazy—absolutely crazy. I tell you . . . George, she's run through all the government funds and is drawing on my personal account. If the taxpayers ever found out what she's spending, they'd drive me out of office . . .' "

Kelley also provides us, through the Senator, one of the very last—and truly ironic—off-the-cuff remarks JFK made before he was assassinated in Dallas on November 22, 1963.

"A few days before his scheduled departure the President flew to Miami with George Smathers to address a group of Latin American newspapers. Returning on Air Force One he said, 'I've got to go to Texas in a couple of days and I hate like hell to make the trip and get into a pissing match with Lyndon [Johnson] and [U.S. Senator] Ralph Yarborough, but I guess I've got to go. Jackie's going with me.'

" 'Hey, that's terrific,' said Smathers.

" 'Yeah, it's about time that she started making some of these damn trips, isn't it? I'm pleased that she'll be along.' "

After the announcement that she was marrying Greek shipping billionaire Aristotle Socrates Onassis. Smathers said tersely:

"I think she did it just so she'd never have to be beholden to the Kennedys again."

George Smathers anecdotes were nowhere as brutal as Kelley's exhumation of the former First Lady's purported bouts with depression. These, according to the author's report, were the "outgrowth of a splintered personality she developed as a child" and which "became more fragmented as she grew up."

Until *Jackie Oh!* was published, no biographer before then— nor since—made the quantum leap that Kelley took in her book with the report that Jackie, early in her marriage to Kennedy, received electro-shock therapy. This was the sensational "dis- closure" in Kitty's unauthorized bio, and became one of the most widely-discussed and controversial points of the book.

However, the consensus of those who know Jackie on the most intimate terms is that she never received electro-shock therapy and the report in *Jackie Oh!* is nothing more than carefully-contrived fiction. It is rooted in the safety of the long- odds that Mrs. Onassis would never sue because, if she did, she'd face excruciating cross-examination on the witness stand about her real—and recorded—psychiatric problems. Those problems arose only after seeing her husband's brains splattered over her in the limousine on that horrific November 22nd. And only then was she finally forced to see a psychiatrist to ease the terrifying memory of the assassination.

What follows is an examination of Kitty Kelley's methodology in creating one particular fiction where the victim had no de- fense.

Kitty Kelley first tells the reader that the strains of living with the Kennedys finally led Jackie to seek relief at a private psychi- atric clinic, Valleyhead, in Carlisle, Massachusetts. This facility specialized in electro-shock therapy, a treatment introduced in this country just at the outbreak of World War II. The treatment had become useful in coping with certain forms of psychoses.

Jackie's visit to the clinic may never have been discovered by her, Kitty claims, had it not been for a set of circumstances that handed the author the professed facts on the proverbial silver platter.

It began, Kitty claims, with a tip from an unnamed "out-of- town friend," described as a physician who'd dropped into the nation's capital for a medical convention in 1976. Kelley claims the doctor invited her to lunch but she declined because she told him that she was facing "the woes of writing a book." Kitty asserts the conversation took this route:

" 'What's it about?' he [the unnamed alleged doctor] asked.

122

" 'You'll think I've snapped.'

" 'You're not writing your memoirs?'

" 'Worse, much worse,' I complained. 'It's a biography of Jacqueline Kennedy Onassis.' "

Kitty has the doctor clearing his throat, saying something about medical ethics, and "how he wished he could help me, but even if he did I couldn't reveal the names, and what good would that do me." Then Kitty goes on:

" 'Besides, it all happened years ago,' he said, 'and you probably know about it anyway.'

" 'About what?' I almost shouted.

"He paused and coughed. 'The electro-shock therapy business,' he whispered. 'My cousin's husband was the anesthetist.' "

Kelley couldn't believe what the doctor was telling her, she continues. She asked her doctor friend whether he "knew for an absolute, certain fact that Jacqueline Kennedy Onassis had electro-shock therapy?" His response, again according to Kitty:

" 'She wasn't Mrs. Onassis at the time,' he replied evenly. 'She was still married to the President.' "

Kelley claims she made tracks to Massachusetts—but not before she boned up on what electro-shock therapy is all about.

Now to draw the reader's attention to this curious fact: none of the above conversation that Kitty Kelley asserts alerted her to Jackie Onassis' electro-shock therapy is in her book. Kitty spelled this out in *Washingtonian* magazine in an article titled "What It Was Like To Write *Jackie Oh!*" This, some six months after she turned in the finished manuscript to her publisher.

"Few would have know of Mrs. John F. Kennedy's trip to Valleyhead if it had not occurred on a weekend when the staff anesthesiologist was on vacation," Kelley writes in *Jackie Oh!* "Substituting that day was an anesthetist employed by Carney Hospital in Boston who worked on a regular free-lance basis at Valleyhead, anesthetizing patients for electro-shock treatments. The man, still employed at Carney, later told his wife that one of his patients that weekend was the wife of John F. Kennedy. Years later, when the office manager, Mrs. Josephine Delfino, was asked about Jackie's visit to Valleyhead, she said, 'I wasn't here at the time, but I remember people talking about it. Poor Mrs. Kennedy. But we had many people more famous than her who came here for electro-shock treatments.' "

Said Kelley in the magazine article:

"Having been hung up on so often [in trying to interview people on the phone], I hesitated calling and decided to visit the anesthetist . . . I begged my friend Don Uffinger to go with me. Uffinger, a former Washington, D.C. policeman, is a private investigator who stands 6-feet-2 and weighs 250 pounds."

Kitty's identification of Uffinger was in error. Actually, Uffinger was a policeman in Fairfax, Virginia, not Washington, D.C. After he retired from the police department in that city as a lieutenant of detectives, he became a private investigator.

I interviewed Uffinger, and his recollection of the trip Kitty speaks about is severely clouded with the mistiness of non-recall. Yes, he told me, such a trip did take place—but he cannot fix in his mind what community in Massachusetts he and Kitty visited. Nor was he able to give any description of the visit to the anesthetist's home, which Kelley portrays in intricate detail for the *Washingtonian's* readers. Kitty also claimed she had used Uffinger on other "investigations"—but the private eye said he couldn't reveal to me what those were because it would violate his client's "confidential matters."

Back to Kitty's electro-shock fable . . .

On an early Sunday morning—no month or year is indicated but it had to have been after the alleged encounter with the doctor-friend in 1976, just after she began research for *Jackie Oh!*—Kitty says she and the sleuth flew to Boston, rented a car, and drove to the anesthetist's house. En route, Kitty claims she was briefed by the detective about how to conduct herself.

"The first thing we do is stop at a drugstore where you buy some rubber bands and put those curls in a school teacher's bun," Kitty tells us Uffinger instructed her. "You don't want to walk in looking like Sparkle Plenty [The flashy lady in the *Dick Tracy* comic strip]."

Kelley says she "pushed" her hair into a "clumpy chignon and continued chain-smoking." She also purports Uffinger told her not to smoke in the house if she didn't see any ashtrays about, and not to "cuss" if there was a Bible in view.

"Timing is very important in this business," she was told, "so once we get there, we'll wait in the car for a while. You never knock on someone's door before noon on Sunday. You'd wake him up and embarrass him for not being in church."

She and her companion arrived at the house at 10:30 a.m., parked outside and conducted a "surveillance." In the car, Uffinger continued to counsel Kitty.

"Now remember," she quotes him as saying. "I'm going to introduce you as Katherine, because you're supposed to be a serious writer from Washington, D.C., who is working on a book and needs a few minutes of time to discuss a very important detail. You smile and get us invited inside. Then you sit down, zero in on So-and-So, say you know he is the guy who zapped Jackie and you'd like to talk about it."

This is what Kitty says transpired once inside the house:

"He [is at the hospital and] won't be home until tomorrow afternoon," Kitty says the anesthetist's wife told the detective after she answered the bell. "But won't you come in anyway and perhaps I can help you."

Imagine! A doctor's wife inviting two perfect strangers into her house instead of directing them to her husband's hospital.

Kitty and her sleuth found the spotless living room barren of ashtrays, and there, reposing on top of the mahogany coffee table, was a leather-bound Living Bible. Kitty, seemingly reluctant, sputtered. "Mrs. So-and-So . . . I had hoped to find your husband home because . . . I . . . well, I wanted to . . . ah . . ."

It's almost as though Kitty had suddenly been anesthetized herself, but her Boy Scout-in-tow Don Uffinger was Johnny-on-the-spot as he stepped into the vacuum of Kitty's uncharacteristic uncertainty of purpose.

"I think what Katherine wants to say is that she has a very confidential matter to discuss with your husband and she wants to keep it confidential without ever revealing his name."

"Yes, I wanted to . . . ah . . . discuss with him . . ." Kitty has herself continue talking in this alien hesitant manner.

"Katherine, I don't think you need worry about Mrs. So-and-So here," she quotes Uffinger. "After all, we know that she knows all about Mrs. Kennedy's electro-shock therapy."

Kitty doesn't resort to the cliche, "You could have heard a pin drop," but she does assert:

"The initial graciousness vanished as Mrs. So-and-So reared back in her chair looking as if she were ready to summon the police."

"How did you ever know about that?" she hissed. "I mean—I didn't even know myself for some time after it happened."

"Well, that's not what you told Miss Kelley's source," Uffinger hammers. "You told him about it the very weekend it occurred."

Picture this scenario:

Mr. So-and-So is filling in for the weekend at Valleyhead for the staff anesthesiologist. No sooner has he administered anesthesia to Jackie for alleged electro-shock therapy, than he's on the phone with his wife to tell her the hot news. Quick as a bunny, Mrs. So-and-So transmits the sensational story to a cousin!

If you believe that, then you'll also believe the following exchange that Kelley claims also happened:

"Oh, God," Kitty has Mrs. So-and-So moaning. "Not my cousin. How do you know my cousin?"

Guess what the bearer of these lip-smacking details did then?

"I [just] smiled sweetly," says our Kitty, who then let Uffinger continue talking:

"And we'd just like to confirm a few details with your husband since he was the anesthetist."

Finally, you are asked to believe this all transpired that Sunday noon somewhere in the Bay State. Kelley, of course, never identifies the community.

"As the interview turned into an interrogation, we learned the treatment had been administered to Mrs. Kennedy at Valleyhead, a private psychiatric clinic in Carlisle, Massachusetts, which was now closed and for sale."

Learned? Just now, finally and at last, Kitty and Don have *learned* that Jackie's zapping took place at Valleyhead? Does that mean that Mrs. So-and-So's cousin, the conventioneering doctor, never mentioned the name of the clinic? Could he have forgotten to do that, yet remembered to betray his cousin by conveniently providing Kitty with her name and address?

Implausible?

No. Unbelievable!

Because it never happened!

Kitty winds down this medical fable by recounting her return to Washington with Uffinger, and that they placed a call the next night to the anesthetist's home, which she says her private eye "tape-recorded for possible evidence, saying Mr. and Mrs. So-and-So might suddenly get amnesia after the material was published came out and forget all they had said."

Note this: Suddenly Kitty has herself, Uffinger and the anesthetist on the phone—yet not a word has been quoted from the anesthetist for her readership in the *Washingtonian*. And not one editor on the magazine had wondered why. The copy apparently was simply shoveled into the hopper with all its gaping flaws and absurdities and set in type to get the issue out.

Kitty closes the make-believe chapter by saying her detective "volunteered to go to court with me, if necessary."

Go to court for what?

We've already made it eminently clear that Jacqueline Kennedy Onassis would be the last person in the world to sue Kitty Kelley for bringing up electro-shock therapy—because it would open a Pandora's box about all of her legitimate sessions in psychoanalysis for real—not imagined—treatment.

127

11

Kitty Kelley offered one fact in her narrative about Jacqueline Kennedy Onassis and electro-shock therapy: Valleyhead did close down in 1977 and its records were committed to storage in a vault in Springfield, Massachusetts. Kitty told her publisher there was "no possibility of retrieving those records without the patient's written authorization."

In other words, according to Kelley, only Jackie could authorize the release of her records.

Another tall tale from the little girl from Spokane.

C. David Heymann, author of *A Woman Named Jackie*, published in 1989 by Lyle Stuart, Kitty's own publisher, went to Springfield and had no difficulty in examining Valleyhead's files. He simply obtained permission to do so from one of Jackie's blood relatives.

Heymann's finding? *Valleyhead never gave electro-shock therapy to any patient named Jacqueline Bouvier or Jacqueline Kennedy. In fact, no treatment of any kind was administered since Jackie had never been a patient at that hospital!*

But Heymann's search for the truth didn't end in Springfield. He pursued the issue of electro-shock therapy and learned what any self-respecting journalist would have uncovered:

"No legitimate mental health facility—and Valleyhead was very legitimate—would perform the sort of treatment Kitty

Kelley described in her book." Heymann told me. "Electro-shock therapy is *never* administered in *one* session in the way Kelley claims, a *quick fix* given on a weekend.

"We're dealing here with a *long-term* procedure that requires the patient's confinement in a hospital or clinic for *weeks*, even *months*. It is apparent that Kitty Kelley didn't research the subject of electro-shock therapy adequately enough to provide the reader with a lie that might be regarded as remotely believable.

"Moreover," Heymann continued, "to receive electro-shock therapy, a patient must be in treatment with a psychiatrist. Kelley states flatly that 'Jackie was well into her forties and living in New York before she began seeing a psychoanalyst regularly. Years after she tried the [non-existent] electro-shock therapy she began treatment with a psychiatrist for an hour a day, five days a week.' "

To further nurture her falsification of facts applying to Jackie Kennedy's mental health, Kelley tells us on page 76 of *Jackie Oh!*: "About the time she [Jackie] was hospitalized at the Valleyhead Clinic, a young St. Louis lawyer . . . Thomas Eagleton was hospitalized for electro-shock therapy at the Mayo Clinic in Rochester."

KITTY TALE: Jackie was electro-shocked at Valleyhead at the same time as Senator George McGovern's running mate in the 1972 Presidential race, Senator Eagleton, was a patient at Mayo.

KITTY TAILSPIN: Eagleton was treated at that hospital in mid-September, 1966, and "given electric-shock therapy for depression," as Kelley wrote—without pin-pointing the date. But Jackie couldn't possibly have "politically embarrassed Jack Kennedy," as the author claims on pages 76-77 of *Jackie Oh!*, if her Valleyhead fable were made known then. *For by that time Jack had been dead for nearly two years!*

KITTY TALE: Or was the author referring to Eagleton's hospitalization in 1964 at Mayo?

KITTY TAILSPIN: If so, obviously she didn't learn that no

electro-shock therapy was administered to Eagleton at that time. He was treated for a stomach disorder. And JFK still could not have been embarrassed about Jackie because he had been assassinated the year before.

KITTY TALE: Or was Kelley alluding to Eagleton's first encounter with electric-shock therapy, in mid-September, 1960?

KITTY TAILSPIN: If so, the records show Eagleton indeed had such treatment then—but at Barnes Hospital in St. Louis, not at Mayo. And Jackie indeed was hospitalized at *about that time*. But, of course, it was not at Valleyhead . . .

****

Kitty could have learned where Jackie was hospitalized if she'd paid closer attention to detail when she cribbed from yours truly's book, *The Hidden Side of Jacqueline Kennedy*, published by Pyramid Books in September, 1967. That book was in one of the cartons of Jackie material Liz Smith turned over to her. It's all there on page 54, with its description of a Thanksgiving dinner Jack and Jackie had at home in Washington on November 24, 1960, after which the President-elect left for Florida to continue his post-election vacation in Palm Beach while Jackie stayed behind because her troublesome pregnancy left her in no condition to travel. Quoting from *The Hidden Side*:

"It all happened shortly after Kennedy left home. Jackie felt labor pains. She called her physician, Dr. John A. Walsh, at 10:15 P.M. and told him. He summoned an ambulance, then went to the Kennedy home, examined Jackie, and ordered her removed to Georgetown Medical Center.

" 'Am I going to lose the baby . . . will I lose the baby?' Jackie cried before the ambulance drove her to the hospital.

" 'Don't worry,' Dr. Walsh replied. 'Everything will be all right.'

"Jackie then broke into a smile that ambulance driver Willard Baucon said was 'like a baby doll.'

"At the hospital, Dr. Walsh directed Jackie to be adminis-

131

tered anesthesia, then proceeded to perform the surgery which delivered the baby at 12:22 A.M.—a healthy, normal 6-pound, 3-ounce boy with brown hair and a howl that the doctor called "very good.' "

As we all know the infant born during that hospitalization was named John Fitzgerald Kennedy Jr.

"Most of the people I interviewed demanded confidentiality," Kelley wrote. "Some insisted they never be alluded to in any way. Pete Hamill [the columnist who dated Jackie] asked that our three-hour interview be entirely off the record . . ."

Kitty broke her word.

Pete Hamill's name appears again and again in *Jackie Oh!*. Kelley betrayed Hamill in the magazine by saying he was one of the sources who didn't want information about Jackie to be attributed to him, yet named him, and in light of what she states in the book—"On-the-record Pete Hamill was too much a gentleman to discuss his private life with a reporter"—Kitty comes up smelling nothing like a rose. Or as Hamill, a former colleague of this author's on the *New York Post*, said in an interview on February 2, 1989:

"I might have met Kitty Kelley at the Lion's Head where her future husband worked behind the stick, but I have no memory of it. Mike Edgley and I were good friends. Many of the writers who drank there were friends with Mike."

How then did Hamill get so tangled up with Kelley as to have her write about him the way she had?

"She called me [from Washington]. It was no trouble to find me. Edgley could get the phone number from guys at the Head. She phoned me at home in Brooklyn on the basis of the friendship with Mike. She told me she was writing a book about Jackie.

"I said I'm not going to talk about any of that stuff [inside dirt on the former First Lady]. It's not my act. I don't talk about anybody with whom I've gone out or whatever.

"So she says, 'Well, can you verify some of these things . . . ?'

"I said, 'Off the record, I'll verify things if you just wanna do that.' And I did, off the record—and it all ended up on the record with a lot of other shit."

Hamill went on to say he "took it as an absolute violation of the friendship I had with Mike" for Kelley to have "used that friendship to get to me, and then say she talked to me, which she did—but she never interviewed me.

"I think her whole technique is scabby stuff. She's a journalistic whore, pure and simple!"

12

"Kitty was persistent, Lyle Stuart said. "She was a pain in the ass to some people, but she really kept at it. Every so often I had to figuratively hold her hand because she felt she couldn't finish the book. For example, she had to do some research in New York City. Some friend let her have the use of her apartment on the East Side. She'd call me repeatedly from there for comfort and assurance."

"I can't do it . . . I just can't do it," Stuart says Kitty would tell him. But he kept reassuring her that she could. "You're going to make a lot of money from it. It'll be a big book . . ."

When asked by Stuart to furnish a rundown on the contents of *Jackie Oh!* for the publishing firm's fall book list, Kitty held back on the explosive chapters of the book. Stuart was annoyed. Stung by his apparent lack of enthusiasm for the work that was two years in the making, Kitty dispatched a long, rambling apology to Stuart. She explained that she had purposely kept out the most sensational disclosures from the catalogue because she wanted to "protect us from plagiarists. All that emphasis is to reassure you that you'll soon be receiving probably the hottest Jackie book written yet, and as you know I'm not given to bragging.

"I've got three more chapters to go and then you'll have everything . . . stories about a pre-frontal lobotomy that the

Kennedys had performed on their daughter, Rosemary, and have never to this day admitted . . . Jackie's trip to a private psychiatric clinic for electro-shock therapy . . . and the most revealing interview yet with JFK's close personal friend, [former Senator] George Smathers, who went into great detail telling me about [JFK's] sex life and Jackie's reaction to it.

"Naturally I didn't put those things in the catalogue description because I didn't think you'd want all that announced, but I got so concerned when I heard about Birmingham's nothing book that I had to dash this off to you . . ."

Kitty was referring to *Jacqueline Bouvier Kennedy Onassis,* another unauthorized biography by Stephen Birmingham, who had written the best-seller *Our Crowd.* In his book, published at the same time as Kitty's, a more compassionate portrait of Jackie Onassis emerges. Birmingham covers Jackie's childhood (totally ignored in *Jackie Oh!*), her reign as First Lady, her marriage to Aristotle Onassis, and her life in the years after Ari's death, when she became a book editor, first at Viking, then at Doubleday, where she still works.

Kitty Kelley's third "scoop"—after the interview with George Smathers and Jackie's non-existent electro-shock therapy—is nothing more than a rehash of what has been told and retold about the Kennedy's mentally retarded daughter Rosemary.

Anyone with an awareness of the Kennedy family's well-documented saga, knows that Rosemary was born mentally handicapped. As Rose Kennedy had written about her daughter in the matriarch's autobiography, Rosemary did undergo a lobotomy. But Kelley debases the surgical procedure, takes it all out of context, and exaggerates it.

Kelley tells us that because Rosemary, who was 23 years old in 1941, was throwing "violent temper tantrums, hitting people and breaking things," her parents decided she had to be reined in. "She was taken to the best doctors available, and they diagnosed her rages as the symptoms of neurological disease. Distressed by her extreme behavior, the former Ambassador to England and his wife finally decided to take a drastic, irreversible step . . . they submitted their daughter for a pre-frontal lobotomy."

Kitty writes that the Kennedys tried to make it seem that Rosemary attended her brother's inauguration, when she hadn't. No such claim appears anywhere.

The truth, as documented in Rose Kennedy's autobiography, was that Rosemary lived in a facility run by the Roman Catholic Sisters of St. Colette in Jefferson, Wisconsin. The surgery performed on her during World War II had not corrected her condition. She was, in short, in need of confinement to a home that could give her around-the-clock attention.

In writing about the pre-frontal lobotomy performed on Rosemary, Kelley describes the surgery in gruesome language. She tells us "holes were drilled in the skull and surgical incisions made in the white matter."

On the other hand, the author makes no effort to shade her story with some compassion for Rosemary's plight. She ignores the preface from the source she borrowed so heavily for this chapter—Rose Kennedy's book *Times To Remember*, which read:

"This book is dedicated to my daughter Rosemary and others like her—retarded in mind but blessed in spirit. My vision is a world where mental retardation will be overcome, where we no longer mourn with mothers of retarded children, but exult and rejoice with parents of healthy, happy youngsters. Then, and only then, can we say, in the words of St. Paul: I have fought the good fight. I have finished the course. I have kept the faith."

Kitty completed the manuscript and finally delivered 470 typewritten pages to Lyle Stuart. These became *Jackie Oh!*, the 352-page clothbound book.

Many threats but only one lawsuit followed publication of *Jackie Oh!*. Stuart was served with court papers because of the words Kitty put into the mouth of Mrs. Betty Spalding, a long-time friend of the Kennedys. Spalding objected to several personal comments attributed to her, violating a written agreement granting her approval on all quotes which the author obtained from her. Kitty ignored that pact. She turned in her manuscript without showing anything to Mrs. Spalding.

Betty Spalding was irate to read that Kitty quoted her as saying that "Jack's and Jackie's relationship was extremely stormy in the beginning because her psychosexual emotional development had been retarded." She found herself describing Jack telling his wife that the "American people aren't ready for someone like you," and having Jackie "burst into tears and run out of the room, sobbing hysterically . . ."

Since Kitty hadn't become professional enough to use a tape recorder, she relied on handwritten notes. She was in no shape to defend against Betty Spalding's complaint that her words were misused. The complaint contained a copy of the agreement Kelley signed. Kitty settled out of court with a cash payment of $40,000. Her attorney's fees came to another $40,000.

Betty Spalding wasn't the only interviewee to hit the roof about *Jackie Oh!*. Senator Smathers became apoplectic at the mention of Kelley's name and her boast of how she got him to unzip his lips.

"Ooooh, what an interview that was!" she exclaimed to *Washington Post Magazine* columnist Rudy Maxa. "I wrote him about 20 letters, made 30 phone calls. I talked to him in his law office, with the door open, feet on the floor and no drinks."

"As far as I'm concerned, her feet will always be on the floor, and the door will always be open!" roared Smathers, who conceded that he finally agreed to meet with Kitty only because, as mentioned previously, she said she had spent some time in a spa with his ex-wife and because she promised her book was going to be "a eulogy to Jack."

Smathers never denied the accuracy of any quotes attributed to him. Scores of others said they were misquoted. Often their words were juxtaposed and out of context. Often things they deny saying were mixed in with their quotes.

Two whom Kitty talked to and who say that what they told the author and what she wrote in the book were far apart, were

Jackie's mother Janet Auchincloss and Jackie's half-brother Jamie.

"It's a deeper blow than the day President Kennedy was assassinated," Jamie said after the book and its revelations about Jackie's past life were put on public display. "We're suffering from the same emptiness in the gut we went through after the President was shot down in Dallas."

Jamie Auchincloss said Jackie had asked the family to ignore the book completely. Yet he noted that "it's difficult for us to wave it away because it's so destructive. There's no reason left to hurt Jackie any more. This is really cruel.

"The book is cleverly done, but . . . it's full of innuendo and half-truths. It should have been twice as long and also brought out all the nice things Jackie has done. Everything put her in a bad light."

Jamie also spoke about his mother's agony over what Kitty had written in what she purported was obtained in interviews with Mrs. Auchincloss.

"My mother categorically denies [she had] five interviews with Kitty Kelley; she denies even having one interview with her," Jamie said emphatically. "She spoke [to Kelley on the phone once], all the time refusing to talk about our family. I'm not denying that I talked to the writer, but I have been badly misquoted. On top of that, the material was taken completely out of context.

"If all the things supposed to have been done by Jackie were true, she'd be worse than a two-headed monster. In fact, she's a lovely person."

Jamie said his mother couldn't believe what she read in the book about her daughter.

"She kept asking me questions and making comments on almost everything in the 352 pages. She was deeply hurt by parts. Jackie telephoned her and reassured her so she wouldn't be so miserable over it. But they didn't talk about the book's contents.

"If the good things had been included no harm would have

been done—but then there wouldn't have been a book. It seems nobody wants to hear the good."

In response to these complaints, Kitty replied:

"Maybe I could have written a more intimate biography had I been part of the privileged circle, but given the human desire to remain inside, I wonder if I would have risked expulsion by writing candidly. As it was, I wrote *Jackie Oh!* from the outside looking in . . ."

When her manuscript was turned into her publisher, Lyle Stuart was puzzled by a section that allegedly took place in a bedroom. It contained an intimate exchange of words between Jacqueline Onassis and Pete Hamill.

Stuart was puzzled. He knew that Kelley hadn't been able to speak to Mrs. Onassis.

"Did you talk with Pete Hamill?" he asked.

"Not yet. But Mike is going to help me reach him."

"So where did you get this conversation?"

"Why?"

"Because only one of these two could have related this. Nobody else was in the bedroom with them and you haven't spoken to either of them."

"They won't sue," she said, smartly.

"I didn't ask if they'd sue. I asked where you got it."

Kitty looked down at her shoes as if studying the condition of their shine. "I made it up," she said. When she looked up, her demure expression was that of a naughty little girl. "They won't sue," she repeated, almost imploringly.

"No good, Kitty! This comes out. You can't make things up! Please don't do this again."

She nodded, albeit reluctantly.

"At the time," Stuart said, "I believed her shock-treatment story. Looking back, I feel I was had and the whole thing was a fable. I doubt that it ever happened. And knowing how she makes things up, I believe she was sure she could get away with it because no one would sue."

13

"Let me tell you about the time we got the book ready for the press and we were preparing the jacket . . ."

Lyle Stuart is talking.

"Kitty Kelley gave me her resume. I don't know why she didn't realize her lies would be challenged. I don't think she's psychopathic. Yet she gave me a resume that turned out to be fiction. She claimed she was an editorial writer at the *Washington Post*, and was Press Secretary for Senator Eugene McCarthy on his 1968 Presidential campaign."

Stuart was only a phone call away from hearing the truth . . .

"Actually, as it later turned out, she was a secretary who did some researching for an editorial writer on the *Washington Post*."

Before taking the next step—checking on the duties his author purported she had done with the McCarthy campaign—Stuart called Kitty to ask why she lied about her work at the *Post*.

"I wrote *an* editorial . . . and I can . . . show it to you," Kitty stammered.

"How will I know it's *your* editorial?" Stuart asked. "Is your name on it? The people at the newspaper say you didn't write *any* editorials!"

Stuart then learned Kitty had also overstated her role with Senator McCarthy.

The tens of thousands of book jackets printed for *Jackie Oh!* had to be destroyed at considerable cost to the publisher. Flap copy was revised to read, "Kitty Kelley left a job at the *Washington Post* to write for a variety of publications, which occasionally published her as a freelance reporter/writer." The jacket copy continued, "Ms. Kelley has lived in Washington, D.C. for twelve years and worked as a Press Secretary to Senator Eugene J. McCarthy for four years.

"As a Washington journalist in the nation's capital, she has covered the White House and Capitol Hill and developed access to valuable sources on the life of Jacqueline Kennedy . . ."

Then—incredibly, in light of what we've discovered thus far about Kitty's methodology in fictionalized and distorted writing—she is quoted:

"President Kennedy once said, 'The greatest enemy of the truth is very often not the lie—deliberate contrived and dishonest—but the myth—persistent, persuasive and unrealistic.' In writing about Mrs. Onassis, I've tried to go beyond the myth to reality."

****

Shortly after the book hit the stores with the first of its two September, 1978, printings, Stuart received a letter from Smith Bagley, a prominent Washington businessman and heir to the R.J. Reynolds' tobacco fortune. At the time, Bagley was publishing *This Is Sunday*, a magazine distributed nationally as a newspaper supplement similar to *Parade*. Unlike *Parade*, it targeted the upscale sophisticated urban markets.

Writing from his offices at 1425 21st Street N.W., Bagley asked Stuart about the "strange wording" on the jacket.

"What's strange about it?" a puzzled Stuart asked on the phone, after deciding the cryptic correspondence called for an immediate response.

"Well, I've got a resume here submitted by Kitty Kelley, who has been working as an editor for my magazine," Bagley replied.

142

"And I don't find what the jacket says jibes with what she claimed in her resume."

"What did she claim with you . . . ?"

". . . that she was an editorial writer for the *Washington Post* and was Press Secretary to Gene McCarthy . . ."

Stuart then recounted his own painful experience with the thousands of dust jackets that had to be trashed and new ones printed.

Bagley himself had endured other idiosyncratic Kelley-isms during the months she worked for him while finishing the manuscript on Jackie Onassis. Discovering that Kelley had falsified her resume was only the latest in a series of vexations Bagley experienced with his troublesome employee.

From the outset, Bagley was uneasy about Kelley and so, before taking her on as an editor, he added a unique amendment to her contract.

"I had it read that she could not write about me personally . . ."

A lot of good it did.

Kitty had no sooner occupied her editor's desk at *This Is Sunday* than Bagley read an item about himself in the *Washington Star*, the capital's second newspaper, and one that Kelley claimed ran stories she wrote as a freelancer, including the one she expanded into her first book, *The Glamour Spas*.

Over the next several months, other items about Bagley appeared in *The Ear*, a gossip column pieced together by Diana McLellan, who later became a columnist for the *Washingtonian*.

"One of those items really shook me up," Bagley said. "It reported on certain legal complications we had encountered with the magazine—matters known only by my wife and the two main people in my office, my vice president, Betty Burke, and Kitty Kelley.

"I knew my wife wasn't invading my privacy," Bagley went on. "And I also trusted Betty implicitly. I knew she'd never betray me. So I decided to set a trap. I took a piece of paper and wrote, 'Betty, just heard that my wife is pregnant, please send her two dozen red roses.' I then crumpled it up, put it in the wastepaper basket and, together with Betty, carried the trash outside and deposited it in the alley.

"By God, three days later Diana comes out with this scoop that Smith Bagley's wife is pregnant, and that he sent her two dozen red roses."

Did Bagley have any clue as to how Diana McLellan came up with that gossip item?

"Kelley had been going through my goddam garbage!" he snapped. "Why don't you ask Diana . . . ?"

"Oh, sure Kitty gave me that item," Diana McLellan admits now, more than a dozen years after the fact, and in her reformed state as a writer of non-gossip. "Kitty is a great garbologist."

Bagley summarily fired Kitty. Soon afterward, his magazine folded. "But no one in the whole wide world can say *Today Is Sunday* failed because Kelley wasn't around to save it," Bagley told the world.

It's a wonder the magazine didn't go under a lot sooner than it did. A source who knew the routines of the office intimately but asked not to be identified because "I'm terrified of Kitty Kelley . . . she is fucking dangerous," told me how Kitty and a co-editor put Bagley's magazine on the skids from the instant they came on the payroll in late 1977.

"This was a time when Kitty was in the throes of writing *Jackie Oh!* and she had to have an income. She had only gotten fifteen-hundred dollars from Lyle Stuart as an advance on signing the contract for the book and would not get the other half of the three-thousand dollar advance until she delivered a completed acceptable manuscript.

"She found a real gold mine at *Today Is Sunday* because she could goof-off all she wanted . . . I mean, she could stay home and write the book from the clips and other material she received from Liz Smith. She hardly ever came into the office. She just wrote all her copy at home and delivered it when the mood moved her—usually on deadline or past it."

The same source from Bagley's office continued:

"She had a co-editor, Dave Leggett, who was no prize either. He was a reporter, a writer in Washington for some years—a beer-drinking good ol' boy who dressed in Bermuda shorts and wore a baseball cap.

"I think it's a fair comment to say that the two of them—Kitty and Dave—contributed to the demise of the magazine. Their being late with deadlines generated monumental cost over-runs."

One of Kitty Kelley's more extravagant assignments was a fashion shoot in Manhattan.

"She lined up models, a makeup artist, and a photographer and took them to a well-heeled society *grande dame*'s pent-house to do a layout for lingerie. Well, when the bills came in, it was not to be believed what she charged the magazine for expenses.

"One item was three-hundred dollars for orchids. Now, you must understand that Bagley is an astute businessman who, despite his great fortune, watches his money very carefully.

" 'What is this about?' he asked Kitty when she returned to the office.

" 'Oh,' she exclaimed in a fluster, 'one of the models touched a satin bedspread with a black ink pen and the woman who let us use the apartment was furious. So I went to the lobby, walked into the florist, and sent her the orchids to atone for the damage.' "

Piling it on seemed to be an art-form with Kitty . . . My source wasn't done yet:

"Bagley watched production costs skyrocket. Everything—photography, travel, charges of all kinds—were going up constantly. It got to the point where a story that ended up in the magazine as a mere column in length, or even shorter, was costing thousands of dollars. It was impossible to operate in the black under those conditions."

One of the conditions of her employment was that Kelley would provide fresh, interesting copy for the magazine's *Gossip* and *Q. & A.* sections.

145

"Bagley knew how tightly wired Kitty was to Diana McLellan and was confident when he hired her that she'd come up with appropriate items that might be in Diana's pockets but may not be suitable for her newspaper column. It didn't happen."

Bagley had to go to an outside writer for gossip. Teddy Vaughn was a theater critic/book reviewer for the *Washington Times*. Vaughn also did gossip for a program on NBC's WRC-TV in the capital.

"Paying Teddy Vaughn as a supplemental gossip source spiraled editorial costs even further. And that was Kitty Kelley's fault, too."

****

CBS-TV's Mike Wallace from *60 Minutes* also figured in the bad taste Kitty Kelley left in Smith Bagley's mouth.

"Kitty went to Miami Beach to cover a royal ball of European aristocracy at the Fontainebleau Hotel—a gathering of phony counts and countesses and the like. She said it would be an exciting story but I don't think the trip went well. When she returned to Washington, she had nothing that could interest the magazine readers. The biggest item she came back with was that some international armaments dealer was involved in a deal that was a decade ahead of the Iran-Contra scandal—but had no appeal to *Today Is Sunday* because the magazine supplement wasn't into hard news.

"So Kitty wrote a letter to Mike Wallace and tried to interest him in doing a piece on her and her forthcoming Jackie Onassis biography in exchange for what she suggested was 'This tremendously interesting information I picked up at the ball.' Wallace declined the deal.

"Meanwhile, in New York, the magazine was doing a feature on Illinois Senator Charles Percy. Kitty screwed up the picture that was being taken of Percy when she mussed up his hair on a Manhattan street corner. She thought she was being cute—but it angered Percy and he refused to comb his hair for another photo."

Bagley, speaking candidly, recalls a multitude of "stupidities" that he attributes to Kitty Kelley while in his employ. But, he grimly observed: "I've been through so much litigation with this horror of a woman that the less I say now the better off I'll be."

Bagley fired Kitty Kelley. For the next two years he was up to his eyelashes in legal suits she generated. Kitty sued for breach of contract. He countersued and accused Kitty of falsifying her resume and failing to perform her editorial duties satisfactorily. The war was on.

In her answering papers, filed by attorney Ian Volner, Kelley denied she lied in her application for the job, or that she had ever perused Bagley's garbage. She also accused her former employer of falsifying the date of her dismissal to avoid paying her severance, which was one of the conditions of employment in the contract. As Lyle Stuart would later be quoted in *Us* magazine: "She even lies about her lies."

Bagley's deposition, submitted to the District of Columbia Superior Court, contained other allegations against Kelley. One of them indicated that she wasn't exactly trusting of her husband.

"I had a conversation with Kitty one day and she asked me to recommend an attorney," Bagley reported. "She said the major reason was that she wanted to draw up a contract which would enable her in every possible way to keep any royalties from the *Jackie Oh!* book away from him."

At the time, Kitty Kelley and Mike Edgley had been married less than two years. Their twelve-year courtship that began in 1965 at the New York World's Fair, stretched into 1976 when, in August of that year, Kitty and Mike took their vows. The wedding was shrouded in mystery for the bride's friends and associates. It took place in Spokane, but Kitty didn't want any of the Washington, D.C., crowd there because she was reluctant to have them see her family. She was anxious that they not learn about her mother's alcoholism.

Nevertheless, Kitty's father staged a classic wedding that far exceeded the little splash his marriage to Delie Martin created.

147

He gave it at his favorite country club and it was the talk of Spokane. Before leaving the capital with Mike, Kitty told people she intended to wear a beige dress.

"I dare not wear white!" she confessed with humor.

But when she returned to Washington and showed the crowd the wedding pictures, Kitty was wearing stark white. "A virgin in dress, a whore in action, and a vampire in actuality," was the way one of her associates called the bride.

After the big reception in her parents' country club, the bride returned with the groom to Washington and held another reception in a friend's garden in the capital that was attended by some one-hundred guests. Kitty and Mike were making it legal and traditional in every sense of the word.

The reception was given by Paul Weick, a Washington correspondent for a group of New Mexico newspapers. Weick also has a carriage house on his grounds which was rented by Mike Edgley, ostensibly as a writing studio for his own failed efforts as a scrivener. He was reported to have taken refuge there to put words together because he couldn't tolerate the criticism Kitty was giving his literary efforts while the manuscript was still in the typewriter at home.

Kitty had no time to encourage her husband, who once again began to rely more and more on the bottle for his sustenance. When he wasn't drinking, he became moody.

Kitty frequently telephoned her publisher from Washington to pour out her heart about her marital woes. There was the evening that the two were going to a social function. Thirty minutes before they were scheduled to depart, Mike said he wasn't going. He didn't like Kitty and he didn't like her friends and he'd be damned if he'd spend time with them.

"But I love you," she said.

"It isn't mutual," he said.

She went to the party alone. Kitty didn't like to miss parties. This further infuriated Mike who totally stopped talking to her for three days.

She would call Lyle Stuart and have long sobbing outpourings about the way he was mistreating her.

"Kitty, I'm not a therapist," her publisher said. "The two of you should see a counselor or something. This isn't my thing and I don't have time for it. Finish your book."

Kitty explained that her "occasional flirtations" with other men were designed to revive Mike's interest in her. But when it came to giving Edgely encouragement about his writing, she stopped short. "He simply doesn't have any talent," she told an acquaintance.

With it all, she found time to encourage David Richards. Richards was drama critic for the *Washington Star*. He took a one-year leave from the *Star* to write a biography of the ill-fated actress Jean Seberg.

The book, titled *Played Out* was published in 1980 by Random House. Among those whose help Richards acknowledges is Kitty Kelley "who listened."

A decade later, Richards became Sunday drama critic for *The New York Times*. Richards, who has known Kitty from the time she arrived in Washington, confessed recently that he was both fascinated and puzzled by the Kitty Kelley syndrome. Even after knowing her all those years he couldn't understand what drove her beyond the point where normal people stopped.

"I don't know of any Kennedy intimate who has ever before opened up the way George Smathers did," Kitty Kelley bubbled enthusiastically in the midst of the one-hundred or more friends at Washington's Sulgrave Club on the night of September 20, 1976. This was the book party for *Jackie Oh!* hosted by Leslie Cantrell Smith.

Kitty was giddy. She floated around the room on a cloud. Overnight, she had become a Washington celebrity. She wheeled in a half-circle, pretending to look for Smathers. "He was invited," she insisted. "But . . . my, my, my. I don't see him any place . . ."

A while later, the tigress of the typewriter lampooned her sources. "This isn't a party for the people who gave me information . . . except . . ."

She hesitated as she stared at Priscilla Crane Baker. Of all the

149

guests present, Baker's was the only name listed as a source in Kelley's Author's Notes.

"Oh, she has nothing to worry about," Kitty purred with a wink at Priscilla. "There's absolutely no way anyone can figure out what she told me for the book."

Baker appeared distressed. She hadn't expected to be listed as a contributor in the book and seemed hard-pressed to explain her role.

"What Kitty did was ask what I knew about Jackie Kennedy," Miss Baker explained. "I told her what I knew and said she'd have to check it out. I didn't go beyond that. After all, the Kennedys are very powerful, and there are a lot of them. I come from Massachusetts, so I know. But no, I've never met any of them."

****

Jackie Oh! broke out of the starting gate at full gallop and left Stephen Birmingham's *Jacqueline Bouvier Kennedy Onassis* standing in the paddock.

Both books were published with modest printings but Stuart went back to press for a second pre-publication run of 10,000 copies, followed by two more returns to the press for a total of 100,000 copies. The competition's book remained frozen at its initial 40,000 printing.

****

When *Jackie Oh!* was offered to mass-market paperback publishers, the Hearst Corporation's Avon Books came in with the high bid of $92,000. Stuart told Avon he wanted a fifteen percent royalty. Avon said they never went that high. Finally Avon Editor-in-Chief Walter Meade sent a message:

"Tell Stuart that if he doesn't give us this book, we won't do any more business with him."

Stuart gave the item to columnists who had a field day with it. Meade had pushed the wrong button. Maverick Stuart had received fifteen percent royalties on several of his best-sellers, including his then recent *The Sensuous Man.*

The story to the press was: "Avon Books told Lyle Stuart that if he doesn't give them the *Jackie Oh!* book they won't do any more business with him. This amused Stuart since Avon hadn't done *any* business with him during the previous twenty-one years."

When word got out about Avon's fiasco, other mass-market houses approached the publisher with new bids for *Jackie Oh!*.

Two of the prime movers and shakers in the field of the giant paperback publishers were among Stuart's new suitors: Marc Jaffe, Editorial Director at Bantam Books, and Richard Krinsley, Executive Editor at Random House and in charge of Ballantine Books, their mass-market paperback arm.

Stuart and Jaffe were long-time friends who respected each other. Jaffe was a legend in publishing. Stuart had never met Krinsley who built Random House's marvelously profitable children's book line.

But it wasn't a children's book that Krinsley wanted to discuss when he phoned Stuart at his apartment overlooking the Manhattan skyline from New Jersey's Fort Lee. This was a Saturday morning in October.

"Would you mind very much if I dropped by for a few minutes to talk with you about *Jackie Oh!?*" Krinsley asked.

The Ballantine executive drove to New Jersey from his home in New York's nearby Westchester County. Stuart opened the door to find a man in casual dress.

"He was wearing tennis shoes, slacks, and a sweater. He made an immediate favorable impression with me—a nice, pleasant fellow. And I was to learn later from him that I came across as an okay guy with him—despite the fact that he'd been led to believe from people at Random House that I was some kind of nut . . ."

No sooner had Krinsley put his proposal for paperback rights on the table, than the phone rang. Marc Jaffe, who Stuart said had never called him at home before, was on the line.

"Marc," the flabbergasted publisher started to say, "you're not going to believe what I'm doing now . . ."

"No, no, Lyle, I don't want to interrupt anything . . . but

since we're having dinner Monday night, why don't we finalize a deal on *Jackie Oh!* before Monday so it's out of the way. Let's have the book . . ."

"Marc . . . Let me get back to you . . ."

After Stuart hung up the phone, he observed that Krinsley was downcast. "He couldn't help but hear my conversation with Jaffe and he wasn't happy. He knew Marc was a friend and he a stranger."

Krinsley cleared his throat. "Look, Lyle, I know Bantam is a large house and I know the temptation to go with them. But I can tell you one thing—Ballantine would do a hell of a job."

"Okay, let me think about it."

Krinsley left with Stuart's assurance that he would consider Ballantine and get back to him promptly.

Hardly an hour went by before the phone rang once again.

"Lyle, I have this suggestion . . . Why don't we co-publish?"

It was Krinsley, who apparently had done some hard, fast thinking on the drive home.

What Krinsley proposed was a venture in which both the author and publisher of the cloth edition receive no advance against royalties from the paperback house. But the deal would be pregnant with the promise of much bigger returns over the long haul for both author and publisher.

In their telephone discussion that Saturday afternoon, Stuart and Krinsley agreed that were Ballantine to do the book, the deal would be a fifty-fifty split between the partners on all income in the joint venture.

What would Kitty Kelley make on the transaction?

"Let's give her a straight fourteen percent on the cover price of the paperback," Stuart suggested.

"That's okay with me . . . whatever you say," Krinsley replied.

"Okay, I'll think about this and get back to you . . ."

"Oh, by the way, one more thing . . . I'd also like to buy *Casino Gambling For The Winner* . . . We'll give you a hundred and fifty-thousand dollar advance on that one."

Stuart was impressed by Krinsley's innovative approach. *Casino Gambling For The Winner* was written by Stuart himself. It would go on to sell 120,000 copies in its $20 cloth edition. But at the time, it hadn't been launched and the offer was a sweet extra.

"Dick, let me think about it . . ."

Next morning, Sunday, Stuart called Jaffe at home.

"Marc, I have disappointing news. I'm giving it to someone else . . ."

Then Stuart phoned Krinsley at home.

"Dick, we have a deal . . ."

"Krinsley," Stuart now says in retrospect, "was smart enough to make me an offer I couldn't refuse—not if I really believed our book would be a genuine big book. At the same time he had enhanced it with the offer for my gaming book.

"So I called Kitty and told her what a great thing we had going—and after I recited the terms and the possibilities, she was ecstatic."

****

At about the time Lyle Stuart had the mass-market deal with Ballantine wrapped up, he heard from Kitty Kelley on a different matter.

"I want to do a biography of Elizabeth Taylor . . ."

"Kitty," Stuart said flat out, "I'm not going to publish a hatchet job on Liz Taylor. With Jackie Onassis, you can love her or you can dislike her. But how can anyone hate Elizabeth Taylor?"

Kelley persisted. She said she had scandalous stuff about the celebrated film beauty. Among the gossip Kitty cited was a wildly circulated rumor that the violet-eyed movie queen had slept with political columnist Max Lerner.

"So what, Kitty. Who cares?"

Despite several more attempts by Kelley to hard-sell the book, Stuart was firm. "No way I'm going to do that book . . ."

At that juncture, Kitty Kelley became a wheeler-dealer. But

not before she was rocked back on her heels by Mel Watkins's review of *Jackie Oh!* in the *New York Times.*

Calling it "an ersatz biography," Watkins went on to say the book "rarely emerges from the muck with which it is pasted together . . ."

Pointing out that the facts of Jackie Onassis's life were well-known by then, Watkins offered the view that something more than just another rehash was needed on this well-known personality—something of much greater depth than Kitty Kelley offered in her book.

"What one expects from yet another unauthorized biography is deeper insight into the personality of a woman who, despite her publicity, has remained enigmatic. The author's groping notwithstanding, no such characterization emerges here; what we get is innuendo, amateurish psychology and airy speculation."

Watkins took great exception to Kitty's descriptions of Jackie after the assassination when she wrote that the grieving widow was "wallowing in self-pity" or, after she speaks about the country's reverence for the First Lady at the funeral, adds the gratuitous observation that the public "had no idea of the imperiousness which lay behind the black veil."

"Even her grief provides an occasion for carping," said Watkins before delivering his final rap:

"*Jackie Oh!* is little more than a compendium of what gossip magazines and previous books have related about Jacqueline Kennedy Onassis, with a dash of rancor to spice it up. To be sure, there are some fresh anecdotes and quotations from sources as varied as Gore Vidal, former Senator George Smathers and Norman Podhoretz. But despite the 'more than 300 interviews' Kitty Kelley is said to have conducted, there is almost no new information here.

"Miss Kelley attempts to portray Mrs. Onassis as a cold, pretentious, plotting woman whose chief virtue is her occasional devotion to her children. Instead, she emerges as a private person, admittedly prodigal, who still resists the unwanted public role into which she was thrust. In short, she remains opaque; only Miss Kelley's intentions become transparent. As for the reader, well, there is an old saying about the inevitability of being soiled if you dally too long with dirt."

14

"Why are you crying?" a puzzled Lyle Stuart asked as he watched tears roll down Kitty Kelley's cheeks. Stuart and Kelley were standing on the steps of the world-famous Plaza Hotel, where the publisher was getting a room for his soon-to-be bestselling author.

New York hotels were fully booked that night. Stuart had gone first to the St. Regis where he was known because of his frequent visits to one of that hotel's celebrity residents, Salvador Dali. The St. Regis couldn't accommodate Stuart's request but, as a courtesy, the manager had called the Plaza and extracted a room as a favor. The next morning Kitty was to begin her media tour to promote *Jackie Oh!* Her first appearance was NBC-TV's *Today* show.

"Lyle . . ." Kitty sobbed, "I'm crying because . . . this will be the first time in my life that . . . I'm staying at a first-class hotel . . ."

"Two months later I would recall this emotional scene," Stuart mused, "when we received the bill from the posh Beverly Hills Hotel. She charged everything from the morning newspaper to a once-a-day visit to the hotel's beauty parlor. The bill for those few days came to nearly two-thousand dollars."

Kitty had become a professional free-loader.

"I should have reined her in," reflected Stuart. "I had already spoken to Bagley—but that was about her lies about her background. We never touched base on the way she handled her expense account."

Somewhere in the not-too-distant past, Kitty had had a falling-out with her agent, David Obst, over royalty payments. Kelley had the notion that *The Glamour Spas* sold more copies than the publisher's statements claimed—and she played hardball with Obst over that belief, demanding that he retain an accountant to audit Pocket Books' royalty accounting. Obst knew the book had bombed, and he said so to Kitty. He decided to drop her as a client because she wasn't a quality writer of the kind he wanted in his stable.

Kitty decided to represent herself.

"Why should I pay ten percent to an agent when I can sell my stories myself?" she'd say to her then-best-friend Janet Donovan. "I've been asked to write a Jackie Onassis biography and have been negotiating with the publisher by myself. Why do I have to have an agent . . . ?"

After he struck the mass-market deal with Ballantine Books' chief Richard Krinsley, Stuart informed Kitty that *Jackie Oh!* would be co-published as a paperback by Stuart and Ballantine, with no big money up front.

Kitty recalled her experience with her first paperback, *The Glamour Spas*, which had netted no royalties beyond the $1,500 advance. She wasn't the big-stakes gambler that Lyle Stuart was, but she had seen him in action and respected his judgment. Also, her contract didn't give her a say in the way subsidiary rights were sold. Kitty was aware of that. Yet she thirsted for a bite of that $45,000 she would have had from the aborted Avon deal.

"She wiggled her butt into my office one day, gave me a long song-and-dance about how she was being screwed financially by Stuart, and asked if I could find an agent to represent her," Smith Bagley told his interviewer. "It was an ironic situation. Here I was hurting from the hideous track record Kitty had set on my magazine, while she was acting like a helpless little female. I went along with the gag. I was marking time then in

my effort to trap her in the act of tattling on me to the columnists. I planned to fire her as soon as I had the goods on her."

(Smith terminated Kitty three weeks later when he trapped
her with the item in Diana McLellan's column about his wife
expecting a baby.)

"I knew a real go-getter," Bagley said. "Lucianne Goldberg
lives in New York City but is very active in Washington. She
represents several writers and authors who live in town. So I
told Kitty to get in touch . . ."

"I don't know why you'd want to write about Kitty Kelley,"
Mrs. Goldberg told this author in our first interview. "It was a
hellish experience to deal with that woman. She constantly had
this attitude—lift me, carry me, clean up my mess. When I
undertook to represent her I had no idea that she came with a
whole trail of enemies in Washington. She turned out to be a
totally negative person . . ."

Kitty and Lucianne were still on the honeymoon of their
author-agent contractual relationship when the agent went to
bat for her newest client. Believing Kitty wasn't getting the best
of it despite the fourteen percent of the paperback pie, Lucianne set out to mine some quick gold.

The hardcover *Jackie Oh!* was at the top of every best-seller
list by this time. Foreign sales were more than merely brisk: the
book was sold in Great Britain to Granada Publishing Limited
for a $100,000 advance and brought another $75,000 from London's *Daily Mail* for first serial rights in the United Kingdom.
Additionally, book and serial rights were sold to such far-away
places as Australia, South Africa and New Zealand. Those commanded a hefty $150,000—in addition to $65,000 paid by
Bertelsmann Publishing Company for a German edition of the
book and $52,000 shelled out by Bunte for magazine serializa-
tion rights in that country.

Stuart stressed how those sales had materialized in just the
short time the book had been on the shelves. Then he hit Kitty's
battle-ready new agent with this salvo in her demand for a new
contract.

"I told her, 'Lucianne, maybe you wouldn't have agreed to let your client sign such a contract. But if she hadn't she wouldn't be making the kind of money she's making now . . . The way I see it is that I'd rather have one percent of Paul Getty than 100% of Lucianne Goldberg."

"Goldberg walked away in a huff after that exchange," Stuart said. "She made no further effort to do battle with me. I was slightly annoyed with Kitty for bringing Lucianne Goldberg onto the scene after the fact. I was more annoyed with a letter she wrote to Carole Livingston [then serving as one of his publishing firm's top three executives.]"

The letter contained a strong expression of Kitty's distaste for the people programming her promotional tour and arranging her stays in such cities as Chicago, Portland, San Francisco, etc.

****

Kitty's first promotional appearances for *Jackie Oh!* were disasters.

"After I heard her on the Bob Grant radio show in New York," Lyle Stuart remembers, "I told her, 'Kitty, you were awful! You didn't mention the title. You gave the listener no reason to buy the book. Improve or we'll cancel the tour . . .' "

That night, Kitty went on the *Long John Nebel* midnight radio talk show for an hour. Afterward, she put in a call to Stuart's home.

"Well, was I better?" she asked in a plaintive voice.

"You were good. That's the way you should come over in all the shows you do from now on. Mention the title. Mention the publisher so they don't accidentally buy that other book. Give 'em reasons to buy it."

Kelley became a competent guest on the talk-show circuit.

"But then we discovered a weird phenomenon about her appearances," recalls Stuart, "one that it took a while to accept. As she went from town to town, the sales of the book invariably dropped after her appearance in a city. She turned people off. Her tour was having a negative impact."

Yet despite the counter-productive vibes she radiated on TV and radio, the book's sales continued to soar overall. Then . . .

"Lyle, dear . . . I have something to tell you . . ."

Her voice was weak, shaky . . .

"I've just been examined and the doctor found a mass in my uterus," she began. "He indicates that it could be cancerous . . . I'm going to have a hysterectomy . . ."

"When does the doctor want you to go to the hospital?" Stuart asked.

"As soon as possible . . ."

"Okay, but you know we have a couple of the morning network shows to do this week and next . . . Do you think you can delay surgery for a few days?"

"Of course! I'd rather die than not do those shows. I already told Mike that I don't care about me. I told him I just want to go out there, do the talk shows and sell my book for Lyle . . ."

The surgery was performed in Washington and was followed by a period of convalescence during which Kitty put herself through a daily regimen of swimming and exercise at a YWCA. In short order she regained her health and vigor and resumed her tour for *Jackie Oh!*

The book continued to sell well. The royalties and subsidiary income were enough to allow Kitty to make a down payment on the elegant, historic house in Georgetown where she still lives today. Ironically, the house was diagonally across the corner from the residence of Jackie's mother, Janet Auchincloss.

Negotiations for the house began in December, 1978—even before the big bucks had cascaded upon Kitty. But seeing them coming, she went after retired Justice Brennan's old mansion.

Writing to Lyle Stuart on January 14, 1979, Kitty poured out her heart about the house, her firing by Smith Bagley, and about an article in the *New York Post* which blew Kitty's mind. There wasn't much to the article. But it exposed publicly, for the first time, that Kitty had claimed false credentials. This upset her.

"These aren't the kind of clips I like to pass on," Kitty stated in her letter to Stuart. "But since you've been out of the country, I wanted to keep you abreast . . . My lawyer is asking for a retraction from the *New York Post*, on the basis that they printed lies . . ."

At about the same time, in an attempt to get herself on *60 Minutes* to promote *Jackie Oh!*, Kitty tried to butter up Mike Wallace. She interviewed Wallace and wrote a puff piece about him for *Today Is Sunday*. In a long, rambling, simpering letter to the CBS-TV mahatma, Kitty wrote, in part:

"I've called my publisher . . . to say you mentioned doing a launch of *Jackie Oh!* on the condition that nothing more appears in print or on film from either of us beforehand . . . Afterwards it occurred to me to mention to you that *Ladies Home Journal* bought the first serial rights . . . you can tell me if this serialization would in any way jeopardize what you have in mind . . ."

In the same letter, Kitty told Wallace about "an assignment" she'd been given to write about the book, then hedges, "But I will hold off until I hear from you." Kelley is referring to the story published in the October, 1978, edition of *Washingtonian* magazine, relating how she zapped the wife of the unidentified doctor who never administered anesthesia for Jackie Kennedy's non-existent electro-shock therapy.

The *New York Post* article which so upset Kelley winds up with a reference to the Kitty Kelley-Mike Wallace fiasco in the form of a quote from The Man at *60 Minutes*:

"We considered it [the *Jackie Oh!* book] and we discarded it."

****

The question of a sequel to the best-selling *Jackie Oh!* remained up in the air as Stuart flew off to the Caribbean for a brief vacation. Until the phone rang in his home in Port Maria, Jamaica.

"Lyle, dear, it's Kitty."

Her voice was honey-coated and she was putting on her Southern accent. Every so often Kitty became a Southerner. "I wasn't exactly in the mood to speak with her," Stuart recalled.

"How is it there, Lyle?"

"Beautiful as always."

"Could you use another house guest? I'd love to fly down . . ."

Silence.

After a telling pause, Kitty said, "Lyle dear . . . what if I do the Elizabeth Taylor book with Simon & Schuster, and then do one for you?"

"No."

"Why?"

"Because the next book you do will get very big money from a paperback house, and I want my share of it. We took a chance on you, Kitty, and I'm entitled to a piece of the action."

Stuart knew the conspiratorial wheels were whirling inside the bleached blonde head at the other end of the long-distance call. He didn't know she'd already offered the Elizabeth Taylor biography to Simon & Schuster via agent Lucianne Goldberg.

S&S came back with an offer of a $150,000 advance.

Under her option with Stuart, the advance would be a nominal $3,000.

"Lyle, dear, you let me write my next one for Simon and Schuster. I really want to write this Liz Taylor book . . . I promise you I'll do one for you after I write that one for them."

"No."

"Then let me out of my contract. You did it for Evelyn Keyes . . ."

Kitty was referring to the former Hollywood film star who could count among her husbands the much-married band leader Artie Shaw and brilliant movie director John Huston, and whose lovers included theatrical impresario Mike Todd, who later married Elizabeth Taylor. Evelyn Keyes had written *Scarlett O'Hara's Younger Sister*, her Hollywood autobiography, which Stuart published and which became a bestseller.

Keyes had phoned Stuart one day to report that literary agent Irving "Swifty" Lazar told her he could get her $400,000 to $500,000 for her next book, which was a novel. She asked if there was any way that she could go with him.

Stuart told Keyes she was free.

163

She asked, "What do you mean?"

He repeated, "Evelyn, you're free."

"Well, what percentage do you want?"

"Evelyn, we love you . . . You're free. I don't want any percentage. I'll send you a letter giving you a complete release."

Kitty was reminding Stuart of the "favor" he'd done for the actress:

"Lyle . . . what do you say . . . will you let me out of the contract . . . ?"

"No way."

Now she was crying.

Stuart recalled that he spoke slowly. "I figured that the longer the conversation, the more she'd have to pay for the call and this was one she couldn't charge to us. As it turned out, the call stretched to about fifteen minutes which was about thirty bucks out of Kitty's pocket."

When Kelley again, through her sobs, reminded Stuart of his release of Evelyn Keyes he responded evenly, "Kitty . . . I did it for Evelyn Keyes because she's my friend and I love her . . . I don't even *like* you!"

The crying stopped abruptly. An icy Kitty said, "Well, that's good to know" as she slammed the phone down.

"And," Stuart added with a smile, "we've never spoken since . . ."

With Lucianne Goldberg breaking ground for her, Kitty went through the motions of living up to her commitment to submit her next work to Stuart. Since he wanted no part of an unauthorized biography of Liz Taylor, Kitty sent the publisher what is known in the trade as an option-buster. It was the completed manuscript of a novel entitled *Reunion*, which she later told friends was actually written by her husband.

It was a literary atrocity.

****

"Well, Lyle, you turned down *Reunion*, but Simon & Schuster didn't . . ."

The voice was Lucianne Goldberg's. She phoned to let Stuart know Kitty was no longer committed to him, inasmuch as the book he rejected was accepted by S&S.

Stuart suspected S&S bought *Reunion* as a ploy to get the Taylor biography.

"They're paying twenty-five thousand," Goldberg told Stuart.

Kitty believed she had outsmarted the publisher. But when she jumped ship, she fell into the drink. For, soon after she broke from Stuart, it was reported that Kitty Kelley returned the $25,000 advance to Simon & Schuster and reclaimed the manuscript.

On what grounds?

"I don't wish it to be published under my name," Kitty announced.

Lyle Stuart had put his ear to the ground, heard what Kelley had done, and nailed her. He brought her into arbitration for breaching the terms of her contract.

"Did your husband write any part of *Reunion?*" Kelley would be asked at the deposition hearing.

"No," was her answer.

Once again, "Did your husband write any part of the manuscript entitled *Reunion?*"

"No," was her answer.

The question was asked again.

"It's hard to answer that, because almost everything I write my husband goes over and edits."

Once again, "Did your husband write any part of the manuscript entitled *Reunion?*

"Possibly . . ."

Kitty went down for the count in the arbiter's ring, and was compelled to pay Stuart a substantial sum.

15

January 5, 1989
Dear Mr. Carpozi:
I regret that I will be unable to do an interview [about
Kitty Kelley] as I feel that there are more important and
urgent matters to discuss in life than to sit and talk about
someone whose existence I do not even acknowledge . . .
Wishing you a very successful and happy 1989.
Sincerely,
Elizabeth Taylor

Some nine years earlier, Elizabeth Taylor Warner, then the wife
of U.S. Senator John Warner from Virginia, and residing in
Washington, sent a letter to Kitty Kelley that could be assessed
as the precursor of the one she sent to me—declining to be
interviewed for the book Kelley was writing about her.

Kitty had telephoned Elizabeth Taylor's representatives incessantly to request an interview with the actress. Failing to
reach Taylor directly, Kelley sought to interview Taylor's
friends. But, as *Washington Post* writer Jonathan Yardley relates, no true friendwould give Kelley the time of day:

* "Does Senator Warner wear a sleep mask to bed?

* "Is it true Elizabeth had three-hundred diamonds sewn on
the bodice of her evening dress just so she wouldn't have a

cheap rhinestone shine when the Kleig lights were beamed on her?

* "What can you tell me about the ostentatious lifestyle of Elizabeth when she was Richard Burton's wife?

* "Tell me about Elizabeth's dogs? I heard she refused to be separated from them and that when she took them to Europe's finest hotels, they ruined every expensive carpet by pissing all over it [sic]. Can you confirm that?

* "Do you know whether Liz suffered menstrual cramps while making *A Place In The Sun*, and after that had a stipulation written into her contract that she'd never work when she had her period?"

Etc., etc., etc. All questions designed to paint an unflattering or unglamorous portrait.

But Kelley's approach to the classier people in Elizabeth Taylor's world—directors, producers, fellow actors—was made on a different, subtler tack.

"Please don't be reluctant to talk about her," Kitty would tell them. "Confide in me because you'll be doing a disservice to Elizabeth if you don't speak up. You can understand how important this is if I'm to make my book as accurate as I possibly can . . ."

In New York, Liz's publicist Chen Sam was drowning in the cascade of correspondence from Kelley requesting—indeed begging—to interview the actress.

Taylor finally responded by writing the polite but positive putdown . . .

****

August 8, 1980
Dear Ms. Kelley,
Thank you for your interesting note—I say interesting because what I have heard from acquaintances (not great friends) reveals you have been asking questions that I find very peculiar and personal. I see no way how your approach could result in a meaningful book since substantial amounts of alleged facts sound fabricated.

Liz Smith I do believe is a valued friend and I value my friendships very much. I have never given interviews about people I know, past or present because I honor "privacy" so much.

Throughout my long association with journalists, I have asked no more than a professional, objective and honest evaluation of my life and career. Your words "a meaningful book, better, fair and more interesting" are, I presume, in that same spirit.

Sincerely,

Elizabeth Taylor Warner

****

Kitty pursued her objective with renewed vigor after receiving the rejection letter. How could anyone expect Elizabeth Taylor would let Kelley interview her after the number she'd pulled on Jackie Onassis? Of course, Kitty herself let the cat out of the bag when she told good friends Janet Donovan and Diana McLellan one day soon after she began her assault on Liz's publicist Chen Sam:

"I'm just going through the motions of requesting the interview so I'll be able to say 'I tried.' I don't believe in my wildest dreams that she'll sit still to talk to me . . ."

In her search for the "truth" about Elizabeth Taylor, Kitty gave this tidbit to *Washington Post* columnist Rudy Maxa:

"Elizabeth Taylor probably will not cooperate with the project. Even if she doesn't, if the book is a best-seller I intend to donate a sizable portion of my royalties to Liz's favorite cause, a children's hospital in Botswana . . ."

Although the book would make a brief appearance on the best-seller lists, a check of contributors to Botswana Hospital in Africa more than ten years after that statement was made, fails to turn up a donation by anyone named Kitty Kelley, Katherine A. Kelley, or Mrs. Michael Edgley.

****

When Kelley was digging into Smith Bagley's trash for gossip column tidbits, she was exhibiting what many view as her deepest compulsion, to dig deeply for dirt. Kitty decided that there was merit in that practice, and if carried far enough could produce a wealth of trashy intelligence about the subject.

Kitty and Mike Edgley observed their third wedding anniversary around the time she signed to do the Liz Taylor book. The former bartender hadn't made any progress in his literary career. But it wasn't for a lack of trying. Kitty occasionally spoke to literary agents and publishers on Mike's behalf.

"Can you get him a contract to write a novel . . . or any kind of book . . . ?"

All to no avail. The highest Edgley climbed on the literary ladder was to work as media director for the National Council on the Aging. But he quit that job in 1980 to become Kitty's first assistant garbologist and Man Friday.

He could be seen standing by in the shadows at book-signing parties for *Jackie Oh!* At home in their Georgetown mansion, Edgley found himself marching to Kitty's drum and suffered her flirtations with others.

"Mike, get your ass over to the *Washington Post* and pick up the clips I ordered . . ."

"Mike, I have to find out [this or that] about Senator Warner at the Library of Congress . . ."

Mike would wear a neatly-pressed suit and carefully-knotted tie on his rounds of researching. But then came the day when Kitty sent him—in second-hand threads—to an address not too distant from the Edgleys' own Georgetown manse—3240 S Street N.W.—the home of Senator and Mrs. John Warner.

"Kitty had me collecting and sorting through John's and Liz's trash," Edgley admitted. "She transformed me into a skilled garbologist."

Speaking with no demonstrable rancor or disgust about his role, "Mr. Kelley," as some cynics dubbed him, described how he performed his "garbage runs":

"On trash collection days, I'd get out of bed shortly after dawn, put on my sweat suit and jog for a couple of miles. Then

170

I'd get into my car and drive to the Warner house to pick up their garbage.

"They'd empty it into cans that were left on the side of the porch, where the garbage collectors picked it up. I'd get there first and sift through the stuff, pick out whatever I felt Kitty would need for the book, and haul it to our place . . ."

Although his early-morning garbage-gathering excursions had been a running joke for Kitty and Mike at social get-togethers, the author didn't think it funny when she learned the practice had been reported by her agent to an editor at the publishing house considering Kelley's proposed next book, a biography of Frank Sinatra.

****

One of Kitty's triumphant information-gathering endeavors occurred when she went to Metro-Goldwyn-Mayer studios and persuaded them to open their files on their one-time fabled star.

From these files, Kitty claims, came whole globs of dirt.

Another of the book's "revelations" was attributed to Max Lerner, octogenarian syndicated columnist who held a chair in history at Brandeis University. Lerner was described as the hottest lover Liz Taylor ever had. Kitty claims Max let his hair down with her and talked at great length about his purported affair with the violet-eyed beauty, and about Liz's other lovers as well.

"I deny everything and anything Kitty Kelley said I told her. She distorted everything I said—she's a journalistic debaucher . . ."

In the book, Kitty gets all the mileage she can out of the overblown Lerner-Taylor encounter.

Page 83 of *The Last Star* introduces the first of the shockers. It concerns Liz's relationship with actor Montgomery Clift, a closet homosexual who co-starred with Taylor in three films, *A Place In The Sun* (1951), *Raintree County* (1957), and *Suddenly, Last Summer* (1959). He had long been rumored to have been romantically attached to Liz. Allusions to Clift's sexual preferences have been made by writers in the past.

Author Thomas Thompson claimed Elizabeth told him she "never made it sexually" with Monty. Truman Capote had written that Taylor told him, "Well, one doesn't always fry the fish one wants to fry. Some of the men I've really liked didn't like women."

Kitty borrowed these quotes as a prelude to her introduction to the statement she attributed to Max Lerner about how "desperately in love" Elizabeth and Clift were with each other:

"She told me they had an affair, but you've got to remember with Elizabeth that a homosexual is a prime sexual target—a challenge to be met. After all, that represents the unattainable, and how better to demonstrate your sexual power than to possess the unattainable? In Monty's case she wanted to make him straight. She couldn't do it."

Kitty goes on to say Liz "settled for the only relationship possible—one that was to become extremely involved and convoluted until Clift's lonely death in 1965 . . ."

While on the subject of homosexuals, one wonders why Kitty Kelley never touched upon the other man in Elizabeth Taylor's life whose bedroom habits with other movie industry men were widely known—perhaps no less so than Montgomery Clift's: Rock Hudson.

Liz's friendship with Hudson began in 1956 when the two appeared in *Giant*, which received ten Academy Award nominations. These included two for Best Actor (Rock Hudson and James Dean) and one for Best Supporting Actress (Mercedes McCambridge). Although her performance was one of her best, Taylor wasn't nominated.

Liz survived this disappointment and remained visibly buoyant in her private life. She sailed through a series of marriages— to hotel heir Nicky Hilton, impresario Mike Todd, and singer Eddie Fisher. It was while she was wed to Fisher that Elizabeth developed the relationship with Max Lerner. The seed was planted by a compassionate column about Fisher's divorce from Debbie Reynolds and marriage to Elizabeth Taylor. Wrote Lerner:

"I like the fact that . . . they are quite frank about their feelings for each other. This is a case where a joyous candor is far better than a hypocritical show of virtue. Where so many people have been desensitized in our world, I welcome this forthright celebration of the life of the senses."

Elizabeth and Eddie were so moved by those words that they let it be known they wanted to meet Lerner.

"I called them at their hotel," Kitty quotes Lerner, "and spent a very spontaneous evening with them, talking and laughing. We all liked each other immediately. Elizabeth was her usual seductive self, and I fell in love [Taylor was 27 at the time, Lerner 57]. She was careful to tell me how stimulating Eddie had been in bed the night before. 'Three-and-a-half times, Max, three-and-a-half times,' she bragged. They were definitely reveling in their sensuality at the time."

By the time Lerner was having it on with Taylor, according to Kitty's version, Max had written eleven books. Liz asked him to write a twelfth that would be titled *Elizabeth Taylor: Between Life And Death*. "I'll do the recalling and you do the heavy thinking," Kelley claims the actress told her cerebral partner, then quickly has Liz and Max producing the book—under the covers and between the sheets. Kitty again allegedly quotes Max:

"We started working with a tape recorder a couple of mornings in bed, but as you might suspect we didn't really get much work done on the book there . . ."

Working on the book, Kitty observes, "was a good excuse for the two of them to spend legitimate time together, but Elizabeth still wanted to allay any suspicions Max Lerner's wife might have."

Asked now whether the affair Kitty reports Lerner had with Taylor was serious, he replies:

"I don't want to dignify any more than necessary the lies about me and Elizabeth Taylor Ms. Kelley perpetrates on her readers. There was never an affair between us—definitely not! *Never!*"

But hadn't Max said he thought about marrying Liz, yet changed his mind because "she would use me the way a beautiful woman uses an older man—as a front while she goes to bed with everyone in sight?" That's what Kitty put in the book.

"I never said that. There was no affair. Period. Miss Taylor agrees with me on that . . ."

Well, he was asked in an interview for this book, what was there between you and Liz, Mr. Lerner? Was there *anything*—*anything at all*—between the two of you?

"There was a romantic friendship," Lerner concedes. "it lasted a brief time. It was never serious."

Lerner will tell the whole story, he promises—when he writes his own book. Meanwhile, he told his colleagues on the Brandeis University campus:

"Kitty Kelley has simply run away from the facts . . ."

Asked if he considers her a "journalistic debaucher," as he is quoted earlier, Lerner nods affirmatively.

"I've said all I'm going to say for now . . ."

Not surprisingly, Kitty Kelley blew steam over Max Lerner's putdown. As she does whenever anyone challenges her writing, she protested loudly:

"I interviewed him several times. I gathered corroboration that an Elizabeth Taylor-Max Lerner affair did occur. I have every confidence in that my account is fair and accurate . . ."

Then Kelley sounded yet another familiar refrain:

"I'm surprised at Max Lerner, both personally and professionally. He told me everything that I said he told me."

During the period that *The Last Star* was in the bookstores, Kitty was interviewed many times. Norma Langley, the Washington Bureau Chief of *Star* magazine, cornered Kitty and managed at the same time to interview husband Mike "The Garbage Man" Edgley, who gave enough exposure about his wife's tactics to command this headline:

How sexy writer used charms to get
the scoop on Liz's secret affair

"I think Kitty uses sex appeal to get certain information," Edgley gushed. "Maybe it's subconscious, but I know I wouldn't have got the same interviews she did.

"Kitty's a genuinely curious person. She'll meet someone at a party, for example, and see they're wearing a beautiful necklace or ring. Then she'll say: 'Gee, that's so pretty' and in five minutes they're talking like long-lost friends.

"A lot of men are flattered by that sort of attention. They think: 'Oh, yeah, she really digs me. She must be trying to get me into bed,' and that's all they can think of. Right away they're blabbing and their whole life comes out.

"That's how she got Max Lerner to tell her about his affair with Liz Taylor."

Kitty had another go at Lerner:

"Max is groveling, saying 'Well, it wasn't exactly an affair—it was a romantic friendship.' I'm sorry, but when a man is in bed with a woman, that to me is an affair, not a friendship."

Kitty took exception to her husband's suggestion that she employs sex appeal to nail down an interview with a man.

"I don't think my success has anything to do with being sexy," she protested. "I believe it all comes down to the questions I ask—and I'm very up-front and blunt when it comes to asking questions."

Before she'd completed the manuscript for the Elizabeth Taylor biography, Kitty Kelley was invited, along with other Simon & Schuster authors, to her publisher's 1980 annual Christmas party in Manhattan. By now Kitty was being given red carpet treatment by the firm's Editor-in-Chief Michael Korda and its Chairman, Richard C. Snyder.

Because she held out the promise of being so bankable for the publishing house, S&S decided to spare Kitty the inconvenience of a one-day's roundtrip between Washington, D.C., and New York. They arranged for an overnight stay following the party in the posh St. Regis Hotel at Fifth Avenue and 55th Street.

S&S editors recall that Christmas party which featured a sumptuous sitdown dinner. Kitty was not the only guest from Washington attending the bash. She'd brought a gaggle of girlfriends from the capital to New York—all on the S&S expense account.

"We found early-on that Kitty Kelley is very demanding and very grubby . . ."

Speaking about his encounter with the free-spending author is S&S Board Chairman Snyder who, in the irony-of-ironies, will surely face Kelley's wrath for what follows:

Snyder spoke disparagingly about Kitty *after* she had jumped the Good Ship Simon & Schuster and climbed aboard over at Bantam Books. Bantam had sweetened the kitty for Kelley's next book, *His Way: The Unauthorized Biography of Frank Sinatra*, in a way S&S didn't want to—after having been burned by *Last Star* whose sales had been a major disappointment.

Snyder relates what happened after Kitty and her girlfriends returned from the Christmas party to the St. Regis:

"We didn't know about it until after we went to pay the bill for her suite. Kitty had called room service and ordered full-course dinners for everyone. This, after that huge sitdown dinner at the party!

"She picked one of every item on the menu. That Babylonian orgy cost us several hundred dollars . . . Kitty did everything humanly possible to run up the bill. She had herself a field day in the hotel beauty parlor with haircut, massage, manicure, you name it. Then she bought practically every newspaper and magazine at the newsstand, ordered shampoo, toothpaste, aspirin and, I can't remember how many cans of Tab. She just went completely wild."

Ten months later there was another party . . .

Elizabeth Taylor: The Last Star was at last off the press and in the book shops. The night of September 30, 1981, a Wednesday, was Kitty's night to purr and meow in ultimate ecstasy. Simon & Schuster leased Washington's West End Circle Theater for the party—and it turned out to be a celebrity-studded celebration.

The party was inside but the people outside had a riotous

A radiant Kitty Kelley at 18 years old in her Holy Names uniform shortly before her 1959 graduation. She was voted Most Popular Girl in the school four years running.
(COURTESY OF THE *SPOKANE CHRONICLE*.)

Kitty (far right) attended by her court after winning the Lilac Princess Pageant n Spokane.
(COURTESY OF THE *SPOKANE CHRONICLE*.)

Kitty greets Rep. Tom Foley (D. Wash)
at the New York World's Fair in 1965.
Since her father had helped elect him to
Congress, the least Foley could do was
invite Kitty to "come on down" to
Washington after the Fair closed.

Kitty Kelley in 1962.

Kitty displays photo of herself with
Senator Eugene J. McCarthy taken
during the Senator's bid for the 1968
Presidential nomination. Kitty was to
have worked "temporarily" in the
Wisconsin Democrat's office, but she
stayed on for four years.

Kitty's father, William V. Kelley, flanked by Kitty and her husband Mike Edgley.

Kitty at work: "Give her a telephone, scissors and paste and with her imagination she'll write you a book." (PHOTO BY CAROLE LIVINGSTON.)

Kelley in her "I defy Frank Sinatra" pose. The singer sued to stop her from misrepresenting that she had his approval.

Nancy Reagan and friend. Even people who disliked her became sympathetic after publication of the hatchet job on her by Kitty Kelley.
(PHOTO BY JON GILBERT.)

The Kelley assault on Sinatra left him
more popular than ever. Here he is with
(left) Luciano Pavarotti. (STAR PHOTOS)

Elizabeth Taylor in a 1988 photo.
Despite the Kelley assault, she remained
unscathed and as popular as ever.
(PHOTO BY ARNOLD BRUCE LEVY.)

The First Victim of Kitty Kelley's
poison pen: Jacqueline Onassis.
(PHOTO BY J. WHALEN.)

Frank Sinatra in action. Although his singing career spanned nearly sixty years and thou‐
sands of recordings including hundreds of hits, Kelley mentioned his voice only twice in
her bitter 700-page biography that attacked everyone from his mother to his butler.
(TED KORYN LIBRARY.)

Moment of Triumph. (PHOTO BY CAROLE LIVINGSTON.)

Kitty and Random House editor Joni Evans at a 1990 Literary Guild party at the Waldorf-Astoria Hotel. (PHOTO BY MAUREEN O'BRIEN.)

Kitty Kelley in repose.
(PHOTO BY CAROLE LIVINGSTON.)

Kitty and Nancy (DRAWING BY VINT LAWRENCE FOR *THE NEW REPUBLIC*.)

time too. It became a gaper's holiday on the street for rubber-necking motorists. There were balloons, placards, still and TV cameras. Tapes of Eddie Fisher singing *Wish You Were Here* and Richard Burton's stentorian voice rendering from the score of *Camelot*.

Kitty Kelley arrived in a chauffeur-driven limousine. She stood in black stiletto heels, giving the unmistakable appearance of having been poured into her black velvet skirt and hot purple blouse.

"Your blouse is insane," her friend, Theodora Hausman, gasped after Kitty made her grand entrance into the theater. She mixed with the crowd sipping champagne from crystal stemware.

"Oh, everyone's spilling all over me," Kelley exclaimed. She craned her neck over the heads in the packed reception area and cracked, "Well, we invited Elizabeth Taylor, but I don't see her royal presence here . . ."

****

"The bad news about *Elizabeth Taylor: The Last Star* is that it does not deliver what the buyer has a right to expect of a 'breathlessly detailed biography by Kitty Kelley, author of the best-selling *Jackie Oh!* [as the book jacket promised].' It does not deliver any hot gossip. The good news . . . well, there isn't any good news. *Elizabeth Taylor: The Last Star* is a bore."

Thus wrote *Washington Post* resident critic Jonathan Yardley in the Sunday edition's *Book World* magazine, and continued:

"Those in the market for lurid new details about the life and loves of the pneumatic Taylor must look elsewhere . . .

". . . Relying almost entirely on secondary sources and the testimony of persons barely within genuflecting distance of the Taylor throne, Kelley has produced a tired, ordinary star bio that reeks of information gathered from old news clips and/or borrowed from other books and articles—few of them identified.

"Kelley comes to her task, however breathlessly, with no

177

clear view of her subject and no evident interest save that of making a bundle—which, since Barnum was right, she will. She has no discernible feeling for Taylor, who, if nothing else, is a certifiably fascinating individual; to Kelley she's just another star, about whom to write just another formulaic biography."

Newsweek published an interesting anecdote: "Did Sen. John Warner really expect to endear himself to Elizabeth Taylor by calling her 'Chicken Fat'? That's one of the giblets about the legally separated spouses that are served up . . ." Actually this review is based on Kitty's story in *Washingtonian* magazine, in which she feeds just some extra juicier tidbits about Liz and John that she hypes beyond what she's already written about in the book. Another Kitty Kelley fabrication, another non-committal review by a major weekly magazine.

People panned: "Liz may be, as Kelley charges, hysterical, spoiled, ill-educated and a hypochondriac, but you can't prove it from this diatribe . . ."

Nineteen days after his October 14th review of the book, Jonathan Yardley reported to his readers:

"For my 42nd birthday, which took place last week, I received a sweater, a pen knife, a picture frame, a casserole dish, a suede hat—and a large plastic bag filled with the severed heads of dead fish. This last, which was delivered to *Book World* at the *Washington Post*, came in a gold Gucci box (a nice touch, at that) and was accompanied by a card reading: 'From the Friends of Kitty Kelley.'

"Happy birthday indeed! Obviously this generous and welcome gift was sent in gratitude for my review in *The Post* of Kelley's new book, *Elizabeth Taylor: The Last Star*, which I had characterized as 'a bore' and 'a tired, ordinary bio'; to make the connection absolutely clear, on the other side of the card accompanying the fish heads was a photograph of the luscious (it was taken in 1961) Taylor that had been clumsily doctored so that it appeared she was giving me the finger. The friends of Kitty Kelley, like the friends of Eddie Coyle, clearly were out for blood.

"So it is with great sorrow that I must tell them—by means of this column, since for some reason they declined to give their names [as evidence in future chapters will show, it could have been none other than Kitty Kelley herself who sent the fish-heads and card to Yardley]—that none has been shed. Sticks and stones may break my bones but fish will never hurt me. To be sure, in nearly two decades of writing book reviews and otherwise expressing my opinions in print, I had not previously been assaulted by a sack of fishheads; but I have had my fair share of slings and arrows from outraged and aggrieved authors, and/or their 'friends,' and I have lived to tell the tale."

Jonathan Yardley's last word on the subject:

"Perhaps the friends of Kitty Kelley . . . are convulsed by their wit or impressed by their boldness. But I am of the view that their behavior is even trashier than their friend's book—and that is saying something."

16

The reviews weren't yet written in late August, 1981. *Elizabeth Taylor: The Last Star* wouldn't reach the shops until November. But already literary agent Lucianne Goldberg was negotiating with Simon & Schuster for Kitty's Frank Sinatra biography.

S&S Editor Michael Korda had visions of a runaway bestseller in *The Last Star*, so he was not the least bit reluctant to offer five times the $150,000 advance he paid for the Liz Taylor book. Seven hundred and fifty thousand was the bid. Actually, it had been Korda's boss, S&S Chairman Richard C. Snyder, who came up with the idea of Kelley doing the book on Sinatra.

"At first blush it looked like a deal no agent could resist," Lucianne Goldberg told me. "Here we had the top man in this mighty publishing empire picking the author and the subject for her next book. It was a dream of a deal . . ."

It certainly was an offer out of fantasyland—especially since Kelley was told she need not provide an outline before contracts were drawn. Kitty let her hair down and told Snyder and Korda exactly what they wanted to hear:

"Oh, you've hit the nail on the head. Sinatra has been on my mind for the longest time . . . What a book I could write about him!"

Kitty then revealed she had "never-before-told dirt" on the venerable troubadour.

"I couldn't have put this in *The Last Star*," she said, "because it wasn't nailed down before the deadline . . . But now I can write about it . . . Sinatra made Liz pregnant and then paid for her abortion!"

Since the Taylor book was coming off the presses and heading to the bindery, the S&S chieftains were delighted to sit on this spectacular news rather than break into the production schedule and have it trumpeted in *The Last Star*.

Snyder and Korda were pleased to learn Kitty had turned up leads on the Sinatra family's early years in Hoboken, New Jersey, that—as Kitty put it to her salivating listeners—"will blow your mind." Among her juiciest discoveries that grabbed the S&S big numbers was Kelley's claim that she uncovered court records which had Frankie's mother arrested for performing illegal abortions.

"Dick and Michael flipped out when I told them about this," Kitty told her agent. "They couldn't believe I had dug up such sensational information."

Mrs. Goldberg could believe it. Seven hundred and fifty thousand dollars without so much as an outline was a juicy offer.

In a euphoric state, Lucianne returned to her Manhattan office and phoned Kitty in Washington with the exciting news.

"Not enough!" complained the author, who, just three years earlier had been thrilled to accept a three thousand dollar advance to write *Jackie Oh!*

Startled by her client's response, Mrs. Goldberg finally found her voice and asked what Kitty was talking about.

"I want a million dollars . . ."

"What!" exclaimed the agent.

"You heard me . . . one million!"

"How did you arrive at that figure?"

"Because I want to be able to say I got a million dollar advance for this book . . ."

"But it wasn't even your idea . . . Dick Snyder suggested that you write it . . . and he's giving you five times what you received for *Last Star*. You're pushing it, Kitty . . ."

"I'm not pushing it. And it makes no difference whose idea Sinatra is . . . I want that million-dollar advance . . . Go to another publisher, but get it . . ."

"Because I felt it was the honorable thing to do," Mrs. Goldberg told me, "I went back to Korda and told him of Kitty's demand."

The meeting in the editor's opulent offices in Rockefeller Center, didn't go well.

"Can't be done," Korda told her. "We've already exceeded the budget planned for such a book. A million is out of the question. Seven-hundred and fifty thousand is our offer and it's generous and that's where we stand . . ."

Lucianne was now free to go elsewhere. She approached Harper & Row, and spoke with editor Larry Ashmead. He was amenable.

Kitty flew to New York and went to lunch with Ashmead. Over the main course, the editor almost caused his guest to fall out of her chair.

"I understand that you employ some clever tactics to get information on the people you write about," Kitty's host declared.

"What are you referring to . . . ?

"The way you sent your husband out to pick Elizabeth Taylor's garbage . . ."

"Where did you hear that!" Kitty screeched, almost choking on the last morsel she'd forked into her mouth.

"From your agent . . . Lucianne . . ."

"Ohhh," Kitty shot back. "Ohhh . . ."

****

"It was all downhill after that," Mrs. Goldberg said. "Kitty, who'd been calling me four and five times a day, stopped phoning. This was around mid-February of 1982. Her silence dragged into the middle of March."

Then Lucianne heard from Benjamin L. Zelenko, a Washington-based attorney and "close friend" of Kitty's.

"He sent a letter asking me to attend a meeting in Kitty's house at which her husband and Zelenko would be present. He offered no clue as to what it would be about."

Goldberg suspects that Kitty wanted to make an issue out of the garbage incident "but she couldn't bring herself to talk about it."

So they discussed other matters of little consequence.

"The only substantive thing that came out of the meeting was that Kitty was furious at the one-thousand dollar fee she was being charged by a lawyer I had recommended to her . . ."

The lawyer, whom Lucianne identified as John Diamond, formerly a counsel at Simon & Schuster, was retained to negotiate a contract with the producer David Susskind, who wanted to adapt the Liz Taylor book as a special for television.

"It's customary for literary agents to retain lawyers or Hollywood agents to work on such arrangements because of their expertise in these matters," Mrs. Goldberg explained. "But when Kitty got his bill, she went out of her mind. She even tried to sue him . . ."

The agent returned to New York thoroughly puzzled about the purpose of the meeting at Kelley's home. In May—after another period of uninterrupted silence on Kitty's part—Goldberg was served with a summons for a suit filed by Zelenko in Kelley's behalf in Washington's Federal District Court.

Now Lucianne Goldberg began to see the light . . .

For some time, Kitty had been bugging her agent about royalties from foreign rights that had been sold for her *Jackie Oh!* and *The Last Star* books. The tattletale author believed the agent was holding back.

"She confronted me with those claims and I told her she was mistaken," Goldberg said. "Kitty was letting her imagination run rampant. True, she had some royalties due her—but publishers overseas are frequently tardy in remitting checks. Kitty was hungry for the money . . ."

Even as she pondered the grounds on which Kitty was suing her, Goldberg got wind of another development . . .

"I heard Kitty was looking around for a new agent. But I wasn't certain of that because she wasn't talking to me . . ."

Kelley developed an almost paranoid distrust of Goldberg and was determined to dump her.

"First I find out she's holding out on my royalties on foreign sales," Kitty told Diana McLellan and other friends at lunch. "Then she badmouths me with the people at Harper by telling them I pick people's garbage. So, to make a long story short, I'm suing her ass . . ."

One of those at the lunch suggested Kitty approach Robert (Robbie) Lantz, a highly-respected New York literary agent. Kelley offered herself to him but Lantz declined. She interviewed several other agents, but either she wasn't impressed with them or they weren't interested in her.

Finally she turned to a giant literary agency, International Creative Management. She was welcomed into the fold and, to show her how much they respected her as an author, assigned Kitty to one of their top agents, Lynn Nesbit.

Nesbit crackled from Day One. She went after Michael Korda and told him she was confident she could find another publisher for Kitty's Sinatra book and that S&S's $750,000 offer would easily be topped by another house. Wasn't Michael interested in keeping this best-selling author in his stable . . . ?

"Okay," Korda finally relented. "Show me an outline, give me a summary of chapters and thumbnail sketches of what'll be in those chapters. Then we'll talk . . ."

Under the terms of her S&S contract Kitty was legally bound to give the publisher first refusal on her next book—just as she had been committed to do so under the earlier agreement with Lyle Stuart. But the problem now, unlike before, was that Korda wanted Kitty to write the Sinatra book while Stuart showed no interest in an Elizabeth Taylor bio.

Kitty's new agent chose not to take refuge in the option-busting tactic Lucianne Goldberg had resorted to with Lyle Stuart. Kelley committed herself to a Sinatra biography and wanted the biggest possible bucks for it. Nesbit's only other course was to go to different publishing houses and return to S&S with a larger offer.

That's what happened. Lynn Nesbit didn't need a cab to convey her the short walking distance from Fifth Avenue to 1230 Avenue of the Americas to break the news to Michael Korda. The agent had just left a huddle with a gaggle of editors at Bantam Books Inc. and departed with their trademark rooster emblem comfortably tucked under her arm. When admitted to Korda's office, Nesbit was restrained as she reported to Korda:

"We've been offered a million five-hundred thousand by Bantam."

"It seems to me that's an offer you can hardly refuse," Korda responded quietly. "I wish you all the best."

It was mid-June and Korda wasn't remorseful at being outbid for Kelley's next book. Reports from the field about *Elizabeth Taylor: The Last Star* were disappointing. The book simply wasn't selling well.

S&S executives felt compelled to direct its publicity people to hype the book.

They were told to stir up a groundswell to give the book the appearance of a best-seller.

Dell was the lollypop. It entered into a bidding war with Bantam Books for mass-market rights to *The Last Star*.

The people at Bantam had no idea how lucky they were when they stood pat on their final offer of $900,000 after the spirited bidding contest. At the end, unbeknownst to each other, only Bantam and Dell were left. Dell got the book for a guaranteed advance of $915,000. It was a Pyrrhic victory.

Listen to Dell's then-president, Bud Tobey, who sanctioned the bidding to the maximum and today is living in tranquil retirement in Augusta, Georgia, far from the New York publishing world's trench wars:

"Kitty Kelley was a total disaster for us. We lost upwards of eight-hundred thousand dollars on the book. It was a very depressing experience . . ."

The reviewers who'd taken the hardcover edition over the

coals hadn't helped. But essentially the book didn't sell because it was dull.

Kitty Kelley wasn't concerned about Dell's loss. She had become Washington's newest millionaire.

Now all she had to do was send her "researchers" to gather the books and newspaper and magazine clippings she'd need to paste up her unauthorized biography of Frank Sinatra.

17

The ink had hardly dried on the agreement between Kitty Kelley and Bantam Books before the irreverent author was rocked by a dispatch from Francis Albert Sinatra himself.

No, the celebrated troubadour wasn't capitulating to Kitty's requests for interviews. Sinatra's song to Kelley was no ballad. He served her with a $2 million lawsuit to make her stop misrepresenting herself as the *authorized* biographer of Frank Sinatra.

The nuts and bolts of the action, filed on September 21, 1983, in California's Superior Court, were machine-tooled to transport Kelley into the legal labyrinth.

Attorney Milton Rudin had been in and out of courthouses on Sinatra's behalf innumerable times in the 40 years he'd been The Voice's mouthpiece.

Rudin had been Frankie's defender for most of the many assault cases he was involved with. The singer's short temper prompted him to slug people at will. Those assaults were almost never committed without strong-armed companions nearby.

Rudin had been at Sinatra's side when Nevada's Gaming Commission revoked his license to own a piece of a gambling casino because of his friendship with a notorious mobster who was entertained at the Cal-Neva Lodge, in which Frankie was a point-holder. And Mickey Rudin was there when, with an assist from President Reagan, the license was reinstated.

The senior member of the Beverly Hills law firm of Rudin, Richman & Appel was at his side when Sinatra had appeared before the House Select Committee on Crime to testify about his association with known underworld figures, as well as investigating his investment in a mob-scarred New England racetrack.

Rudin also went into combat for Sinatra when the House UnAmerican Activities Committee unraveled testimony alleging that Ol' Blue Eyes "acts as a front" for Communist organizations. Rudin quashed that un-American allegation in triple time.

Rudin also handled Sinatra's three divorces: from Nancy Barbato (the mother of his three children), Ava Gardner, and Mia Farrow.

So Mickey Rudin was no Philadelphia tangle-jaw. Suing on behalf of Camden Enterprises Ltd., the Nevada corporation holding the right to be "exclusive licensee . . . to commercially exploit the name and likeness of Frank Sinatra including the right to publish the authorized biography or autobiography of Sinatra's life," the complaint he filed called for:

". . . damages for unlawful business practices; misappropriation of name and likeness for commercial purposes; and for injunction."

Rudin delegated his firm's libel attorney, John D. Forbess, to confront Kitty and her judicial seconds in court.

The court papers stated that in his more than four decades in show business, Frank had become "one of the best-known and successful entertainers alive today," thus generating "a great deal of interest by the public worldwide in the events, both public and private, of Sinatra's life."

Because he had "chosen to keep private many of the private events of his life . . . a mystique of sorts has grown up over the years and decades as to the 'real truth' or the 'inside story' about numerous events and personalities" attending his life—thus "the commercial value of an unauthorized biography or of Sinatra's autobiography [which the papers said he planned to write someday] has been greatly enhanced."

Now the case against the author, and why Sinatra was seeking to enjoin her from doing his story:

"Defendant Kitty Kelley is an individual who is engaged in the business and profession of writing books about famous and widely-known individuals. In her books, defendant focuses primarily on those events of the subject person's life which are sensational, scandalous, and deprecating . . ."

The primary complaint against the author was that she "engaged in unfair competition and unlawful business practice, in violation of California Business and Professional Code Sections 17200 and 17500," and that she also violated California's Civil Code Sections 1710 and 1711 because she made "false and misleading statements . . . to members of the public . . ."

Attorney Forbess based these charges on events that Kitty Kelley had initiated in early 1983 when she trekked to Los Angeles with her companion, the *Time-Life* photographer who was to receive this dedication in *His Way*:

"To Stanley Tretick, whose tireless efforts on behalf of this book disprove his theory that photographers are a shiftless lot."

Once in L.A., she established a beachhead at the Beverly Hills home of Hollywood Free-lance correspondent Jack Martin, who allowed Kitty to occupy his place rent-free for four months while he visited England. Martin also let Kitty use his 1976 American Motors two-door Pacer.

"Defendant has . . . attempted to interview numerous individuals who are friends, acquaintances, or associates of Sinatra who have or might have 'inside' knowledge of the private aspects of events of Sinatra's life. In securing, or in attempting to secure, interviews with said individuals, defendant has . . . made representations and statements, orally and in writing, to said interviewees which are false or misleading, in an attempt to obtain such interviews . . ."

The complaint further accused Kitty of issuing press releases that suggested she was gathering material for the biography "with the blessings of Sinatra, and that he (Sinatra) and his attorneys and other representatives are aware of her project and approve or do not object to the interviewees disclosing the 'inside' facts to her."

Moreover, the charges went on, Kitty went so far as to tell people Sinatra's office was cooperating with her by feeding her the phone numbers of Sinatra associates. A number of those who were persuaded to give interviews, it was charged, did so because they believed her false representations; on learning the truth they withdrew their consent to be quoted in the book.

In no instance anywhere in the 10-page court document is it suggested that Kelley had approached any member of Sinatra's family for an interview. Yet when the book was published 11 months later, the Author's Note in the front of the book tells us:

"My sources made the most important contributions to this book. Some were too frightened of reprisals from Frank Sinatra to speak on the record; others, because of their positions in the entertainment industry, law enforcement, and the White House, cannot be thanked by name, but I am grateful to all of them for their help . . . I appreciate the time and consideration of everyone who cooperated, including *several of Frank Sinatra's relatives, who so generously shared their recollections.*"

The emphasis is mine. The naked truth is that, after *His Way* was published, Kitty confessed in an interview with *Baltimore Sun* writer Alice Steinbach that "the *only* member of Sinatra's immediate family who talked to her was his son, Frank Sinatra Jr." He later denied he'd spoken with Kitty.

Junior, depicted by Kelley as the "forgotten child in his family," complained bitterly that the book was "nothing but vicious lies . . . Any facts are coincidental."

For pretending she had the singer's authorization in her quest for interviews, the suit demanded Kitty Kelley pay Sinatra $10,000. A mere pittance compared with the $2 million being demanded as punitive damages for "misappropriation of name and likeness for commercial purposes."

The excitement Kitty Kelley felt on learning about the suit from the news media was profound. "The whole idea is prior restraint," she said. "The last time someone tried this was when President Nixon tried to get an injunction against the *New York Times* and the *Washington Post* to suppress the Pentagon Papers."

Kelley was never as vocal in any cause as she was in this one that concerned her so personally—and ostensibly as she wanted us to believe, threatened her $1.5 million project.

My colleague Norma Langley, Washington Bureau Chief for *Star* magazine, was one of the first to interview "an angry" Kitty Kelley:

"Frank Sinatra has intimidated many, many people through the years," Kitty told Norma. "But I have no intention of being one of those who cave in.

"Sinatra is going to have to back off. I'd hate to countersue, but I'm sure I could.

"I didn't think I would get sued before I even wrote the book. This isn't the Soviet Union.

"I thought there was a possibility of Sinatra suing me afterward, but I had no idea it would be before. There is such a thing as the First Amendment and freedom of the press in this country. He's got to realize that."

What upset her, she said, was Sinatra's accusation that she'd sold herself as having been anointed by Ol' Blue Eyes to do a biography of him. "They haven't been able to come forward with one person who can say I have misrepresented myself.

". . . They claim Peter Lawford, whom I interviewed, was deceived in some way. If he was deceived, why did he talk for *eight hours* running his mouth about Frank Sinatra . . ."

The truth is that Kitty Kelley didn't speak to Peter Lawford for more than *ten minutes*, and even those ten minutes were obtained by deception. She used Stanley Tretick's *Time-Life* press credentials to fraudulently gain entry into the actor's house.

"I bristle because it is a terrible thing to accuse someone of misrepresentation," Kelley's interview with the *Star's* Langley continues. "There is something ugly about it.

"When these bugs crawl out of the woodwork making these

accusations against me, they had better have proof. So far I have shot down every accusation they have made.

"It's Sinatra's ballgame. His first accusation is that he owns the story of his life—that's the two-million-dollar claim.

"But that's against the law. He's a public figure and the First Amendment allows a writer to write about whomever they want—as long as it's not libelous.

"I would love to see the law suit go ahead and give me a chance to take a deposition from Sinatra. That would be just as good as an interview. Sinatra has just got to back off . . ."

Kitty found it easy to choreograph a chorus of support from authors and journalists. She turned the case into a First Amendment issue. The media paid scant attention to the main complaint charging Kelley with misrepresenting herself as the crooner's sanctioned biographer. Instead, a huge contingent of writers' organizations became vocal in defense of Kelley's right to write.

Most cacophonous in the aria of protests was the Washington Independent Writers, an organization Kitty had joined as a charter member in 1975 when she was still dreaming of making her first literary score. What brought the WIW charging to her defense was Kelley's own loyalty to the organization. Unlike other literary lights who drifted away from the group after they attained success, Kitty remained close to the WIW's hearth after she obtained fame and fortune.

"She served on committees, helped with our fund-raising activities, and campaigned for our causes, such as tax reform," noted Executive Director Isolde Chapin. "She even opened her house for meetings, hosted a spring party for our Writers' Conference. Despite her success, she's always had time for us."

So the WIW threw itself wholeheartedly in support of Kitty as she mobilized for battle. Sinatra's attack turned the spotlight on Kelley as no public relations stunt could have done.

"In attacking her, Sinatra gave Kelley respect and credibility," wrote the *Washington Post's* Gerri Hirshey. "The celebrity 'scalp hunter' suddenly became Joan of Arc, leading a mighty Fourth Estate charge."

Some of the nation's most prominent journalists rallied to her defense . . .

The *New York Times'* William Safire led the pack by protesting Sinatra's contention that only he and nobody else can write his life story without his permission.

"If that legal theory were sound, farewell to the First Amendment," the columnist wrote. "Fortunately, Howard Hughes [the eccentric billionaire industrialist and Hollywood mogul] lost that argument in 1966 [when a court overruled his efforts to stop a biography about him by a former associate.]

"Somewhere, some judge will throw this private attempt at prior restraint out of court. The decision against the reclusive Hughes established that nobody's 'life' is his own. But here is what such legal maneuvering does:

"First, it sends the word out to everyone who has known or done business with Sinatra that he frowns on cooperation with Miss Kelley's research in any way. Curiously, the California complaint was made public in Hollywood, yet no copy was mailed to Miss Kelley or served on her . . .

"More important, the Sinatra suit suggests to people of wealth and power a new way to harass journalists: Before you can drag me into print I'll drag you into court . . ."

Safire suggested that if moneyed people were to wage prepublication battles against those writing about them, then it would encourage others to "generate enough legal expenses to close down any small paper or magazine or broadcaster that dared to take on the powers that be."

Others who came to Kitty's defense were the *Baltimore Sun* with a supportive editorial, and political cartoonists Garry Trudeau and Jules Feiffer, wielding their drawing pens like stilettos that opened gaping wounds in Sinatra's thin skin.

On October 8th—17 days after the suit was filed in the Santa Monica courthouse—Kitty Kelley stood on the dais in the crowded ballroom of the National Press Club in Washington. She was flanked by representatives from writers' organizations. The author of celebrity gossip-biographies was being projected as a victim of celebrity vengeance, and she wallowed in it.

This was a news conference called jointly by the Reporters Committee for Freedom of the Press, the National Writer's Union, and its Washington chapter, the American Society of Journalists and Authors, along with Washington Independent Writers. Kitty turned a tightly-tuned ear toward WIW president Michael Whelan as he read the coalition's statement:

"Frank Sinatra's suit is an assault upon this author's—and all writers'—constitutionally protected freedom of expression and should be dismissed on its face. His apparent goal is to scare Ms. Kelley away from her investigation and, ultimately, force her to scrap the book . . . That is an abuse of the judicial system and a chilling example of how a powerful public figure using money and influence can orchestrate what the public should know about him."

Then Kitty was given the mike.

"Mr. Sinatra's attack on me is an attack on all of us," she told her listeners. Although the suit had been filed on September 21st, she had yet to be served in the complaint. Actually, Kitty had been dodging the process servers for all of the days and weeks since September 21st until the night of November 6, 1983, when the elusive author was finally "papered" with the summons and complaint.

While she was hurrying around corners to avoid being served, she kept bleating away at how unfair Frank Sinatra was to her and vowed defiantly that she'd write the book despite the crooner's "efforts to stop me." Others at the rally spoke of their intentions to back Kitty "to the limit" and would file *amicus curiae* briefs to show the California court that they were in her corner all the way.

The writers also tossed a legal defense fund-raising party for Kitty on the night of November 6, 1983—and it turned into an historic event.

For six weeks Kitty had played her cat-and-mouse game between New York and the nation's capital. The paper-chase began the day after the suit was filed in Los Angeles. Rudin's law firm enlisted the services of one of the nation's best-known subpoena-servers, Irving Botwinick of Serving By Irving. Botwinick operated from headquarters in New York's first skyscraper, the 55-story Woolworth Building. Listen to Botwinick's recital of the goose chase:

"I gathered a team of my best process-servers. For days we laid siege on the apartment complex where Kitty was staying with a friend. But Kitty knew we were there and she eluded us. We were convinced she was using wigs and other disguises.

"One of our best methods of serving a subpoena on an elusive target is to climb the building's fire escape and slap it on the person through the window. This building had no fire escapes. And the guards in the downstairs foyer were too alert to let me or my people get into an elevator.

"Finally, I came up with this brilliant thought. I had read in a newspaper item that Kitty was having lunch with Harper and Row's editor Larry Ashmead. I phoned his office and spoke with a secretary.

" 'I'm very embarrassed,' I said. 'I have a luncheon engagement with Larry and Kitty Kelley and I inadvertently misplaced my calendar. Can you tell me where Larry and Kitty are lunching . . . ?'

" 'At the Russian Tea Room,' the secretary replied.

"So, off we went to the Russian Tea Room, took a table before the lunch crowd streamed in, and waited. And waited. And waited . . .

"But Ashmead and Kelley never showed. I found out later that the secretary had a pang of conscience and mentioned my call to Larry. He knew Kitty was being sought for the serving and, so, took her to lunch at another restaurant.

"I was left holding the bag—make that holding the *service notice.*

"Back at the office, I called Mickey Rudin and told him what happened. I also informed him that I'd heard Kelley was returning to Washington in a couple of days. I suggested I tail her to the capital and slap the papers on her there."

"No thanks," Rudin said to Botwinick. "Your rates are too

high. I'm gonna get somebody in Washington to do the serving,
Irving . . ."

****

We now return to the night of November 6th and the legal
defense fund-raising party for Kitty. Greatly emboldened by the
support the writers were giving her, the brash author stood
seemingly unconcerned in the doorway of Herb's Restaurant,
where the bash was being held. She was all smiles, greeting the
guests with handshakes and kisses, until suddenly, a tall, handsome man of about forty appeared before Kitty, smiling.

"Do I know you?" Kitty asked.

"I don't believe you do," the stranger replied, still smiling—
but now reaching into his breast pocket.

"Are you Miss Kitty Kelley?" he asked.

"Of course I am . . . who are you . . . ?"

The smile grew broader on the stranger's face as he pulled a
legal-looking document out of his jacket and said, "I have something for you . . ."

With that, he touched Kelley with it. It was the service
notice. Frank Sinatra had finally made it all legal for Kitty—46
days after the complaint was filed in court.

After she swallowed hard, Kelley became giddy.

"Oh! What's taken you so long?" she managed to quip with a
forced smile. "Won't you come inside and have a drink with me?"

"By golly, I think I will . . ." the process-server responded.

"But not before you pay the fifteen-dollar entrance fee," Kitty
growled.

The man dug into his pocket and handed the money over to
the banquet manager.

"I hope you charge that fifteen dollars to Frank Sinatra," Kitty
cracked as she accompanied the stranger to the bar.

****

The voices of protest from the press section weren't the only
dividends accruing to Kitty by the ill-advised lawsuit.

Kelley found Bantam Books was determined to give her aid

and comfort—and to put its money where its mouth was. The beleaguered author was summoned to a meeting in New York with Vice President of Publicity Stuart Applebaum and the company's editorial board.

"We called you in to give you every assurance we're standing behind you all the way," Applebaum said. "We're going to back you with every resource at our disposal against this action."

Kitty thanked the Bantam executives for their support, then:

"I have Sinatra just where I want him now. He has given me something much better than an interview . . ."

Bantam's brass stared at Kitty in puzzlement. They didn't understand.

"I'm going to force Frank Sinatra to answer each and every question I intended to ask him if he'd given me an interview. I'll ask him everything about his entire life."

Applebaum interrupted the author. "How will you do that, Kitty . . . ?"

"Before we go to trial, my lawyers [she had retained the Los Angeles law firm of O'Melveny & Myers] tell me there will be a deposition hearing at which Sinatra must testify under oath. That's when I'll zap him, but good. He'll have to respond to every question the attorney's put to him—and, boy, you just have no idea how many questions I intend to have them ask. If you say a hundred, better come up with a higher figure . . ."

But Kelley soon learned that the prospect of facing Sinatra one on one, and with the star under oath, was far-fetched. She'd been on the phone constantly with one or another of her west coast lawyers. Her main contacts at O'Melveny & Myers were attorneys William W. Vaughn, Robert C. Vanderet, and Diane Pritchard.

Among the assurances they gave Kitty was that Sinatra was unlikely to go through with the suit; that it was a harassment tactic. They didn't believe he'd be foolish enough to let himself be deposed. His track record showed that he'd always been reluctant to testify at public hearings, such as those held by Congressional committees. Was he likely to let Kitty's lawyers pepper him with questions about his personal life?

The odds were against it.

Kitty wasn't happy to hear this. Since Sinatra started the suit, Kitty had become a media darling, all the time sparring with a phantom Frank Sinatra in print and on the air. She relished every moment of it. Miss Nobody had become big-time. Learning that Sinatra might not be willing to meet her face-to-face was a letdown.

What questions had Kitty Kelley prepared to give her such confidence in what was now beginning to look like an improbable confrontation with The Voice?

Kitty's "laundry list" of questions became common knowledge in Washington and soon coursed its way to the Penthouse at 9601 Wilshire Boulevard in Beverly Hills (the offices of lawyer Mickey Rudin) as well as to 70588 Frank Sinatra Drive in California's Rancho Mirage (the crooner's official residence).

Kitty's "laundry list" of questions for Sinatra included:

* *Mr. Sinatra, were you ever arrested for rape?*

* *Was your mother an abortionist?*

* *Did she ever take an unborn baby's life in your presence?*

* *Did your mother ever abort a girl or woman whom you made pregnant?*

* *Did you ever have an affair with Elizabeth Taylor?*

* *Did you make Elizabeth Taylor pregnant, tell her you couldn't marry her, then pay to have the baby aborted?*

* *During your marriage to Nancy Barbato, your first wife and mother of your three children, did you cheat on her by sleeping with showgirls, women of ill-repute, or other floozie types?*

* *While married to Mia Farrow, did you abuse her by slapping and beating her?*

* *Is it true that you are friends with some of America's most feared underworld figures?*

* *Can I ask what you did when you went to Havana in 1947 and carried a suitcase there with what was said to be a large sum of money for Charles "Lucky" Luciano, the Mafia Godfather of that era?*

* *Did Luciano, who ran the prostitution rackets in New York*

and was eventually convicted and imprisoned as a pimp and panderer, ever arrange sexual encounters for you with ladies of the night?

* *Let me now ask you about your marriage to Ava Gardner. Did you know whether at one point when she was bearing your child, she became so outraged at your behavior as her husband that she vowed not to ever give birth, and had the baby aborted because she didn't want you to be its father?*

* *Mr. Sinatra, I would like to return to the business of your association with gangsters and ask whether you introduced the Chicago mob boss Sam "Momo" Giancana to Mrs. Judith Campbell Exner?*

* *Did you arrange to have Mrs. Exner sleep with President John F. Kennedy?*

* *Is the report true that you and Mr. Giancana had an orgy with Marilyn Monroe on at least one occasion?*

* *Was your father, Martin, ever charged with receiving stolen property?*

* *Your uncle, Gus, is said to have been arrested for running numbers. True or false?*

* *While on the subject of your relatives, was another uncle, Babe, charged with taking part in a murder and sent to prison?*

These were the questions but the deposition was not to be. . .

****

Although Kelley's lawyers believed Sinatra wouldn't chance a court fight, they nevertheless prepared to do battle. So a motion was filed in U.S. District Court in Los Angeles to move the proceeding from the California state court to the federal legal arena, an obvious delaying tactic.

Their grounds: "This is a case in which the district courts of the United States have criminal jurisdiction under Title 28, Sections 1332 (a) (1) and (d), in that it is a civil action between citizens of the state of California [Sinatra's residence] and Nevada [Camden Enterprises' home offices], on the one hand, and a citizen of the District of Columbia [where Kelley lives], on the other . . ."

The petition hung on a technicality—that while Camden also has offices in California, it has no mailing address in Washington, just as Kelley didn't have one in the Golden State. Thus Kitty couldn't be tried in the state court because jurisdiction clearly fell to a U.S. district court.

These legal maneuvers would prove moot. The questions Kitty prepared for the deposition and leaked through the grapevine brought Sinatra to the conclusion that he didn't need the trouble.

Before Sinatra made that decision, Kitty had two further significant encounters with Mickey Rudin's troops.

First came an affadavit from Sinatra's side claiming that his musical arranger Nelson Riddle had been interviewed by Kitty, and the questions she asked suggested she was writing a "negative book."

Kitty huffed at that claim: "My lawyers told Mr. Sinatra (actually they spoke to his lawyers, not to Frank) that it was not against the law to ask tough questions."

But is it within the law to leave a message on a telephone recorder saying: "Hi, I'm Kitty Kelley, the *authorized* biographer of Frank Sinatra, and *Frank asked me to call you* . . . ?"

The tape was played by Sinatra's lawyers to Kitty's legal eagles. Ostensibly Kelley was allowed to listen to it because she was to claim later:

"The voice obviously wasn't mine. It sounded like Boy George doing an imitation of Joan Rivers."

Next in what was now rapidly becoming a three-ring circus under a collapsing legal tent, came a letter from attorney John Forbess proposing to drop the suit—but only if Sinatra were allowed to bow out gracefully. The letter reportedly read:

"She [Kelley] certainly does not have to admit guilt, but I would rather go to court, win or lose, than just walk away from it with Kelley pronouncing complete vindication. I must have at least enough to prevent the headline, 'Sinatra Gives Up.' "

Despite all his influence and resources, Sinatra could not prevent that headline on September 18, 1984—just three days shy of a year following the filing of the complaint against Kelley.

This carefully-worded press statement was distributed by Frankie's legal battery:

"Mr. Sinatra wishes to correct the impression that he sought to enjoin Miss Kelley or in any way stop her from writing a biography . . ."

Meanwhile, only a few weeks after Frank's process server found her, in November, 1983, Kelley's suit against former agent Lucianne Goldberg finally went to trial. In the suit, Kitty charged that Goldberg had not paid her for foreign sales in six countries and sued the agent for "breach of contract, breach of fiduciary duty, and fraud . . ."

In testimony given before a six-member jury and Judge Oliver Gasch in Washington D.C.'s U.S. District Court, Kitty first claimed she was owed more than thirty thousand dollars, and the agent was refusing to pay that amount or provide a proper financial accounting.

"Actually," Mrs. Goldberg told me, "I had gotten in the foreign royalties after a period of time had passed following Kitty's early complaints about not receiving these moneys. So I sent her a check for that exact amount, thirty-thousand and two-hundred forty dollars.

"But the check was returned to me uncashed. Kitty claimed, through her lawyer, that in the pre-trial discovery process the amount had grown to approximately $60,000 . . ."

On November 29th the trial ended with a jury award to Kitty Kelley of $60,000 plus $640 in punitive damages against the agent.

Immediately afterward, Kitty swaggered out of court and smiled impishly as her lawyer made a heady victory speech to reporters:

"The decision will help protect authors who depend on the integrity of their literary agents to remit the full amount due them after deducting their commission."

Goldberg's attorney, David N. Webster, asked the court to set aside the verdict. Judge Gasch took the motion under consideration and then really shook up Kitty by cancelling the $60,640 award.

Gasch set aside the jury's verdict which had found the agent guilty of fraud in handling Kelly's royalties on *The Last Star* and awarded her *exactly* the amount Goldberg said Kitty had coming to her: $30,240. He further ordered Goldberg to pay an additional $11,167 for lost interest and extra commission.

Kelley couldn't have been happy over having $19,233 lopped off the award. Nevertheless she grabbed the money and ran all the way to the bank.

A smiling Lucianne Goldberg had the last word on this caper with her former client:

"Kitty's suit would probably rate a good chapter in an unauthorized biography of Kitty Kelley . . ."

In the 509 pages of *His Way: The Unauthorized Biography of Frank Sinatra* which Kelley published in 1986, there is virtually nothing written about Sinatra's half-century in show business, his unique and marvelous voice, or his talent as a superstar singer and entertainer. Nothing about the thousands of songs he recorded, the hundreds of songs he made hits, the many starring roles in his movies, or the millions and millions he earned. Instead, she concentrates on his foibles, packing in all the alleged dirt surrounding his three failed marriages, his friends in organized crime, and his escapades. Her first attack begins right on page one:

"The night of December 22, 1938, two constables from Hackensack, New Jersey, headed for the Rustic Cabin in Englewood Cliffs to arrest Frank Sinatra."

The arrest came after a girlfriend of Frank's, one Toni Francke, decided to "punish" him and, on November 27th, had sworn out a morals charge warrant alleging he had had sexual intercourse with her on November 2nd and 9th and caused her to become pregnant.

Here are the errors in Kitty Kelley's report about the first arrest warrant obtained by this self-styled virtuous married woman, who claims that she was "a single female of good repute for chastity . . ."

*CLAIM: She was single.

*FACT: She was married and separated from her husband.

*CLAIM: She was chaste.

*FACT: Not unless she spent her honeymoon and the approximate two years of her marriage in a nunnery.

*CLAIM: Frank Sinatra promised to marry her before the alleged seduction.

*FACT: Such a promise was unlikely because at the time Kitty claims he made it he was already engaged to Nancy Barbato.

It was common knowledge long before he made the engagement official, and long before the Summer of '38, that Frank was going to marry Nancy. If Toni Francke didn't know it, she must have been wearing blinders and had ears full of wax.

Everyone even remotely acquainted with the Sinatra family in Hoboken knew of Frank's long-running courtship of Nancy and that he'd slipped the ring on her finger in early September, just after she returned from a two-week vacation at a relative's seaside Summer retreat in Long Branch on the Jersey shore.

The couple met in 1934 at that same Summer playground where Frank's aunt Josephine "Josie" Garavante Monaco, his mother Natalie's sister, also had a cottage. The romance became serious in 1936 when Frankie took Nancy to the Paramount Theater in Manhattan's Times Square. First they saw a movie. Then the spotlights went on and the elevator stage rose to its full height. The band struck up a tune and Bing Crosby crooned. Afterward, Frank turned to Nancy and told her:

"I'm going to be a singer. And I'll make enough money so we can marry."

It took Sinatra two more years to obtain the engagement ring [from his mother] for Nancy's finger. Then Frank launched his singing career at the Rustic Cabin and was "moonlighting" during the daylight hours as a crooner over WOR, the radio outlet in New York.

Nancy was also working—in a Manhattan department store. Between them they were earning $50 a week—enough for a married couple to live on.

Frank was twenty-three and Nancy twenty when they took

their vows on February 4, 1939, in Jersey City's Lady of Sorrow Catholic Church.

But Kitty Kelley persists in trashing Frank and Nancy through Toni Francke, this yet-to-be-divorced "single female of good repute."

She has Toni phoning the Rustic Cabin sometime prior to November 27, 1938, and has Nancy Barbato—by now Frank's most loyal fan at the club—picking up the receiver.

"He's my boyfriend and I want to know why you want to talk to him," Kelley has Nancy say, making the caller so angry that she hops into her car, drives to the nightclub, barges in, grabs Sinatra, and threatens to make a scene. Suddenly, Nancy materializes. Toni screams at Nancy. Nancy turns to Frank:

"What is this? Another whore?"

A perfectly proper question. It spotlights what's been observed about Frank Sinatra's relations with women before. Richard Gehman, author of *Sinatra and His Rat Pack*, has one of Frank's friends put it this way:

"Frank is just plain broad-nuts. He can no more not look at a dame than he could stop singing. Say he's in a restaurant and there's a pretty waitress. Suppose he jokes with her a little and she doesn't give him a tumble. It drives him right out of his mind. Nine times out of ten after he leaves he'll send somebody back to pick her up for him.

"It's pathetic in a way. Once I heard him talking about a girl he'd been out with the night before. She wasn't much, but the way he talked about her, you'd have thought he couldn't begin to understand it. 'You know, I think that girl really did like me.' How do you figure? Here he's had broads after him by the thousands . . . and he doesn't even know what they see in him."

When I was researching my Sinatra book, I was given the notes of a colleague on the *New York Post* who'd interviewed Fred Tamburro, one of three young men Sinatra worked with in 1937. Tamburro, who had known Frankie since 1934 when he was 19, was asked about Sinatra's girlfriends—especially the ones he had met before he met Nancy.

"All I know is that he could get all the tail he wanted,"

Tamburro said. "This guy had an appetite for sex like no one I ever knew. We called him Little Lord Fauntleroy because of the fancy clothes his mother made him wear. He would screw a snake if he could hold it still long enough . . ."

Tamburro was speaking about the Frank Sinatra of 1937.

"Frank didn't seem like he had been to bed with anyone before," Kelley writes. This quote Kelley attributes to Toni Francke in describing her first purported sexual encounter with Sinatra. "He was kind of shy. He wasn't all that good because he was thin. But he was very gentle with me. He did not grab me the first night. He could have, but he didn't."

After more alleged exchanges between Nancy and Toni and after Toni rips Nancy's dress in the Kelley-related nasty scene, Kelley writes:

"Taking Toni by the hand, Frank led her into the lounge. That's where he said, 'I have to marry Nancy. Otherwise her father will kill me. She's pregnant.' "

If Nancy were pregnant prior to November 27, 1938, the night Toni had Frank arrested on the morals charge, then that pregnancy must stand as one of the longest on record. For Nancy Barbato, who suffered no miscarriages after the vows she took in Lady of Sorrows Church on February 4, 1939, did not give birth to her first child, Nancy Sandra, until June 7, 1940.

"So what?" Kitty now has Toni replying to his statement that Nancy was carrying his baby. "I was pregnant and you didn't break your neck for me."

Toni then "stormed out of the Rustic Cabin and drove home, wondering how she would ever tell her friends in Lodi that Frank wasn't going to marry her."

That was when Toni decided to bring the law down on Frank. How can we reconcile that Toni had sexual intercourse with Sinatra for the first time on the 7th of November, subsequently on the 9th, as his accuser clearly states in the warrant Kitty Kelley offers, and then "within six weeks" she was pregnant? A six-week period of pregnancy brings us to December 22 when the constables reacted and slapped the cuffs on him at the Route 9W roadside inn perched on the Jersey Palisades. In lodging that allegation on November 27 and causing Frank's first arrest that clamped him in jail for 16 distressful hours, Antoinette Della Penta Francke had to have been clairvoyant.

"When she broke the news to Frank [that she was six weeks pregnant], he did not say anything for the longest time. Then he said, "Well, I'll have to marry you.""

After quoting Toni's response, "Don't do me no favors, Frank," Kelley relates:

"She [Toni] said that there were no fights or arguments over her pregnancy and that Frank did not suggest an abortion. But Frank's mother Dolly bore down so hard on him for continuing to see Toni that the aggravation contributed to her miscarriage in her third month."

A miscarriage in the third month?

If we count the time since November 7-9 when Toni claims Frank made her pregnant to the day she supposedly lost the baby—on or about February 7-9—she'd have been transported through a time warp to approximately February 4, 1939.

That's the day Francis Albert Sinatra walked down the aisle with Nancy Barbato!

Are we to believe that Frank returned to Hoboken after his four-day honeymoon, which Kelley describes in a later chapter, and rushed to Toni's side to promise he'd marry *her*?

The Kitty Kelley Profusion of Confusion marches on . . .

****

In Chapter 4, Kitty Kelley continued her assault on the Sinatra family in particular, Italians in general. She quotes an Irish-American neighbor named Agnes on the house Frank's mother and father settled into some 14 years after they were married. "The house was full of what our parents called Guinea furniture, but they thought it was all wonderful." Continuing the assault on Frank through Sinatra's mother, Kitty resorts to new smears from her earlier source, Toni Francke:

"He hid his face when I got mad [during a purported bitter argument with Sinatra] and called his mom an abortionist. He was mortified by her baby-killing."

Kelley then states:

"The shame that Frank carried over his mother's abortion business intensified when he moved to Garden Street."

Keep in mind that when Dolly and Marty moved with their only offspring to the first home of their own, a four-story $13,000 clapboard multiple-family dwelling at 841 Garden Street, the year was 1932.

"That was where the real trouble started," Kelley quotes another Hoboken paragon of historical backwash on Frank Sinatra. She is identified as Marian Brush Schrieber, "Frank's pretty red-haired neighbor who became his Garden Street girlfriend."

Kitty proceeds to put these words in Marian's mouth:

"Dolly did an abortion there in her basement [of 841 Garden Street] on a girl who almost died. The girl had to be rushed to the hospital and was in critical condition when she arrived. She barely survived. Dolly was arrested and had to stand trial. She was put on probation for five years and had to go down to the probation office every week to sign in. I remember how mad she'd get every time she had to go. She'd say it was a 'goddam inconvenience' and that she had better things to do. She wasn't a bit embarrassed about it, but the Irish-Catholic neighborhood we lived in was scandalized. What she did was considered worse than murder. It was awful hard on Frank."

None of this is from any official record. All of it cascades from a woman Kitty tells us was Sinatra's Garden Street girlfriend.

None of this is believable, especially in the harsh light of another flaw in the author's reporting:

Kitty claims Toni Francke made Frank hide his face when she accused his mother of being a baby-killer. Kitty further tells us "the shame Frank carried over his mother's abortion business intensified when he moved to Garden Street." And Kitty has reported earlier in this same Chapter 4 that the family moved to Garden Street in 1932. In that year, Frank celebrated his 17th birthday on December 12th. From what Kitty has said in Chapter 1, Toni had her affair with Frank in 1938, which was when she claims *she met him for the first time* at the Rustic Cabin. In

1938, Sinatra was 22 years old going on 23. Kitty Kelley's report has a gap of five unaccounted for years!

****

13th September 1989
  Dear Mr. Carpozi,
  Thank you for your letter of September 2nd [requesting an interview about Kitty Kelley].
  Since I have never had the misfortune to meet the 'lady' in question, nor have I read any of her rubbish, I have nothing to contribute to your book.
  Yours sincerely,
  Ava Gardner

On October 5, 1986, Alice Steinbach, Washington correspondent for the *Baltimore Sun*, quoted Kelley's Ava Gardner material in an article entitled,

"IS KELLEY'S
SINATRA
FOR REAL?
Biographer defends her accuracy
in face of criticism and denials."
"In Ms. Kelley's book," writes Steinbach, "Ava Gardner is alleged to have told the wife of cameraman Robert Surtees that she had an abortion in London because 'I hated Frankie so much. I wanted that baby to go unborn.' The statement has been widely reprinted in magazines and newspapers."
The article continues with a Kelley interview:

Q. This is one of the most hurtful remarks in the book and, if not true, a very destructive thing to print. Do you have any other confirmation that Ava Gardner really said this or are you just taking at face value the word of a man who said his wife told him this?
A. That isn't the only source. It's also in the MGM legal file as well. It's also been printed before, too.

210

Q. But does that mean it's true? Haven't you ever had something printed about you that wasn't true?

A. You're right. It doesn't mean it's true. But it's in the MGM files.

Q. You mean there's something in those files that has Ms. Gardner saying, "I hated Frankie so much, I wanted that baby to go unborn?"

A. Oh, no, no, no. That quote is not in the MGM legal files. The abortion business is in the files. The quote comes from Mrs. Surtees. And that part has not been quoted before.

Q. So you really only had the say-so of one woman. And you accepted it at face value?

A. Oh, no, no, no. I tried with Ava Gardner. I sent a letter with that part in it, among other things.

Q. But when you got no answer and couldn't corroborate the remark, you decided to go ahead and print it, trusting that the information given to you by one source was true.

A. Yes, I did.

Steinbach continues: "Some of the people [Kelley] didn't talk to—or to put it more precisely, some of the people who *wouldn't* talk to her—are taking issue with the material presented in the book.

"Elizabeth Taylor, for instance—responding to the charge that she had an abortion after Mr. Sinatra got her pregnant— told columnist Liz Smith that Kitty Kelley 'is not . . . a writer but a fabricator.'

"And Mia Farrow, through her publicist, said that 'the references to how Frank Sinatra treated me are absolutely untrue.' The book claims that Mr. Sinatra was resentful of her career and acted violently toward her."

Kitty was asked to respond.

"I don't think anybody's denied anything," she told Steinbach.

One writer who gave Kitty high grades for getting the goods

211

was author Ovid Demaris, who was pleased with the credit he receives in Kelley's Author's Note. He had given her material from an unpublished interview he had with Bobby Garcia, owner of an illegal gambling club in Palm Springs frequented by Sinatra. Demaris, who has written often about Frank over the years, also gave Kelley a list of people to contact.

"I don't know of a name I gave her that she didn't call or pursue," Demaris said. "And they were all impressed with how thorough she was."

Steinbach came up with an unnamed Washington journalist who allegedly said Kitty's research "was probably pretty good" but who went on to object to the methods she used to obtain the material:

"What she does is she gets her claws into people and exploits them. She charms them and wheedles them and pretends to be their best friend. Then when she's got what she wants, she dumps them."

While Steinbach doesn't identify the journalist who gave her that assessment of Kitty, several writers have agreed that that's the most accurate description anyone can give of Kelley. Among them are Rudy Maxa, Diane McClellan, Dan Moldea, Teddy Vaughn, and Gerri Hirshey.

The point Alice Steinbach made in her story about the way Kitty charmed people was repeated by Demaris, but in kinder words:

"Kitty becomes your best friend. She flatters you. She does things to get you to open up."

The words of writer Dan Moldea aren't nearly as flattering because he has bitter memories of the treatment he received from Kitty—after he opened dozens of doors that provided her with information about Frank Sinatra's reported connections and activities with underworld figures.

Author of three books on the Mafia and the corrupt International Brotherhood of Teamsters union, Moldea had considered Kitty Kelley a friend when she approached him for help on her book.

In mid-1982, Moldea learned that his father was dying of cancer. He left Washington and went to comfort his parent.

"Now and then Kitty phoned and asked how things were going, and how dad was. Besides the earlier impressions I had of her—that she was charming and witty and fun to be with—I found now she was also quite caring."

His father died June, 1983, and a short time later Dan Moldea returned to Washington—just as Kitty was digging into Sinatra's mob ties. Aware of Moldea's works on the Mafia, Kitty asked him for whatever help he could offer.

"Besides giving her the names of people to contact for information, I invited her up to my place to let her riffle through my files without any censorship whatsoever. I also know that she got in touch with people I steered her to. So I had been of some help to her."

Kitty's Author's Note lists Moldea as "one who contributed help and advice throughout the project . . ."

Months after he let Kitty see his files, Moldea signed a contract with Laurel Publishing to produce a book entitled *Dark Victory: Ronald Reagan, MCA, and the Mob.* The thread that Moldea wove through the manuscript was the link the underworld had with Hollywood movie studios and their unions— and of the way then-Governer of California Ronald Reagan was assertedly aiding and abetting the mob's activities through the all-powerful theatrical agency, Music Corporation of America.

As he set out to develop his book, Moldea heard that another Washington author had undertaken to write on a similar theme. This writer, whom Moldea wouldn't identify, was known to him as a close friend of Kitty Kelley's.

"Don't ask me to put my finger on why I had become suspicious of Kelley. All I can tell you is that this gnawing feeling took hold of me all at once—that she couldn't be trusted . . ."

Kitty had been plying Moldea with endless questions about his book:

"When's your pub date . . . ?"

"Who's the publisher . . . ?"

"What have you got on President Reagan . . . ?"

"Are you going to crucify him . . . ?"

"Does he have direct ties with the mob . . . ?"

Questions, questions, questions. Always more questions . . .

Moldea became convinced that Kitty was pumping him so she could convey the answers to the rival author. Moldea learned the other writer was encountering tough sledding on his tour of the country in search of information for his book—while it was an open secret that doors were ajar for Moldea because he knew his way around. After all, he had written about the mob in three prior books.

In 1984 Moldea became so uneasy about Kitty that he no longer invited her to his parties.

"He was afraid she'd make off with his manuscript—as she had done with mine," said Barbara Howar.

Moldea decided to test Kitty to determine her trustworthiness. He would ask her for a favor—to dig into her own files and tell him what she could about the background of Los Angeles labor attorney Sidney Korshak.

Korshak's name had been surrounded by scandal for years.

"I want you to pay attention to Korshak." This is what convicted labor racketeer and extortionist Willie Bioff once testified that Capone gangster Charley "Cherry Nose" Gioe told him when he was introduced to the lawyer. "When he tells you something, he knows what he's talking about. Any message he might deliver to you is a message from us."

Moldea was aware of that testimony. He had a file of material on Korshak that spanned the two generations of his law practice and oft-chronicled involvements with the mob. He didn't really need Kitty's help. His request was, as Moldea said, a "test." And Kitty didn't disappoint.

She responded "by sending me one lousy newspaper clipping about Korshak," Moldea told me. "I knew then that she was shafting me."

The *Baltimore Sun* interview by Alice Steinbach continued:

Q. Did you talk to Ava Gardner for the book?

A. Oh, yes. I did have someone talk to Ava Gardner. Yes, I did. (Writer) Michael Thornton. He did the interview with Ava in London.

Q. He did the interview specifically for you? For this book?

A. Yes. He also used a lot of the material and had it published in a London paper.

Q. Did Ava Gardner know Mr. Thornton was doing these interviews for you?

A. No. No. I got them afterward.

Q. In other words, this was really his interview and he gave you parts.

A. Exactly.

****

How did Kitty Kelley get the interview that she claims was obtained for her book by Michael Thornton? Here is Michael Thornton:

"Kitty had started research on her Sinatra book and, like the *Daily Express* before her, had moved heaven and earth to get into contact with Ava Gardner, entirely without success. Ava was unrelentingly hostile towards all biographers of herself and of anyone connected with her. In my earliest interviews with her, she roundly cursed two previous Gardner biographies— [by] David Hanna ('a friend who turned out to be a shit') and Charles Higham, whom she persisted in calling 'Mr. Hig-ham.'

"That very month of my interviews [in December 1982], a Gardner fan in Britain sent her yet another biography [Published by W.H. Allen], which he had signed, "hoping it gives you pleasure." It most emphatically did *not* give her pleasure. On about page 78, in fact, her furious eyes fell upon a reference which seemed to hint at a lesbian relationship between herself and Lana Turner, and this produced a characteristic Ava outburst:

"'He hopes it gives me pleasure! Jesus Christ! The fucking, goddam sonuvabitch . . .'

"At the same time, Frank's daughter, Nancy Sinatra, whom

Ava clearly did not like, had written asking for help with her book about her father, and Ava's reaction to that was cold and caustic.

"Kitty Kelley, therefore, had met with a wall of silence, and [*Daily Express* Editor] Peter McKay, who was amused and intrigued by Kitty, had directed her to me as a possible source of help.

"Early in 1983, I received a letter from her in a scarlet envelope, telling me that she had read my *Daily Express* articles on Ava and considered them 'easily the best thing ever written about her'—which was very far from being my own view."

Michael Thornton was irate over the editing on his series and had had repeated clashes with Peter McKay's successor at the *Express*, Felicity Green, "an aggressive veteran woman newspaper executive . . . who had clawed her way to the top of British journalism and meant to let everyone know that she was the boss. We disagreed about the Ava series from Word One. When it finally appeared, around December 11-13, 1982, the layout appalled me. The best parts were missing, and I felt that the whole thing had been ruined. Ava herself was equally appalled, hated the series, blamed me for it, and went back into her shell with a vengeance.

"I contented myself with telling Miss Green what I thought of her, which is quite unprintable, and returned to Minorca [island off Spain] determined *never* to do newspaper work again."

When the letter from Kitty Kelley arrived, Michael Thornton knew only what everyone else knew—that she'd "written controversial unauthorized biographies of Elizabeth Taylor and Jackie Onassis, and that Liz was so furious she foamed at the mouth at the mere mention of Kitty's name . . .

"Accordingly, I sent Kitty my original Ava scripts and various notes which were not included in them, and told her the general background to the series. I gave her Ava's private address—34 Ennismore Gardens, London S.W. 7—and private telephone number (London 581-8374), but warned her that the latter would almost certainly have been changed.

"I later heard, from a mutual friend of Ava's and mine, that

Ava had refused to answer Kitty's letters, not only because she had promised Sinatra not to help her in any way, but also because of her friendship with Elizabeth Taylor, with whom she had filmed *The Bluebird* in Russia, and about whom, said Ava, Kitty had written 'a lousy, stinking bunch of lies.' "

Several months passed after Michael Thornton sent his Ava interviews to Kitty Kelley in Georgetown. Then:

"She wrote back a letter of profuse gratitude for my help, enclosing a cheque for 100 dollars, which I at once returned. While appreciating a kindly-meant gesture, I am not poor and never accept any sort of payment for helping other authors, as so many have helped me over the years.

"In her letter, Kitty said the book was proving to be a mammoth and exhausting task, and that the walls of her Washington workroom were piled high from floor to ceiling with files bulging with material on Sinatra.

"By the time I heard from her again, in another technicolor envelope—this time turquoise, I believe—she was in Los Angeles on the second leg of her research. By this point, she was clearly under pressure. She said that her *life had been threatened repeatedly* [the emphasis is the author's] and that there were grounds for believing these threats originated from Sinatra's Mafia connections. She also complained of meeting lines of turned backs and closed doors in Hollywood from former associates and friends who had been ordered by Sinatra not to talk to her. She was dispirited by this but clearly not daunted, and she said it made her all the more determined to battle on."

Without at first even realizing it, Thornton was encountering Kelley in fine form. Simultaneously, she was lying to him about her life having been threatened, preparing to lie to others about his work having been conducted originally on her behalf, and milking him for every last drop of information.

****

"The abortion business is in the files." That's what Kelley insisted to Steinbach. But nowhere in the files showcased in her book does Kitty offer her readers a quote from the documents

217

about the abortion. As we'll soon hear, the truth, the whole truth, and nothing but the truth will out—from Ava Gardner herself.

The "I made it up" girl was in action again.

Although she doesn't list cameraman Robert Surtees as a source in her Author's Chapter Notes for Chapter 14, Kelley nevertheless quotes him directly on Page 196 to make it appear that she got the statement from him. She employs the trick of having Surtees' first words rebutting Ava's statement to writer Joe Hyams: that even though her marriage to Sinatra was "shakier every day, I didn't care. I wanted a baby by him." She fabricates the intro for Surtees:

"That isn't the way it was at all," Kitty has Surtees saying.

Again, no source for this statement. Then she has his wife, whom Kitty never names, tell him Ava had the abortion because she didn't want to bear Sinatra's baby.

Kitty Kelley apparently never checked out Surtees or his wife. I did. Nor did she attempt to interview him. I did.

Records of the American Society of Cinematographers, of which all Hollywood cameramen must be members, show Robert L. Surtees was born August 9, 1906, joined the ASC in November of 1942, and died at the age of 78 on January 7, 1985.

His wife, whom Kitty never names, was Maydell Surtees—whom I was told by the ASC, is also dead.

Also dead since 1981 is Morgan Hudgins, the MGM publicist whom Kitty Kelley involved in an exchange of cables.

It appears everyone whom Kitty Kelley quotes on the Ava Gardner "abortion" story is dead.

****

On January 8, 1990, I spoke with MGM/UA legal counsel Herbert Nusbaum, whom Kitty thanks in *His Way* for having given her access to the studio's legal files. Here's a distillation of my interview with Nusbaum:

Q. Kitty Kelley credits you with having allowed her to look at MGM/UA's legal files. Is that true?

A. Actually, she got permission from someone else. When she came here, I got the files for her. Why?

Q. Because Kelley says in her book that Ava Gardner had an abortion, and quotes from a series of cables dispatched between Nairobi [Kenya] and MGM in Hollywood wherein [Ava Gardner] is trying to get leave to go to London to get the abortion. I called you because nothing in those cables substantiates such a situation. I'd like to know, is what she said true or false?

A. I would have no earthly way of knowing now [the MGM film library and legal files were sold to Turner Broadcasting in March, 1985, and many documents, deemed "no longer necessary to keep," were destroyed].

Q. But did she get access to the files?

A. Yes. And the telegrams back and forth were in the files. But I'm not certain the telegrams make mention of an abortion. I don't know where [Kelley] got that information. There are no such references in the files.

Nusbaum said he would not have given Kitty Kelley permission to look at the Ava Gardner files if it were not for clearance granted by someone "above me." Furthermore, he wouldn't have let Kelley peek into those records because of an earlier unpleasant experience with her when she was "researching" *Elizabeth Taylor: The Last Star.*

"I had a set-to with Kitty Kelley when she was working on the Elizabeth Taylor book," Nusbaum explained. "She had been given permission one previous time to look at those files. Back then, as always before and since, we had a policy that applied to people who did research jobs. We wanted to look at the proposed product to see whether or not anything detrimental was said about the studio. We didn't think if we gave permission for this writer to look at the studio file that, in turn, the studio should be stabbed in the back by some unfavorable comments.

"And, someone had warned me about Kelley and her yellow journalism technique. So, when she came I prepared a little agreement, which I had made with all other writers orally. This provided that they could not quote from the files without permission, and they would let us see what they were writing about the studio. In Kelley's case, I prepared a written agreement for her to sign.

"After she had gone through the Elizabeth Taylor files, she vanished—without signing the agreement. Then sometime later she asked permission to quote some other parts of the file on Elizabeth Taylor. I replied that I would consider the request only when she signed my agreement. She flew into a rage. She said that her permission to look at the files was without any conditions.

"That prompted me to call the publisher [Simon & Schuster] and explain to them MGM's policy. They understood. In the end, Miss Kelley sent me page proofs of that part of the Elizabeth Taylor book that concerned MGM. I found a number of 'facts' weren't correct, and I pointed those out."

Q. Did you find that the corrections were made in the book?

A. I can tell you flatly that they were not made. Miss Kelley just went ahead and let stand what she wrote about Elizabeth Taylor, wrong and distorted as her statements were.

****

Some truth surfaced in the last of the make-believe cables Kitty used as props for her Ava abortion fantasy—when she quoted Director John Ford's message to MGM: that Ava is "REALLY QUITE ILL SINCE ARRIVAL AFRICA DEEM IT IMPERATIVE LONDON CONSULTATION OTHERWISE TRAGIC RESULTS STOP"

Ava herself will tell us such a plan was dispatched by Ford—at her request. But can anyone believe such nonsensical literary crafting—that with the wealth and majesty of MGM behind him, John Ford could resort to such a paucity of unpunctuated gibberish to the studio mahatmas on a matter so urgent as superstar Ava Gardner's health? Here's how I reported Ava's medical problem in my book, *Frank Sinatra: Is this Man Mafia?*:

"Ava was flown to London on November 25th, 1952, [not the 23rd as Kitty incorrectly reports] and confined to a nursing home suffering from a 'sort of dysentery' she'd contracted in Kenya, where *Mogambo* was on location. The drinking water in Africa evidently didn't agree with Ava. Or, as other reports had it, she had a miscarriage. When she returned to location she brought her own supply of drinking water with her."

What Kitty Kelley never expected when she wrote about Ava and the fabricated abortion was that Gardner would put the lie to the wicked wordsmith.

Just four months after she wrote to me that she would not sit for an interview about Kitty Kelley, she contracted pneumonia. She died in London on January 25, 1990 one month after her 67th birthday, and was buried on January 29 in her family's plot in Smithfield, N.C., not far from Grabtown, her birthplace.

How safe the author must have felt now that her fiction could not be challenged by the primary participant. But Kelley could not have foreseen that the very publishers of her Frank Sinatra book, Bantam, would have commissioned Ava to write her own book. And that in September of 1990—eight months after she was laid to rest, Miss Gardner would break her silence.

In her autobiography Ava offered vivid details about her trip to Nairobi and of the way she "discovered that I was pregnant." Note that Ava herself says she found out about the pregnancy only *after* she arrived on the African Continent—*not* five weeks earlier, in mid-October—after a big blowup at Lana Turner's house. That was when Ava walked out on Frank and threw "their plans in ruins—their trip to Ava's home in North Carolina, their trip to Africa, their baby . . ."

"In Nairobi, while making *Mogambo*, I discovered I was pregnant. Frank, who'd been visiting me, had gone back to Hollywood to test for *From Here to Eternity*. *I hadn't told him and I wasn't going to* [the emphasis is mine]."

"I had the strongest feelings against bringing a child into the world. I felt that unless you were prepared to devote practically all your time to your child in its early years, it was unfair to the baby.

"Not to mention the fact that MGM had all sorts of penalty

221

clauses about their stars having babies. *If I had one, my salary would be cut off* [again the emphasis is mine].

What did Kitty tell us in *His Way* about Ava Gardner and MGM and pregnancy? Let's read Kelley's version:

"The next contractual battle was over inserting a pregnancy clause that would protect her [Ava] from penalties should she be unable to work due to pregnancy. *She had already announced that she and Frank wanted to have a baby* [my emphasis once more]."

Ava wanted a baby?

According to fiction-writer Kitty Kelley, yes. But according to actress Ava Gardner, then in the prime of her career—and Frank at the lowest ebb in his own (he hadn't yet made it back as Private Angelo Maggio in *From Here to Eternity*)—his wife wanted nothing less than to have a baby. Listen to her true feelings in her own words:

"So how would I make a living? Frank was absolutely broke and would probably continue to be (or so I thought) for a long time. My future movies were going to take me all over the world. I couldn't have a baby with that going on. With that decision made, the most agonizing I'd ever have to face, I went to see my director, John Ford."

Ford "tried desperately to talk me out of it." She quotes Ford as saying that aborting the baby would break Sinatra's heart because he's a Catholic. Ava responds, "He isn't going to find out . . ."

Ford agreed to Ava's departure. She went off to London and had her pregnancy terminated. Any mention of the dribble Kitty reported to her readers? Ava Gardner never said, "I hated Frankie so much, I wanted that baby to go unborn."

The final word on the abortion business comes from the actress herself. Wrote Ava:

"Frank came back to Africa in time for Christmas—and my thirtieth birthday—full of enthusiasm and joy. The test had been successful and the part of Maggio in *Eternity* was his.

"And then, of course, the silliest, stupidest, and most natural thing happened: I got pregnant again.

222

"This time Frank did know, and he was delighted. Yet despite his feelings, I reached the same decision about my second pregnancy as I had about my first . . ."

MGM had cast Ava for another movie, *Knights of the Round Table*, which was to be filmed overseas, causing another lengthy separation from Frank.

"I think Frank, in his heart, knew what I was going to do. But it was my decision, not his. Clearly someone told him about what I was doing, because as long as I live I'll never forget waking up after the operation and seeing Frank sitting next to the bed with tears in his eyes. But I think I was right. I still think I was right."

****

Some last words on the MGM legal files come from Atlanta, Georgia, where communications giant Ted Turner has corporate headquarters for his cable TV and film empire. Setting the record straight is the company's President Roger Mayer:

"Since we have owned the library, Kitty Kelley has not asked permission to look through the files. And if she were to ask, we would not grant it. MGM legal files are not open to public scrutiny any longer."

18

"Ava Gardner and Frank Sinatra stated today that having reluctantly exhausted every effort to reconcile their differences, they could find no mutual basis on which to continue their marriage. Both expressed deep regret and great respect for each other. Their separation is final and Miss Gardner will seek a divorce."

This pronouncement by an MGM publicist on October 29, 1953, marked a critical milestone in the stormy two-year marriage. But by no means was it the end. Ava and Frank saw each other from time to time for the next four years—until July 5, 1957, when a Mexican divorce was finally granted.

Immediately after the MGM announcement, Kitty has Ava proclaiming that she is leaving for Rome to make *The Barefoot Contessa* with Humphrey Bogart. Then the author tells us that Frank is devastated by the breakup and declines to take the advice of an unnamed friend to phone Ava for a reconciliation. The same unnamed friend tells us that Ava is "as miserable as Frank."

Kitty attributes these words to Sinatra:

"Then why is she going to Rome to make a picture? How are we going to make up if she's going to be so far away?"

Kelley adds that Frank never phoned Ava and:

"A few nights later the newspapers reported that Ava was seen dining quietly with Peter Lawford at Frascati's in Los Angeles. Knowing that Peter and Ava had dated before, Frank flew into a rage and called Lawford, threatening him."

Kitty reports what she says the English-born actor told her many years later:

"Oh, God, he was furious with me for going out with Ava. He screamed, 'Do you want your legs broken, you fucking asshole? Well, you're going to get them broken if I ever hear you're out with Ava again. So help me, I'll kill you. Do you hear me?' Then he slammed the phone down. I was panicked. I mean I was really scared. Frank's a violent guy and he's good friends with too many guys who'd rather kill you than say hello. I didn't want to die, so I called [songwriter] Jimmy Van Heusen and said, 'Please tell him nothing happened. Please.' Jimmy said not to worry. That Frank would get over it. He knew we'd been friends since 1945. Well, Frank got over it all right, but it took him six years!"

The date of this statement attributed to Lawford, will not be found by consulting the Author's Chapter Notes from *His Way*.

Kitty claims she interviewed "Peter Lawford on May 15 and June 2, 1983." If she had, then why didn't she include a direct quote from Lawford—instead of resorting to a comment Peter purportedly uttered "many years later?"

I have examined numerous sources for the possible genesis of that quote and traced it to its origin—a story published February 17, 1976, in the *Star*. The procurer was Steve Dunleavy, the Australian-born journalist. Dunleavy came to America in 1967 and quickly established himself as one of the country's intrepid investigative reporters. *Newsweek* hailed him as "Mr. Blood and Guts." In 1976, shortly before moving to the *New York Post*, Dunleavy cornered Peter Lawford for an interview that ended the actor's silence on his stormy friendship with Sinatra and the way it climaxed.

In the first of a two-part "world exclusive" revealing Frankie's tantrums and curious underworld friendships, Lawford told Dunleavy how he met Sinatra and what really precipitated the threat from Ol' Blue Eyes. Note the similarities between this narrative and the one in *His Way*—but above all note how Kelley's version differs, and how she manipulated material to fit her own agenda:

"I first met Sinatra in 1944 when he came to Hollywood, fresh from his triumphs at the Paramount. He was a smiling gregarious kid, very low key, and thoroughly charming.

"We stayed close, partying and drinking together, and going out on double dates with his lovely and still loyal first wife, the former Nancy Barbato.

"He split from Nancy, took up with the beautiful Ava Gardner and the whole world heard about that extremely stormy romance. She eventually dumped Frank and Frank never really got over it. He was always carrying a torch for her and that led to our first split.

"Ava took off to live in Madrid and she returned to Hollywood. Her first night back she dined with her agent at the Villa Frascati, a popular Italian restaurant on The Strip.

"I was with my manager and I saw her. Ava and I had been great pals from our days together at Metro. Anyone who went through that together had a common bond.

"Anyway, I gave her a big friendly wave across the room a big 'hi there.' That was all.

"Well, in those days Hollywood lived and died by the Gospel according to Louella Parsons and Hedda Hopper.

"Two days later, the headlines screamed: 'Ava Dates Peter Lawford On First Night Back In Country.'

"I was staying at my parents' home, that's how much of a swinger I was. Anyway, I was in bed at three in the morning and the telephone rings. Close to death, I groan into the telephone.

"Then comes a voice at the other end of the telephone from New York, like something out of a Mario Puzo novel: 'What's this about you and Ava. Listen you creep. You wanna stay healthy? I'll have your legs broken, ya bum. If I hear anything more about this with Ava, you've had it.'

"I rang New York back the next day to Jimmy Van Heusen

and told him: 'For God's sake, tell Frank I wasn't even at her table. This is ridiculous.'

"Jimmy said: 'He won't speak to you now. Let him cool down. You know what he is like. Let him cool down.' "

That's the way Lawford stated it in 1976. And Peter never denied the story. "Borrowers" often trip over words they've lifted while laying down a smokescreen to camouflage the pirated material. Kitty did this when she put words in Lawford's mouth that supposedly were uttered by Sinatra:

"Do you want your legs broken, you fucking asshole?"

Is it likely Peter Lawford's memory of what Sinatra told him was better on May 15 and June 2, 1983, when Kitty claims she interviewed the actor, or seven years earlier, in 1976, when the 1951 incident was fresher in Lawford's mind? By the time Kelley claimed she talked with him, Lawford was approaching a state of vegetation from advanced states of an atrophied liver, brought on by a lifetime of heavy drinking.

This crippling disease took Lawford's life on Christmas Eve of 1984.

Kelley wrote that Ava announced she was leaving for Rome to make *The Barefoot Contessa* in the immediate aftermath of MGM's statement about the divorce, which was made October 29, 1953. That's fact. Okay, Kitty, so far, so good.

Then she wants us to believe that a "few nights later the newspapers reported that Ava was seen dining quietly with Peter Lawford at Frascati's in Los Angeles . . ."

The restaurant where Peter and Ava had their encounter, according to what Lawford told Dunleavy, was Villa Frascati "a popular Italian restaurant on The Strip."

That's Sunset Boulevard in *Hollywood*—and it's not Frascati's as Kitty called it. There is no Frascati's, never was.

Had Kitty carefully read the piece she cribbed from Dunleavy, she would have gotten the facts straight—that the encounter between Ava and Peter was not *before* Ava left for Rome, as Kelley writes, but as Steve himself quoted one of the gossip headlines: ". . . Ava Dates Peter Lawford On First Night Back In Country"—many months later than Kelley reported; it happened *after* the sultry screen temptress returned from film-ing on the Continent. A bad blunder, because Kitty seems to have cut and pasted this one without bothering to read it.

In Chapter 19, Kitty offers her version of how Sinatra and Lawford reconciled. She quotes Lawford:

"He [Sinatra] threatened to kill me and then didn't speak to me for five years. He got over it one night at Gary and Rocky Cooper's dinner party. I had married Patricia [Kennedy] by then, and she was his dinner partner. I think we were very attractive to Frank because of Jack [Kennedy], who had been elected Senator from Massachusetts and was getting ready to run for President. Anyway, that night at the Coopers got us back together again, and we started seeing Frank all the time. We went around the world together, we named our daughter after him [Victoria Frances], we set up corporations to produce each other's movies, and we went into the restaurant business togeth-er, but even Pat, who adored Frank, was still scared of his temper."

Note that in Peter Lawford's asserted statements, Kitty has him saying first that Frank got over his mad—"but it took him six years"—and then in the above paragraph, fifty pages later, she has Lawford tell us "he didn't speak to me for five years."

Obviously Kitty didn't sort out these discrepancies before the book went to press—and neither did Bantam's editors and attorneys who are reported to have sifted out dozens of obvious mistakes and removed several pages of obviously libelous mate-rial for which Kitty could provide no substantiation.

But as Peter Lawford told Steve Dunleavy, "It took from 1951 to 1959 for Frank to cool down."

Here is another inconsistency:

Do we accept Kitty's version of how Frank and Peter reconciled—at the Gary Coopers' place in Holmby Hills, as she wrote in *His Way*—or Peter's explanation to Dunleavy—as well as to writer Malcolm Boyes—that Sinatra and Lawford ended their no-speak relationship in Monaco?

"Pat Kennedy [President John F. Kennedy's sister] and I had been married for five years by then [1959]," Lawford told

Dunleavy, "and we were on our way to Monaco to take part in a benefit put on by Princess Grace. Frank was in on it, too.

"I don't know whether it's a bit harsh to say so, but by that time the Kennedy machine was in full swing. Only bad luck would keep John Kennedy from being the next President. And Frank could see a bandwagon coming.

"In Monaco he sat next to Pat at dinner and relationships suddenly thawed. We decided to go to Rome together after the benefit. Frank and I were getting chummy again."

So, once again Kitty served up fiction rather than fact. Certainly Kitty's version—that Peter and Frank smoked the peace pipe at the Gary Cooper dinner in Holmby Hills—cannot be true, when we have Lawford, in two interviews, given four years apart with two *legitimate* reporters, saying that their friendship was renewed on the swing through Monaco and Rome!

Many years later—just before his death—Peter Lawford married another Patricia, who'd been his live-in love for nine years.

We meet Patricia Ann Seaton Lawford on a day in 1983 in this couple's Hollywood apartment.

Patricia's encounter with Kitty occurred at a time when Stanley Tretick, the photographer, was wearing two hats. He was lugging his cameras around the country for *Time-Life* and at the same time acting as gofer for Kitty Kelley. Tretick was almost always at her side with the clout of his *Time-Life* credentials, lending undeserved prestige to Kitty.

Pat Lawford told me that Tretick phoned Peter in late 1983 and told him *Life* was doing a 20th anniversary story about the death of John F. Kennedy. Peter knew Tretick from JFK's White House days when he worked for United Press International.

"The day of the interview," Pat Lawford said, "I left for the beach, telling Peter I was going out to get some sun and would be back in a few hours."

"Peter reminded me that Stanley Tretick was coming over that afternoon. The appointment was for five o'clock. I said I'd be there."

230

Some twenty minutes after five, Patricia returned home, out of breath, prepared to offer apologies until . . .

"I saw Kitty Kelley sitting on the couch. I knew who she was because I'd seen her on television during interviews for her Onassis and Taylor books . . .

"Seeing her in our apartment and realizing she was next to my sick husband while he was doing an interview with Stanley Tretick blew my mind. I couldn't imagine how Kitty Kelley could figure in the story for *Life*, which was supposed to be about Peter's remembrances of John Kennedy. Of course I was very well aware what Kitty was up to because Peter had received a letter from Sinatra's lawyer, Mickey Rudin, saying he understood she was going around claiming that Frank was cooperating with her for the book—which was not true."

Pat Lawford's antenna shot up at the sight of Kitty Kelley.

"Immediately I became a mother hen. I was always protective of Peter because he was very ill. I tried to play it cool. I said hello to everyone and gave my husband a kiss. He said to me, 'Oh, hello, this is Kitty, er . . . Kitty, er . . .' He had no idea who Kitty was.

"*I stuck around in the living room for about five minutes, looking like a dummy but taking it all in. Tretick would ask a question about Kennedy, such as 'What was Jack like?' and then Kitty would interrupt, point to a picture, and say, 'Tell me about this picture of you and Frank, what were your feelings toward him then . . . ?'*

"*When I had heard enough and saw the trick they had played on Peter, I started for the other room, saying, 'Excuse me, I just came in from the water and am going to change.'*

"*I closed the door behind me and went to the phone. I called* Life *magazine in New York and asked, 'Do you have Kitty Kelley in your employ?' They said no. Then I asked, 'Has Kitty Kelley been assigned to do a story on John F. Kennedy with Stan Tretick?' They said no.*

"*So I went into the bathroom and deliberately knocked something over. Then I called out, 'Peter, can you give me a hand in here!'*

"He came shuffling in and asked, 'What's the matter with you?'

"I whispered, 'Peter, do you know who she is? . . . She has written very unflattering things about people you love . . . about Elizabeth Taylor and Jacqueline . . . Why is this woman here? I called Life and . . .'

" 'You did what . . . ?'

" 'Yeah . . . She's not here to interview you about Kennedy . . .'

" 'Well, that's strange, because every time Stanley says something the questions go back to Sinatra . . .'

" 'All right, you just let me handle it . . .' "

Peter returned to the interview. Patricia quickly changed her clothes, then returned to the living room, where Kitty was asking, "How long has it been since you and Frank spoke?"

Kelley never got her answer. The interruption was instantaneous and electric.

"Miss Kelley," Pat said angrily, "you do not work for Life and I know you don't."

Pat turned to Tretick. "Stanley, I don't know why you brought her here. I think it's very unprofessional . . ."

Lawford was speechless, according to Pat, who described the scene that ensued:

"They got so upset with me, especially when I told them Peter would have nothing more to do with them. I said, 'Leave right now. Get out of my house!'

"Kelley then said to me, 'Look, Missy, I don't need to take this shit from you . . .'

"I said, 'Fuck you! Get out of my house!'

"And that was that. They left."

As they went out the door, Patricia turned to her husband.

"Peter, how much did you say in those twenty minutes that I was late getting back from the beach?"

"Nothing. But she kept bringing the questioning back to Frank . . ."

"Well, Peter, do you know how unprofessional that is . . ?"

That evening, Lawford phoned Tretick at reporter Jack Martin's house, where Stanley and Kitty were staying, and told him:

"Stanley, I'm really pissed off at you. I wouldn't give an interview to Kitty Kelley about Frank. I'm writing my own book.

"How can you do such a thing," Lawford continued.

"Let's talk about it," Tretick said.

The next day, Tretick, with Kelley tagging along, met the Lawfords in the Hamburger Hamlet on Sunset Boulevard.

"It was a very friendly meeting," Pat said. "We sat and we each had a glass of white wine. Then Kitty said—and I swear this on a stack of Bibles:

" 'I will never print anything you said about Frank. You have my word. I'm sorry. Don't upset Stanley. Don't report him to *Time-Life*. I promise I'll never print a word that you said about Frank.' "

Patricia Seaton Lawford's last words to me:

"The reason that I call Kitty Kelley unprofessional is that she sneaked in. She didn't say to Peter, 'I'm here to do an interview about Frank Sinatra.' She didn't say that at all. You don't creep into a home behind somebody else who is there to do a totally different interview. You can't do that!

"I'm so terribly annoyed with this woman for what she did. I was so upset when the book came out and saw what she wrote about Peter. I went to attorney John Forbess [he had signed the court papers in the Sinatra suit] and told him how unhappy I was about the things Kelley put in that book—and how she lied to Peter, who was now dead and could not defend himself against this miserable bitch."

Bottom line: *Time-Life* had not assigned Tretick to take pictures of Peter Lawford posing next to JFK's bust, nor to shoot any other photos of Lawford/Kennedy. The magazine featuring the 20th anniversary remembrance of the martyred President published its October 1983 edition showcasing some 30 photos. Only one was credited to Tretick, and that was a shot of Kennedy at a political rally during the 1960 Presidential campaign.

This was a stock photo obtained from Tretick's former employer, United Press International. Clearly, Tretick's approach to Peter Lawford with the line that he was on assignment to do a Kennedy retrospective was a lie.

In her Author's Notes, Kelley lists the dates on which she says she interviewed Peter Lawford in seven chapters, from April 13, 1984, to and including January 5th, 1985.

"It was impossible for Kitty Kelley to have interviewed my husband on the dates she lists in her book," Patricia Ann Seaton Lawford told me. "On those dates Peter was lying in bed at home or in the hospital near death . . ."

On the last date Kitty tells us she talked to Peter Lawford, January 5th, 1985, the actor was ashes. Lawford had died twelve days earlier.

19

Years later George Jacobs confirmed that Frank had indeed tried to commit suicide that night over Ava Gardner. "Thank God, I was in there to save him," he said. "Miss G. was the one great love of his life, and if he couldn't have her, he didn't want to live no more."

—Page 169, *HIS WAY: THE UNAUTHORIZED*
BIOGRAPHY OF FRANK SINATRA

According to all available evidence, Ava had returned to L.A. after spending a couple of days with Frank and some of his friends at Lake Tahoe's Crystal Bay. Upon her departure, Frank broke out in a "rash" and Hank Sanicola, Sinatra's long-time associate, called for medical help. Dr. John Wesley Field, the nearby Brockway Hotel's resident physician, went to Sinatra's suite. Field learned that Sinatra had taken sleeping pills and was feeling "lousy."

Kitty Kelley tells us the doctor induced Frank to vomit. Then she goes on to enhance her narrative with an edited quote:

"I did not try to commit suicide," said Frank. "I just had a bellyache. Suicide is the farthest thought from my mind. [. . .] What will you guys think of next to write about me?"

Note the key sentence Kitty omitted: "Ava and I are the best of friends," Sinatra's full statement went on. "We plan more nightclubbing and boating excursions. Believe it, it wasn't a suicide attempt . . ."

Now, let's hear it from Miss Gardner herself, in *Ava: My Story* . . .

"I could tell from the sound of Hank Sanicola's voice that this was for real. 'Oh, my God, Ava. Hurry back. Frank's taken an overdose!'

"A car rushed us [Ava and Mearene Johnson, called Reenie, her maid and confidante] to the L.A. airport. A car rushed us from the Nevada airport to the house at Lake Tahoe [actually a chalet on the sprawling grounds of the Cal-Neva Lodge]. Hank met me at the door.

"I ran through into the bedroom. I looked down at Frank and he turned his blue eyes to look at me.

" 'I thought you'd gone,' he said weakly.

"I wanted to punch him. I really did. Frank had tricked both Reenie and me back to his bedside. He'd had a fine rest. The doctors didn't even have to pump his stomach—he hadn't taken enough phenobarbital tablets for that.

"I could have killed him, but *Frank's mock suicide dramas* [my emphasis] were, at root, cries for help."

At least once before Sinatra "faked" a suicide. It happened in New York's Hampshire House, an elegant hostelry where guests heard gunfire on the night of March 15, 1950. That's when Ol' Blue Eyes triggered two .38-calibre bullets into a pillow of the 33rd-floor suite he and Ava were sharing. Earlier, they had a quarrel and Ava left in a huff. Still later, they were arguing hotly on the phone when Frank, to feign his self-destruction, fired the gun—which brought Ava rushing to his side for yet another reconciliation in their tempestuous roller-coaster romance.

Ava writes about Frank's "down period" with forthright incisiveness and understanding, touches which completely elude Kitty Kelley.

"He was down, way down," Ava sympathetically reports about the time Sinatra's career bottomed out. "His contracts were being canceled. His wife's [Nancy's] lawyers were intent on getting every possible dollar out of him. He'd been the idol of millions and now he was being taunted as a washed-up has-been."

"Our love was deep and true, even though the fact that we couldn't live with each other any more than we couldn't live without each other sometimes made it hard for outsiders to understand. All I know is that if Frank had lost me or I'd lost him during those months, our world would have been shattered."

There it is. The truth about Frankie and Ava—not the stick-it-to-him tale concocted by Kitty Kelley in her mostly make-believe biography!

****

In *His Way*, Kitty Kelley has George Jacobs on the job as Frank's faithful valet more than two years before he actually began the job. After establishing this erroneous time frame, she feels free to put words in the valet's mouth to shore up the framework of her fiction. Kitty jumps into the deception with:

"Years later George Jacobs confirmed that Frank had indeed tried to commit suicide that night over Ava Gardner. "Thank God, I was there to save him," he said. "Miss G. was the one great love of his life and if he couldn't have her, he didn't want to live no more."

****

"In October of 1986, defendants printed, published and circulated, or caused to be printed, published and circulated the book entitled *His Way: The Unauthorized Biography of Frank Sinatra*, in which defendants, on pages 168, 169, 257, 261, 267, 286-87, 302, 319-320, 336-37, 356, and 382-83 falsely and maliciously and with intent to injure, disgrace, and defame plaintiff used and published the following language of or concerning plaintiff:"

This, then, is how George Jacobs responded to Kitty Kelley and her publisher, Bantam Books Inc.—a suit for damages claiming libel and stating emphatically and unequivocally that the venom vented against Sinatra through the lips of his valet was total fabrication.

"These interviews [on which Kelley allegedly based her account] between plaintiff and KELLEY never occurred and thus all statements which are attributed to plaintiff in defendant's book are fraudulent and were published with the intent to expose plaintiff to hatred, contempt and ridicule. Therefore, plaintiff seeks an award of punitive damages as against defendant, KELLEY in a sum according to proof at the time of trial."

The papers, signed by attorney Cristina Lenz, sought "general damages, special damages, punitive damages, costs of litigating the suit, and whatever further relief the court may deem proper."

****

One of the passages that Jacobs objected to involved a wide-ranging interview with Peter Lawford by British journalist Malcolm Boyes in 1982. By then the English-born actor had been divorced from the late President Kennedy's sister Patricia, and for the preceding six years had been living with another Patricia (Seaton) whom he would marry in July, 1984, when she was twenty-six and he was sixty.

One of the anecdotes Lawford spun for Boyes told of a New Year's Eve outing Peter and his first wife went on with Robert Wagner and Natalie Wood. They joined Sinatra for dinner at Romanoff's in Beverly Hills. Afterward, Frank asked the two couples to accompany him to Palm Springs and spend New Year's Day with him.

"As the evening dragged on into the small hours of the morning, the ladies tired and decided they wanted a night's sleep before driving to Palm Springs," Boyes quotes Lawford. "This, of course, did not fit in with Frank's plans and he left in a huff."

In *His Way*, Kitty relates this incident in far greater detail and with considerable embellishment before she spins further quotes from George Jacobs—that he insists didn't come from him—*and from Peter Lawford, based, according to Kelley's chapter notes, on interviews with Lawford on November 5 and 6, 1984, and January 5, 1985, the former being when the actor was on his death bed and the latter twelve days after he died.*

Kelley allegedly quoting Lawford:

"Well, he went absolutely nuts. 'If that's the way you want it, fine,' he said, slamming his drink on the floor and storming out of the restaurant. I rang him the next morning and his valet, George Jacobs, answered and whispered hello. He said that Frank was still asleep because he hadn't gotten to bed until five A.M. Then he said, 'Oh, Mr. Lawford. What happened last night? I better tell you that he's pissed. Really pissed off. He went to your closet and took out all the clothes that you and your wife keep here and ripped them into shreds and then threw them into the swimming pool.' "

Malcolm Boyes, who knew Lawford intimately, told me it was inconceivable that Peter ever described this scene to Kitty Kelley in the words she attributed to him. Note how Kitty brought George Jacobs into the swimming pool episode through Peter Lawford, who is no longer alive to protest. Certainly Boyes didn't have the valet saying Sinatra was "pissed" nor did he have him ripping Peter and Pat's clothes into "shreds" and throwing them in the swimming pool. All that Boyes says Lawford told him about his conversation with Jacobs was that Sinatra took the clothes out of the closet and "kicked them all into the pool where they were now floating!"

That's not all that George Jacobs finds offensive and injurious to him in Kelley's book . . .

****

"I feel like I raised those kids," Kelley quotes George Jacobs as saying. "For a while when Frank and Nancy weren't speaking to each other I was the go-between. Young Frankie and I got to be real good pals. He's a sad little guy, but sweet. A nice kid. I'd drive around with him, and when I'd bring him back home, Nancy, Sr., would be there, asking, 'Well, what did Frankie say? What did he talk about? I don't want you teaching my son no jive.' I never did tell her what Frankie talked about and I never told Frank either, because I didn't want to break the kid's confidence. With all those damned women around, he needed some man to talk to, and his dad just wasn't around that much."

On October 31, 1951—some two years *before* George Jacobs came aboard as Frank Sinatra's valet and began his sixteen-year association with the crooner, Judge Cecil Rhodes in Santa Monica granted Nancy a generous separate maintenance settlement and interlocutory decree of divorce.

How could George Jacobs feel "like I raised those kids," or be "the go-between" when "Frank and Nancy weren't speaking to each other?" How could he "drive around with him [Frankie Jr.]" and bring him home to Nancy and have her asking what conversation the valet had with her son when by the time Jacobs came to work for him, Frankie had been married almost two years to Ava Gardner? (He took on his second wife only days after he was divorced from the first.)

"How could this writer put words in my mouth the way she has when *I never even spoke to her?*" Jacobs complained. "I have no idea how she drummed up all that bull about my having been a father to the kids when I never said any such thing to anyone—*when nothing like that ever happened?*"

****

Jacobs charges that he was further maligned by Kitty Kelley when she dragged him into her sketch of President Kennedy's fondness for Sinatra because Frankie "told him a lot of inside gossip about celebrities and their romances in Hollywood." The Kelley narrative goes on to describe Sinatra's amiability as a host when JFK stayed in Frank's Palm Springs pad after a big Los Angeles fund-raiser, then drags the manservant into the plot once more:

"George Jacobs, Frank's black valet, served Kennedy what he called the house special. 'With Frank it's spaghetti for breakfast, lunch, and dinner,' he said. 'I was serving him by the pool and

Frank told JFK to ask me about my stand on civil rights. I didn't like niggers and I told him so. They make too much noise, I said. The Mexicans smell and I can't stand them either. Kennedy fell in the pool, he laughed so hard.'

In the Author's Notes section for Chapter 20, which is where this sketch appears, Kitty lists *two* interviews for February 22, 1978: George Jacobs and former Senator George Smathers ("who told the author how much Frank liked making it with colored girls"). Unless she chartered a Concorde for a special Miami-to-Los Angeles flight, Kitty couldn't possibly have interviewed Smathers, who was in retirement from politics in Florida, and George Jacobs, who by now had left Sinatra's employ and was working as a carpenter and handyman in California, on the same day!

****

In Chapter 25, Kelley takes us to Las Vegas for Frank Sinatra's marriage to wife No. 3, Mia Farrow, on July 19, 1966.

Minutes before the ceremony, Kelley says Sinatra took George Jacobs aside and said, "Call Miss G," their code name for Ava Gardner. But, Kitty goes on, Jack Entratter, entertainment director of the Sands Hotel in Las Vegas "tried to dissuade George from making the call, but George insisted." Then Kitty, who assures us in her author's notes that Jacobs was one of three persons she interviewed on October 24 and November 1, 1983, puts this response to the nightclub impresario from George's mouth:

"It'll be my ass if I don't get hold of that lady before someone else does, and I'll find her if it's the last thing I do." As he heads for the phone, Kelley claims Jacobs added: "She's the love of his life and you know it."

The valet says that statement is a total fabrication which Kitty manufactured only to hurt him.

His last complaint against the author is that Kelley says that Jacobs's falling out with Sinatra was over an incident on the night before August 16, 1967, when Mia Farrow's Mexican

241

divorce was granted. Kelley puts Mia in the Daisy, a nightspot in Hollywood, where George Jacobs then walks in with his date, and the soon-to-be divorcee "grabbed him for a dance."

Now Kitty really lays it on Jacobs when he returns to the Sinatra house as she has him saying:

"The maid came to me and said, 'Mr. Sinatra wants you to get out of the house,' " said Jacobs. "This was the day of the Mia divorce. Frank had locked himself in his room and wouldn't come out. I banged on the door and said, 'What's wrong? What's going on?' He wouldn't open the door. 'Mickey will tell you,' he said. 'Call Mickey.' So I called Rudin and waited an hour for him to get back to me.

"He told me that the stuff [columnist] Rona Barrett reported really stirred Frank up, that I'd better take a few days off and, in the meantime, move all my belongings out of the house. I tried to explain that I didn't do anything. All I did was walk into the Daisy with my date and see Mia, who was sitting there stoned. She wanted to dance so we danced a couple of times. That was it, but everyone around the old man—Jilly [Rizzo] and all of them—poisoned his mind until he actually believed that his valet was sleeping with his wife. I couldn't believe that he'd ever think I'd do something like that to him. After *fourteen* years together he dropped the net on me just like that and he couldn't even look me in the face to do it. He couldn't fire me in person. He had to have his prick lawyer do it for him.

"I was so mad afterwards that I threw away everything he'd ever given me—two-thousand-dollar watches, suits, sweaters, shirts, shoes, coats, cameras, radios—everything. I didn't want anything from the bastard around. I got twelve thousand dollars in severance pay and blew it, and then I sold all my shares in Reprise Records [Sinatra's record company].

"I had been so close to that man. I even signed his name better than he did. In fact, I did all the autographs. 'Just give it to George,' Frank would say whenever someone wanted a signed Sinatra picture. I went everywhere with him. I nursed him through his suicide attempt in Lake Tahoe. I helped him get through Ava, who was the only woman he ever loved. I was

242

even the nurse after his hair transplants from Dr. Sammy Ayres,
who had done Joey Bishop first and then Frank. I drove all the
girls to Red Krohn [Dr. Leon Krohn] for their abortions, and I
treated each one of those dames like a queen because that's
what he wanted me to do. The women that man had over the
years! I still remember Lee Radziwill sneaking into his bedroom. How do I know? I heard her. I always had a room next to
Frank so he could slap the wall for me if he needed anything.

"Yeah, I was at Cal-Neva with [Chicago Mafia leader Sam
"Momo"] Giancana, and I was with him a lot when he visited
Frank in Palm Springs. The guy was great with tips. I knew
them all—Sam and [mob boss] Joe Fischetti. I even knew
[mobster] Moe Dalitz when he was calling himself the Entertainment Director of the Desert Inn. Don't that beat everything? The Entertainment Director!"

Kitty interrupts the alleged dialogue to interpose: "Devastated by the firing, Jacobs reminisced about the years he worked
for Sinatra, saying that what he missed most was the riotous
merriment." The author then purports the valet described those
happy times in these words:

"We had some funny, funny times together because Frank
was always doing numbers on people. He loved practical jokes.
Like the time he walked in when Milt Ebbins [Peter Lawford's
personal manager] was shaving, and said, 'Let me see that,
Milt.' Wham! He threw the razor out of the window. 'What time
is it, Milt?' He'd take Ebbins's watch off his wrist and throw that
out the window too. He was always doing crazy stuff like that.
Years later [after the break with Frank] I thought I'd write a
book about those funny times and I sat down with Joe Hyams.
We got about thirty-two pages written before the word got out
and oh, God! Rudin hit me with a letter you wouldn't believe. I
told him I'd never hurt Frank. I loved the guy. I just wanted to
write about the good things. Not the bad stuff, nothing about
the Mafia, none of that stuff. I even said they could have the
galleys and if there was anything they wanted to take out of the
book, it would be cut out, but Rudin wouldn't hear of it. Man,
when that word got around I couldn't get anybody to hang out

with me. They thought they'd be shot in the knees because Frank was mad."

Once again, Kelley's Chapter Notes fail to report when she claims to have spoken with George Jacobs.

"She doesn't say so," commented Jacobs in conversation with sources close to his case and anxious to guard his best interests, "because it *never happened.* Just let me point out things this monstrous fraud said about me that are out-and-out made-up:

"How could I say I worked fourteen years for Frank Sinatra when the fact is I was with him from 1953 to 1969—which is sixteen years? Could I lose two years out of my life just like that?

"Do I look dumb enough to throw away two-thousand-dollar watches, suits, sweaters, shirts, shoes, coats, cameras and other possessions if indeed I had been fired by Frank—which in itself isn't so? Of course, all of that's a big damned lie.

"I didn't—and never would—characterize Mickey Rudin as a 'prick,' as this irresponsible lady has me saying. I've known this lawyer for all the years that I was with Frank and never had a reason to speak an unkind word about him. I just like the guy all the way.

"Let me tell you right here and now, there's no way in the world I could have ever described Frank Sinatra as a 'bastard' as Kitty Kelley said I did."

The last word from Frank Sinatra's valet was this: "I'm looking forward eagerly to meet the no good bitch in court. That's when I'm gonna really stick it to her for putting all those dirty words and filthy lies in my mouth . . . ."

****

After angling a $1.5 million bite for *His Way: The Unauthorized Biography of Frank Sinatra,* Kitty Kelley trawled her biggest catch—a $3.5 million advance—from Simon & Schuster for an unauthorized biography that would savage Nancy Reagan. Then, inexplicably, the relentless essayist went casting in a small literary lake and hooked a $100,000 fish that soon smelled as it started to rot.

Agent Lynn Nesbit, still at International Creative Management, sold *People* magazine on an article in which one Judy Imoor Campbell Exner would tell Kitty everything. She would reveal information about her relations with both President John F. Kennedy and Chicago Mafia overlord Sam "Momo" Giancana.

Although her 1977 book, *My Story*, detailed her sexual encounters with JFK as well as with the powerful underworld leader, Exner never suggested that there was any link between the President and the mobster. The only connection between those two lovers, as she told the story then, was that Frank Sinatra—she claimed she slept with him, too—introduced her, on separate occasions, to both the President and the organized crime boss.

The book grew out of her appearance in 1975 before the Senate Select Committee on Intelligence, which investigated the CIA plots to assassinate Cuban Prime Minister Fidel Castro. In its final report, the Committee concluded pretty much what the President's brother, Attorney General Robert F. Kennedy, had surmised about Exner: she was just a party girl who went around telling everyone that she'd slept with JFK and Momo but knew nothing about the conspiracy to poison the Cuban dictator's food and his Havana cigars. This was the plot labelled "Operation Mongoose," supposedly a joint venture between the CIA and the Mafia. The latter wanted to get even with Castro for shuttering their gambling casinos in Havana after the revolution.

Only four months before she was summoned to Capitol Hill, Judith Campbell married golf pro Dan Exner. But that conjugal hookup didn't deter her from offering herself to the public as the sexual playmate of both JFK and the recently murdered Chicago overlord.

Exner came to the hearings saying she was concerned about her safety after reading newspaper accounts out of Oak Park, Illinois, chronicling how Momo had been dispatched to gangster heaven the day before he could testify in Washington.

The sixty-five-year-old mobster was shot once in the right corner of the mouth and five times in the neck (not "seven times

245

in the head" as stated in Kelley's *People* story). Caretaker Joseph DiPersio, 82, found the body face up on the kitchen floor in the basement of Momo's mansion in that western Chicago suburb. DiPersio told authorities he last saw Giancana at 10:30 p.m. on June 19, 1975, when he looked in on Momo. Half an hour later he was dead.

Another Mafioso bigshot from the Los Angeles-Las Vegas precincts, Johnny "Don Giovanni" Roselli, Giancana's West Coast lieutenant, made it to Capitol Hill without a scratch, and testified under subpoena with seeming reluctance. One year later, his mutilated remains were discovered in a weighted 55-gallon oil drum floating in Miami Bay.

Great mystery surrounds the conclusion of the Senate hearings in 1975 because the Committee didn't call Frank Sinatra as a witness after learning that he had introduced Judith Imoor Campbell (she was not yet Mrs. Exner) to both President Kennedy and Giancana.

Kitty Kelley resurrected that episode in *His Way*. Kelley created several curious miscolorations about Exner's assignations with JFK and Momo to buttress her onslaught on Sinatra. Most significantly, the author, after contending that she conducted 857 interview for her book, is remiss in offering even a single new quote from this "scarlet woman" who professed to have bedhopped from the whorehouse to the White House.

Surfacing on page 538 is the first suspicion about the authenticity of Kelley's sources on this aspect of the book. It looms with unmistakable clarity in her Author's Notes for Chapter 33 when she states:

"The author consulted the transcripts of the Nevada Gaming Board's 1981 hearings and conducted extensive interviews with one of the Board's investigators, who requested anonymity, on June 6, June 29, and September 1, 1983. Information on Sinatra's finances was taken from the financial statements submitted by Sinatra to the Board." It was this hearing that led to the restoration of his gambling license which had been revoked after revelations that he consorted with Momo Giancana and other unsavory characters. The chapter is taken in its entirety from the Nevada Gaming Board hearing transcript. This is a public record and accessible merely for the asking. Kelley had simply done her usual scissor-and-paste job, not adding a single exclusive or previously unpublished fact.

Kitty dragged Judith Exner in by the heels after noting how Mafia squealer Aladena "Jimmy The Weasel" Fratianno refused to cooperate with the Gaming Board after he announced that he was "insulted" by Board Chairman Richard Bunker. The passage continues:

"So did Judith Campbell Exner, former girlfriend of President Kennedy and Sam Giancana. Having been introduced to both men by Frank Sinatra, she could have told investigators about their triangular relationship, but she refused because she felt that the hearings were a sham.

" 'What difference would it make?' she said later. 'It was a foregone conclusion that Frank was going to get that license no matter what anybody said. They [the Board] didn't want to believe how close he was to Sam.' "

Although Kelley lists Exner as a source, the chapter contains only this solitary reference to Judy. The quote is taken from a statement Exner made after the hearing to a publication—but never to Kelley!

Said Exner, "I never spoke to Kitty Kelley for the Sinatra book. The first contact I had with her was in 1987 after I phoned Liz Smith and asked her if she could recommend a writer who'd sell a story about my role as a courier between the Chicago underworld and the Kennedy White House. Liz then put Kitty in touch with me to do the story that was sold to *People*."

By late 1987, Judith Exner, approaching fifty-four and facing a "death sentence" from terminal cancer, decided to "spill her guts." She was low on funds and her mounting medical bills required that she make a fast buck some way.

She contacted Barbara Walters and offered her story for TV's *20/20*. The distinguished reporter offered to interview Exner to determine if her story merited airing. But there was one catch. Judy demanded a chunk of cash. Miss Walters told Judy she didn't practice checkbook journalism.

That's when Exner called Liz Smith and that's when Liz brought Kitty Kelley into the picture.

Kitty phoned Exner in early October of 1987. Judy was aware of how Kitty had written smear jobs. She wanted Kitty to do a similar number on JFK and Momo, but she wanted big money for her story.

Kitty wanted to know what new information could Exner come up with in 1987 that she hadn't already bared to Congress in 1975 or in her book in 1977?

Just this: that sometime in 1960 President Kennedy had asked Judy to convey a message to Momo Giancana in Chicago. After that, she said, her role became that of courier between the White House and the mob in the Windy City.

"At the President's request," Exner told Kitty, "I carried envelopes back and forth between Kennedy and Giancana—as well as Johnny Roselli . . ."

Exner brought Kelley to Nirvana when she added that beside the nearly dozen trips she made on her rounds between 1600 Pennsylvania Ave. and Oak Park, Illinois, JFK and Giancana had at least ten face-to-face meetings—and that one of them, in 1962, took place in the White House.

Kelley couldn't believe her ears. She dialed agent Lynn Nesbit, repeated what Exner had told her, then sat back to await a contract to write the story.

Nesbit cut a $100,000 deal with *People*. The arrangement, which the participants were to sign, stipulated that all parties must give their consent before any word was leaked out about the price *People* paid for the story. The magazine's editors had asked very pointedly that no mention of payment to Exner be broadcast.

The hitch in the transaction was that there were to be only two participants in the contract-signing: *People* magazine and Kitty Kelley, represented by Lynn Nesbit. The only document Exner was given to execute was a "Waiver of Liability," which meant that should her story result in libel suits, she would not be held responsible for the inaccuracies. The contract, dated October 16, 1987, excluded her completely, so it was small comfort to Judy that she was being indemnified against possible litigation over the story.

"What a farce," Exner said. "I was going to talk about my experiences with Kennedy, Giancana and Roselli. Those were the main characters in my story. They were all gone now. How do you libel a dead man? What were they protecting me from?"

Not only was the contract between *People* and "Author"—Kitty Kelley—but the copyright was to be in Kelley's name alone.

Even without an agent to guide her, Exner sensed the unfairness of the agreement.

"This was my life story," she protested, "and my name wasn't even on the contract as co-author. Nor would I own the rights."

Judy took the unsigned contract to lunch at Barbara Walters' house in Bel Air. Walters advised Exner to demand a new contract which would make her an equal partner with Kelley.

Ultimately, the fuss Exner raised did result in a new arrangement that gave her a fifty-fifty cut of all income from her story.

Then began interviews with Kitty Kelley. Exner met the writer for the first time. Judy had agreed beforehand to have her words tape-recorded. Kelley met Exner on two occasions in November at the Four Seasons Hotel in California's Newport Beach. Because of doubts about Kitty's integrity after the contract fiasco, Judy insisted that her friend, Felicia Folina, be present at both interview sessions.

"We met for a total of fourteen hours," Exner explained. "And I'm glad that I brought Felicia along. I knew that I needed a witness any time I had a conversation with Kitty."

The first interview went smoothly enough. Exner provided calendars, plane ticket stubs, hotel bills, and other documentation for verification of the trips and meetings she claimed she took at President Kennedy's behest. This same "evidence" had been provided earlier for Judy's 1977 book. It is of greatest significance now to note that those documents—however true or false they may have been—were not trumpeted in her book a dozen years ago as travel expenses incurred as JFK's courier.

The package given to Kelley also included a log of 70 phone calls Judy claimed she made to the White House.

The second day of her meeting with Kitty proved to be a disaster. According to Exner:

"She wanted more episodes of explicit sex. She told me *People* demanded that. She wanted a description of Frank's [Sinatra's] bedroom. All of this [the JFK-Giancana meetings, which was what the story was about so far as the magazine was concerned] had nothing to do with him."

The rapidly deteriorating rapport between interviewer and interviewee exploded into a shouting match between the two women after Kitty pressured Judy for information about the paternity of a child she bore out of wedlock in 1965.

Clearly, the baby couldn't have been JFK's since he had died long before the mother's nine-month gestation period began.

Whether or not Kelley was trying to shape a story that Giancana or Sinatra might be the father is a matter of conjecture. Yet, as a story, it certainly was pregnant with possibilities which held every promise of another gush of gold for Kitty from a publisher.

Exner's main gripe:

"She kept pressing me for information on the paternity of my child whom I gave up for adoption after he was born. I couldn't understand what Kitty was driving at. Why was she so adamant about learning details about a very sensitive situation that had nothing to do with the story she was getting from me?

"We're dealing here with a child's life. I had always guarded details about his birth and who his father might be to protect the boy's privacy. But Kitty insisted over and over again that I tell her what I was determined she'd never learn . . ."

[Late last year, Kitty Kelley finally learned of Exner's son's identity when she read all about the way David Bahrer, then 24, found his mother and reunited with her. Liz Smith broke the story exclusively and gave Kelley another reason to bite her nails in the smoldering feud the scribes had going between them, which wags referred to as "the battle of the lady and the tramp."]

"I had brought my own recorder to these sessions and I was clicking mine on and off as frequently as she was turning hers on and off while we argued back and forth. Kitty was impossible. She'd scream at me. 'You're going to have to address this situation. You're going to have to answer this question.' "

Exasperated and physically depleted by the interrogation, Judith Exner finally exploded. Then she leaped to her feet, gathered her papers and tape recorder and stormed out with friend Felicia Folina. On arriving home, Judy tried to reach Kitty at the Four Seasons Hotel but was told she had checked out. After that and for the next month, Exner phoned once or twice a day to Kitty's Georgetown number but all she got were Frank Sinatra recordings of *I Could Write A Book*, *My Way* and other songs on the answering machine—but nary a response from the person she was calling or any other living human being.

Finally Judy appealed to the editors of *People* magazine. She spoke with Assistant Managing Editor James Seymore Jr., a driving force in the negotiations for the story and now the head honcho in putting the piece together for publication.

Meanwhile, Kitty Kelley's finished manuscript arrived at *People* Christmas week of 1987. It almost floored Seymore, who had boned up on Judith Exner's background by reading her *My Story*. Seymore couldn't believe this was the manuscript submitted to the magazine for $100,000. The story was supposed to give chapter and verse about Judith Exner's role as President Kennedy's courier to Momo Giancana—yet the main thrust of the piece centered primarily on inordinately lengthy sexual details involving Frank Sinatra.

There was no question in Seymore's mind that the story had appeared, almost in toto, in Exner's 1977 book which he'd just finished reviewing. It had been lifted almost word-for-word from that eleven-year-old book.

In purloining from her own co-author's text, Kitty Kelley was practicing the safest form of plagiarism . . .

Not only couldn't Judy Exner sue for the theft of her own words in the deal she struck with Kitty and *People*, but Kelley now had the freedom seldom available to her in past exercises in literary plunder.

Seymore would have none of it. His magazine wasn't going to pay one hundred-thousand dollars for a rehash. He demanded Kelley deliver the story contracted for. He told this to Lynn Nesbit. The agent conveyed the message to the author.

This was the situation at the time a furious Judy phoned Seymore.

"Kitty Kelley hasn't returned my phone calls. I don't have any idea of what she's writing. This is my story—and I demand to know what was going on." Seymore sent an amended contract to Lynn Nesbit. He asked for "substantial revisions" in Kelley's unacceptable manuscript and threatened to cancel the deal if Kitty failed to produce in a reasonably short time.

A fortnight later, Kelley submitted a revised manuscript to *People*—and didn't send a copy to Exner before giving it to the magazine. As she had done before, Judy phoned Seymore and blew her stack. *People* had sent a copy of the manuscript to Exner—and what she read didn't make her happy.

"It's still terrible! It still is all wrong!" Judy protested.

She was assured by Seymore that no story would be published until it was right.

Now Kitty, still in a stew, got on the horn with Exner and attacked her for bitching to *People*.

"You have a goddamned nerve complaining after all the work I put into this story!" Kelley screamed. "I will not rewrite it again! I will not!"

Jim Seymore threw up his hands in disgust and decided on another avenue as a way to salvage the story . . .

People then unleashed a team of reporters and researchers. They rechecked Exner's documentation, only to discover large holes and missing links. Something like fifty percent of Kitty Kelley's manuscript had to be left on the editorial cutting room floor.

"It was one large horror show," said one staffer who inputted copy on a word processor. "It was a paragraph this way one minute, a sentence that way another minute, then it was re-do the whole thing. I had a headache for a week after working on that mess."

Changes in the text—even major subtractions and additions of data—weren't enough to revive Kitty Kelley's $100,000 abomination. *People* dispatched researcher Jane Sugden to California to meet with Exner and her lawyer. In what turned out to be a six-hour conference, Sugden came away with a set of facts almost completely different from what Kelley had in her original manuscript.

Back in New York, editor James Seymore pushed the staff to rework Judith Exner's piece. Before it was done, *People* people had rewritten the story in its entirety. Both the text of Kelley's first manuscript and her rejected second version were virtually unrelated to the cover story finally published under the title, "The Dark Side of Camelot."

Just before *People* went to press, Kitty Kelley was accorded the courtesy of "approving" the version the magazine's editors— and lawyers—finally passed for publication. She came to New York and read the manuscript "line-by-line," as Seymore put it. "She was upset that we'd rewritten her," he told the *Washington Post*'s Gerri Hirshey. "We thought it was livelier, better written and certainly more accurate. We omitted her errors and made it a better piece."

For a time, Seymore revealed, *People* considered withholding payment to Kitty for the story. But in the end a check was issued for $50,000 and another $5,000 for expenses. Exner was also paid $50,000.

"We held up payment [to Kitty] for a day," said Seymore. "But we decided it was more trouble than it was worth. Our dealings with her had been so unpleasant that our feeling was 'Let's just get rid of her . . .'

"We bought [the article] from what we thought was a legitimate journalist. After her work we backtracked on every detail, corrected errors and rewrote it to make it publishable."

The warfare waged in the editorial offices of *People* didn't make the public print. But the $50,000 fee the magazine had agreed to pay Judith Exner for her story did. In spite of signing an agreement not to divulge the money deal with Exner, Kitty Kelley revealed the terms to a reporter from a newspaper, then on television as well, without consulting either *People* or Exner.

The august *New York Times* carried the story under this headline, which touched off charges of "checkbook journalism" and embarrassed *People* editors.

"Author Cites $100,000 Fee For Kennedy Article"

The story, published in the February 23, 1988 edition, read:

"Judith Campbell Exner, who told *People* magazine she arranged more than ten meetings between John F. Kennedy and Sam Giancana, Chicago mob boss, in the early 1960s, was paid about $50,000 for the interview, the author of the magazine article said today.

"Author Kitty Kelley, who also wrote a best-selling biography of singer Frank Sinatra, said Mrs. Exner demanded to be paid for her story which she told in thirty-five hours of conversation."

Kelley had more than doubled the number of hours Judith Exner told us she spent with the author over a two-day period of interviews. Exner had said, "We met for a total of about fourteen hours . . ."

"In a telephone interview from Washington," the *Times* story continued, "Miss Kelley said she first arranged to talk to Mrs. Exner about Kennedy and Mr. Giancana in 1983, but the plans fell through after Mrs. Exner demanded payment.

"'I told her I don't pay for interviews,' Miss Kelley said. 'But I didn't get the story because I wouldn't pay. This time *People* did.'

"Miss Kelley said she and Mrs. Exner split a fee from *People* published by Time Inc., for about $100,000. She said the payment was justified now because Mrs. Exner has terminal cancer and the story was a little piece of history.

"Elizabeth Wagner, publicity manager at *People*, said the magazine would have no comment about the fee.

"In an appearance before the Senate Intelligence Committee in 1975, Mrs. Exner said she knew of no relationship between the two and that Mr. Kennedy never knew of her friendship with Mr. Giancana.

"G. Robert Blakey, professor of law at the University of Notre

Dame and an expert on organized crime, said he found Mrs. Exner's story incredible. 'The President of the United States directly dealing with a mobster and no one knowing about it?' he asked."

The *Times* story went out over the Associated Press, United Press International, Reuters and other news service wires and made its way into hundreds of newspapers around the country.

People was taken over the coals by CBS News in a highly critical story that riled Jim Seymore, who finally spoke out:

"We were quite upset about her unilateral decision to reveal the fee," Seymore said. "Even worse, because of Kitty Kelley's misrepresentations to the press, we were made to look like an outfit looking for the most lurid story, then throwing money at someone to say it."

People could have seen evidence that the Sinatra-JFK-Giancana-Roselli connection Judith Exner was trying to sell to *People* was fiction by examining the Justice Department record compiled from FBI wiretap operations. In one passage in the FBI tape Roselli assesses Sinatra's clout at the White House in a conversation with Giancana:

"He's got big ideas, Frank does, about being ambassador, or something. You know Pierre Salinger and them guys, they don't want him. They treat him like they treat a whore. You fuck them, you pay them, and they're through. You got the right idea, Moe [one of Momo's several nicknames], go the other way. Fuck everybody. We'll use them every fucking way we can. They [the Kennedys] only know one way. Now let them see the other side of you."

Another clue in Kitty Kelley's *His Way* confirms that Exner's story was a fake. Kitty Kelley was well aware Giancana never took credit for JFK's primary victory in West Virginia in 1960, as the *People* story contends. It was in Chicago and Cook County where the mob, at Frank Sinatra's urging, conducted a muscular, arm-twisting get-out-and-vote campaign upon the natives on Election Day—and it was this effort that Giancana maintained helped Kennedy carry Illinois by a slim 8,858 votes to win the Presidency.

Here's the tell-tale paragraph, and it follows a rambling preamble in which Giancana swears Sinatra off with a long string of abusive curses and labels him a liar:

"If he [Kennedy] had lost this state here he would have lost the election. But I figured with this guy [Sinatra], maybe we will be all right. I might have known this guy, this mother —. Well, when a son of a bitch lies to you . . ."

If Kitty Kelley's Judith Exner story in *People* had any validity whatsoever as the Bermuda Triangle of President politics, why didn't Momo say to Johnny:

"Hey, walyo, watsa matta widda you. Why you fool aroun' widda dat scoongeel [Sinatra]? Why you no senda message in envelope to da Prez, eh gibrone? Don't ya rememba how we useta passa da envelopes back an forthwidda dat boutan [whore] . . . whatsa her name . . . yeah, yeah, Judy Campbell . . . ?"

Why, indeed! Because there were no envelopes. No White House visits by Giancana. No meetings with the President. No conversations either. Nor any communications carried by the U.S. Postal Service, Judith Campbell Exner, nor any other courier. The whole story was a fairy tale. And it was published because *People's* editors were eager to publish a sensational story as a circulation builder.

****

In her *Jackie Oh!* Kitty Kelley reports, "She [Exner] . . . remembers Kennedy telling her that his marriage was not too happy. Without ever criticizing Jackie, he indicated that their relationship was far from satisfactory. 'There will be some changes in my life if I don't get the nomination . . .' he told her.

" 'That's all he would say at that time,' said Miss Campbell, 'and I didn't press it. Later, through various conversations, I got the impression that it was Jackie who was planning to leave him if he didn't become President.' "

Observe how Kitty and Judy hype the anecdote to suit the purposes of the story they pawned off on *People* magazine:

"Kennedy met with Giancana at the Fontainebleau [Miami Beach] on April 12. 'I was not present,' says Exner, 'but Jack came to my suite afterward, and I asked him how the meeting had gone. He seemed very happy about it and thanked me for making the arrangements. He then stayed with me for an hour or so, and we talked about the campaign. Jack told me that if he didn't get the nomination in July, he and his wife would get a divorce. He didn't say he was leaving her for me or any other woman, or that Jackie was leaving him for any other man. He simply said that their marriage was unhappy and the divorce was a mutual decision between them."

To Kelley, the Exner story for *People* represented quick profit for only a lick and a promise. Practically no research and little legwork were required. All she had to do was listen to Exner and type the story up. But Kelley was too well informed not to know, or at least suspect, that Exner was lying. And the fact was Kitty couldn't care less.

20

"You can say anything about an Italian—but you don't attack his mother . . ."

This is former Washington, D.C. Police Inspector Joseph W. Shimon talking. He offered that observation because Kelley phoned him one day after *His Way: The Unauthorized Biography of Frank Sinatra* had climbed to the top of the best-seller lists and asked concernedly:

"Do you think Frank Sinatra will break my legs for what I wrote about his mother?"

Shimon said he didn't know.

"But I don't think you should ever stop looking over your shoulder, Kitty," he added. "You never know what can happen . . ."

Perhaps the most succinct—and incisive—description of Kitty's desecration of Mrs. Sinatra is to be found in Barbara Grizzuti Harrison's 1,680-word essay in the November 2, 1986, Sunday Book Review magazine of *The New York Times*. In her unflattering assessment of the book, Mrs. Harrison immerses Kitty into a cauldron of hot marinara sauce for failing to understand Italian immigrant life in Hoboken, N.J., where Frank was born and, as the esteemed critic quotes from the book: ". . . where the air smelled of garlic." Then:

"Mr. Sinatra's mother, Dolly (to whom he was intensely loyal), was, Ms. Kelley alleges, an abortionist as well as a big mouth and a power in New Jersey politics.

"What conclusions are we to draw from this?

"What did Dolly Sinatra's son draw from this?

"What does Ms. Kelley make of this? (Does Ms. Kelley not approve of abortion? Or does she not approve of abortion when Mrs. Sinatra is the abortionist?). Ms. Kelley, because of her ignorance of immigrant life, fails to place Dolly Sinatra in context. She was profane! She swore! She called some of her son's women whores! So, exactly, what? Southern Italian immigrants of Dolly Sinatra's generation lived dangerously; the surrounding society gave them little choice. Their cursing was often a measure of their affection: 'Okay, you bastards. Into the kitchen. I've made some linguini.' Very crude and unladylike of Dolly Sinatra. But ladies did not, as a rule, migrate to Hoboken . . ."

Shimon's response caused Kitty apprehension.

"Do you really think he'll harm me?" she asked.

"How can I know?" Shimon repeated. "All I can tell you is that you wrote things about his mother that you shouldn't have. Italians sometimes take years to retaliate . . ."

Shimon reports:

"Suddenly Kitty's voice sounded frightened.

" 'What shall I do . . . how can I find out?' she asked."

"I'll tell you what I'll do for you," Shimon came back. "I'll call my old pal Ed Becker out in Vegas. He knows Sinatra and he can give you a reading on what's likely to happen . . ."

****

Becker is former Vice President of the Riviera Hotel and Casino in Las Vegas and now heads Ed Becker Associates, an investigative agency based in Los Angeles and Las Vegas. This veteran impresario was a good source for a reading on Frank Sinatra's level of anger.

Becker had known Sinatra since 1956, an association that began through a Sinatra cousin with a different last name who, coincidentally, married an orchestra leader named Ray Sinatra, no relation to Frank until the happenstance of marriage brought him into the family. Ray Sinatra conducted the Riviera Hotel's band and Frank often dropped in for the show.

"That's when I first became acquainted with Frank," Becker told me. "And we've been friends ever since. And although I didn't discuss the Kitty Kelley book directly with him, I heard from people close to him that he wasn't going to comment on it. Yet I also learned that he was outraged at the treatment his mother got."

Shimon called Becker in late November of 1987.

"Kitty Kelley's beside herself," Shimon said. "She wants to talk to you. She wants to know if she's in physical danger."

Becker responded that he'd be in Washington sometime after the New Year on one of his periodic visits to friends, many of whom are writers.

"Although I know a number of authors in the area, I'd never run into Kelley," Becker conceded. "I only knew her by reputation."

After arriving in the capital, Becker phoned Kitty and was greeted by a recording.

"Frank Sinatra was singing *My Way*. I broke out laughing. I thought it was funny—but also pretty stupid. Then I started leaving a message:

" 'I'm Ed Becker. I've just come in from Las Vegas. I know you want to see me . . .' "

All at once a voice broke in.

"Oh, oh . . . ah . . . ahhh . . . This is Kitty Kelley . . . Hello there, Ed. I'm so glad you called . . ."

"The voice sounded like honey oozing through the phone," Becker recalled. "She asked me what I was doing. She let me know right away that she'd heard I was writing a book on Johnny Roselli. She wanted to know how I was progressing.

"I told her I was doing real well because I'd known Johnny in Las Vegas for almost all the years he'd been there. But it seemed like what I was saying was falling on deaf ears. I didn't realize why until I caught her piece on Exner in *People* magazine. I never read such bullshit . . ."

When I spoke with Becker on June 17, 1988, he voiced annoyance at Kelley for diddling him on a matter he was all too familiar with.

"I thought it was ludicrous for her to tell me about the legwork she'd done for the Exner story," Becker said.

"I've got a great piece of information for your book," Becker quotes Kelley. "I checked the archives on the Kennedy assassination but I didn't have it in time for my article on Judith Exner [for *People*]. I found that there'd been phone calls from Roselli's phone number to the White House . . ."

Kitty didn't know at this stage that "The Dark Side of Camelot" had made Jim Seymore and the other editorial brass at *People* so unhappy that she'd be asked to rewrite the piece twice.

But because of those delays, Kitty was able to offer her alleged information about the seventy calls from Roselli's phone to the White House. Becker didn't tell Kelley what he thought of her information.

"I never heard such crapshit," he told me. "Roselli was too smart to allow any record to show such a connection. Obviously he wasn't aware that Judy Campbell was calling the White House from his phone. He never looked at the long-distance calls charged on his bills. If he'd known the calls were to the White House, he'd have stopped them cold."

"Roselli," added Becker, "was too smart to ever allow any record to show such a connection with the President, if indeed there was one. Of course we know that in the old days Johnny played golf with JFK's old man, Joseph Kennedy, in Palm Springs [when Roselli was THE overlord of Las Vegas's underworld, and JFK's father was greasing the palms of labor racketeers to prevent strikes at his RKO film studio in Hollywood].

"Johnny was too smart to let his ego get in the way. He'd never go around saying, 'I know President Kennedy.' He might have used him, if he could. I'm not saying he did. I just don't know. But he'd never show himself so blatantly.

"And most certainly on that other utterly ridiculous story that envelopes were changing hands, as Judy Exner now claims,

Johnny would certainly not have trusted a lowly wench like that one to be his courier."

What advice did Becker offer Kitty about her fear of a Sinatra backlash?

"She was concerned that Frank would never give up seeking some kind of revenge on her. But I told her flat out: "'Kitty, he doesn't even give you a thought. What do you think of that? Moreover, [Barbara] wouldn't allow him to do anything to you. And the way I see it, the only thing he's probably annoyed about is what you did to his mother. I don't believe he himself will do anything to you . . .' "

"Then . . . is . . . someone else . . . likely . . . to?" Kitty stammered.

Conceivably the counsel Joe Shimon gave her still may have been fresh in her mind: that attacking an Italian's mother isn't the right way to go.

"Kitty, Italians don't forget," Shimon had told her. "They can take years to retaliate. You just have to be careful. There are trashy people in his crowd. You wrote a book about a trashy guy. These trashy people worship the ground he walks on and they have long memories."

21

On Sunday, October 12, 1986, Kitty Kelley's *His Way* premiered on the *New York Times* best-seller list in the No. 1 position.

At the break of dawn that Sunday, the newspaper was delivered to 3037 Dumbarton Avenue, N.W., in Georgetown. In mid-morning, the paper was taken in. Over breakfast, Michael Edgley stared at the bestseller list in the *Book Review*. His wife's fondest dream had come true.

But there was no joy in the Georgetown mansion, Mike was holding a lonely vigil while his wife was checking in at one hotel after another across the country as she toured for her book. We don't know what thoughts went through the former bartender's mind as he fixed his eyes on the list. He might have reflected on the years he spent as Kitty's garbage-picker and gofer—a career that, happily for him, had recently come to an end. Almost at an end as well was his 11-year marriage to the celebrated mud-slinging author.

He'd had his fill of being used for the most demeaning chores. He was further frustrated by Kitty's long absences during the years she excavated dirt on Frank Sinatra. What grated Mike more than anything was that his wife's travels that took her to far off places were almost always in the company of her ever-obedient tag-along Stanley Tretick.

Once, weeks before, Kitty had returned from her travels to face a husband whose fury was volcanic. He'd had all he could take of Frank Sinatra. For months he lived and breathed the crooner's name inside and outside the house. What finally made him flip was The Voice's voice on the stereo. Kitty was at her typewriter banging out closing copy on the book. She found it soothing—as well as inspirational—to hear Sinatra singing while she wrote. That was the last straw for Mike. Unable any longer to listen to the sound, Mike upped and wrecked the stereo!

That was the opening round. In the days and weeks that followed—up to the book's publication—Kitty and Mike fought incessantly. Kelley had never appreciated the puppy-dog faithfulness of her aggrieved spouse in the twenty odd years he'd been tied to her.

While he beat her regularly all through their tumultuous life as live-in lovers, and then as a married couple, Mike had always been a loyal paramour and husband—more so than Kitty. She had readily and frequently shared other mattresses in her clumsy efforts to further her career in journalism. On this particular Sunday morning, as Edgley sulked in his solitude at home, Kitty was flying high. Actually she'd been on a high for ten days—since October 2nd, when an interview she was giving was abruptly interrupted in her suite at the Charles Hotel in Cambridge, Mass., by a Bantam Books Vice President who burst into the living room, with the announcement:

"You're number one on the *New York Times* best-seller list next week!"

A shrill scream pierced the smoke-filled air. Kitty was elated. She ditched a half-smoked Parliament and with an unsteady hand lit another. The shakes had overtaken Kelley in her excitement.

"Oh, are you . . . telling me the truth?" she stammered.

The publishing executive convinced Kitty it was no mistake, that it was all real.

Kitty returned to her interview with the *Boston Globe* reporter.

"I don't fear for myself now," she bubbled. "Frank Sinatra's retaliation against writers is ugly. But it's more vocal than violent."

Bantam was going back to press to add significant numbers to the initial printing. Sales had been helped considerably by the two excerpts of *His Way* that were published in *People* magazine on September 15th and 22nd, so when the book was released to bookstores sales were brisk.

The book's highly-successful launch would keep Kitty Kelley on the road for more than six months, promoting a product that would make her famous and rich.

She relished her commercial success, but Kitty was wounded by the book's reviews. In general they were bad ones.

"I find this [the attack] on Frank Sinatra's dead mother, [calling her an abortionist] unforgivable and cheap," wrote Kay Gardella, TV critic of the *Daily News* in New York.

"True, in the course of history mothers of famous people figure in biographies, when one is trying to understand what makes a person tick. In this case, it's not an attempt so much to understand a famous person, as it is to hit below the belt."

The *New York Post*'s Op Ed Page columnist Dorothy Rabinowitz described *His Way* as "biography the way graffiti is art. What sort of biography can it be, after all, that will fail to offer a word—except in passing at the end—about the power of a talent that has spanned generations?"

Time's John Skow asked: "Assuming that this biography of one of President Reagan's 'Medal Of Freedom' winners is accurate, is it also fair? . . . What *His Way* acknowledges, but cannot really convey, is the gift that made Sinatra famous and kept him that way."

The *New York Times* listed *His Way* No. 1 on its Best-Seller list, but its 1,680-word review was anything but No. 1. Writing under the headline "Terrified And Fascinated By His Own Life," author Barbara Grizzuti Harrison condemned *His Way* in harsh terms:

"Miss Kelley is an evangelical writer, her vocations being to pen unauthorized biographies of people she has little affection and no empathy for, precisely those people who wish least to be written about and who have the power to exact silence from those who know and love—or fear—them best. Jacqueline Onassis and Elizabeth Taylor were Ms. Kelley's previous marks. She scribbles with what can only be called a sense of retributive get-all-the-damning-facts-and-print-'em mission. I have enormous respect for facts. Do facts make up a life? Of course not. They don't even make up a story of a life. Facts, unsupported and uncolored by nuance, wrenched out of context, uninformed by lively wit, intelligence (or love), constitute, at best, a story about a story—in this case, a story about the story of an icon.

"Unless one believes Frank Sinatra Jr., Mia Farrow (Frank Sinatra's third wife) and Elizabeth Taylor (one of his lovers)—all of whom have made public statements attributing to the author inaccuracy and cupidity—Ms. Kelley is a good reporter. A good reporter can tell a lot about Angola, inside trading on Wall Street, the new fall fashions; a good reporter, unless she is capable of an imaginative leap into someone else's consciousness, does not have access to the human heart. (One cannot apply to the Justice Department for access thereto.)

"Ms. Kelley is no leaper. Even if one were to suppose that facts are in and of themselves truth, could one then say that Ms. Kelley has command of the facts of Mr. Sinatra's life? No. Any one fact is dependent for its weight and significance on the facts that surround it. And for every one person Ms. Kelley interviewed—a host of scorned lovers, cast-aside friends and disgruntled former hangers-on—we may safely assume there are scores she did not . . ."

A surprising review was from the *Washington Post's* Jonathan Yardley, whose assessment of the latest Kelley book on November 17, 1986, would not command another delivery of dead, smelly fishheads in a Gucci box, as he'd received after his harsh putdown of Kitty's *Last Star*.

This time around, Yardley crowed: "Now we know why Francis Albert Sinatra was so desperately afraid of what Kitty Kelley might write about him that he filed suit three years ago in an attempt to prevent publication . . ."

Yardley hadn't read the court papers or he'd have known that Sinatra was only trying to stop Kitty Kelley from misrepresenting herself as his "authorized biographer." ". . . Kelley's portrait of Sinatra is so devastating that, with nearly a million copies of *His Way* in print and heaven knows how many more to come," Yardley continues, "one can only wonder if Sinatra will have the chutzpah ever to show his face in public again."

****

The reviews notwithstanding, an ebullient Kelley was on her nationwide tour. After Boston and other points east of the Mississippi, was her own hometown, where she addressed the Spokane Club. She explained to her father's fellow members how difficult Sinatra had made it for her.

What made this whistle stop on Kitty's tour different from other places she laid over to promote the book was that she was accompanied by Mike Edgley. It was to be one of the last times her husband would be at her side.

On returning to Georgetown, the couple had yet another of their domestic brouhahas and Mike was sent packing. The story went around that she bestowed a dowry of a million dollars on her husband—he hadn't worked at a salaried job for eight years. He immediately flew to a south seas island. There he could pursue his two favorite pastimes, scuba diving and spearfishing.

After eighteen months of this activity, Mike returned from exile and took up a curious residence in the Washington domicile of his estranged wife's Man Friday, Stanley Tretick.

His stay there lasted until the divorce became final. Late in 1989, Kitty and Mike ended their twenty-four-year relationship that included twelve years of marriage by agreeing to settle their differences quietly and without publicity.

One part of the deal was said to be an ironclad prohibition against Edgley writing a book about Kitty Kelley.

That agreement prompted Mike to give this answer when asked by *Washington Times* gossip columnist Charlotte Hays if he was writing such a book.

"Anything is possible," he replied, "but there are more inter-esting things I'd rather write about . . ."

So far as is known, the only writing Mike Edgley has done since the divorce was to scroll his name on the dotted line of a contract for the purchase of a handsome 10-room residence in Alexandria, just across the Potomac in Virginia. He closed the reported $500,000 transaction with real estate entrepreneur Peggy Thompson, who then went to live there with Mike after they fell in love and married.

****

Kitty planned her next book project: a hatchet job on former First Lady Nancy Reagan.

The proposal was taken by her literary agent, Lynn Nesbit to Bantam. They declined.

Bantam's editors—and even more so the publisher's lawyers—were unhappy with Kitty. For nearly four months after she turned in the Sinatra manuscript intense legal check-ing, or "vetting" was necessary. Kitty was challenged to support her charges against Sinatra with evidence.

The legal queries caused Kitty to lose her cool repeatedly. She vented her anger about the legal profession to friends and acquaintances.

"I hate the fucking lawyers . . . I hate their grimy guts . . . !"

Her dialogue with Bantam's legal battery reached such a heated state that Vice President Stuart Applebaum stepped in as a peace-maker.

"Why don't you let the legal eagles come down to George-town and talk matters out with you in the comfort of your own home?" Applebaum implored.

Kitty consented and the lawyers trekked to Georgetown, where the sessions often ran almost around the clock for the next several weeks. They prodded the author relentlessly to verify her sources.

Kitty couldn't verify much of the information in the book. After her experience with Lyle Stuart, she was smart enough not to repeat her confession, "I made it up."

In May of 1986—well beyond the book's original scheduled publication date—Dan Moldea, the prolific author of books on the Mafia, received a telephone call from an exasperated Kitty Kelley.

"Can you help me? she asked. These bastard lawyers demand all kinds of confirmation. Where can I get it . . . ?

"Sit tight, Kitty, I'll see what I can do . . ."

Kitty was put in touch with author Ovid Demaris, another organized crime expert who helped in rounding up original sources for many of the book's underworld anecdotes about the mobsters named as Sinatra's purported friends—which Kelley had lifted bodily from other works. She seems to have made little attempt to confirm these tales independently.

"She asked me to get her proof that the things she wrote about Sinatra's underworld friendships were true," Demaris said.

Even Demaris himself couldn't be certain about much of the "rough gangster stuff" that he read in Kitty's manuscript. He culled the script and found huge gaps requiring corroboration. Meanwhile, Moldea phoned and told Kitty he'd arranged a session for her with Scott Malone, an author and producer who was knowledgeable about Mafia activities. According To Moldea:

"She wanted especially to confirm the CIA-Mafia plot to assassinate Cuba's Fidel Castro. Malone helped her here. He saved the day for her on that aspect of her book."

One big question remains: If Kitty Kelley had *really* consulted the FBI files that she claims she obtained under the Freedom of Information Act, why couldn't she have exhibited photocopies from those files to the battery of Bantam lawyers?

****

At first, all Bantam Books had to contend with was the libel suit brought by Sinatra's former valet, George Jacobs. Then came a $2 million suit for damages filed in California's Superior Court in Los Angeles by Lor-Ann Land, a film secretary in Hollywood. Miss Land received less than a dozen lines of type in a single paragraph of Chapter 16. Yet she was offended by the words Kitty claims to have heard her say on July 15, 1983.

"Over the years prostitutes became a staple in Sinatra's life, and not just in Las Vegas. 'I remember when Frank and the Rat Pack were doing *4 for Texas* [in 1964] . . . and a whole gang of prostitutes—shipped up there to the boondocks . . . they were also going to act as girls sitting at a bar in the movie, and the man in charge, an older gentleman, very moral and proper, who had to handle arrangements was so upset,' said Lor-Ann Land, a secretary on the film. 'He had to pay them more than scale and he didn't know how to figure it all out. How to designate what they were *really* being paid for . . .' "

According to Miss Land, "I never said any of those things to that woman. She made up the whole thing!"

After the flak from these lawsuits threatened to ruffle the rooster's feathers at Bantam, Stuart Applebaum was heard to say, "We got off very lightly. For all the damaged goods Kitty tried to pass by us . . . we were lucky. Our lawyers very deftly carried us through the landmines the author had strewn so irresponsibly. They saved us from an apocalyptic fate . . ." And that was why, like Simon & Schuster and Lyle Stuart before them, the people at Bantam weren't interested in Kelley's next book. But greed is a major part of what makes Paramount's Simon & Schuster run, so they returned to the playing field and negotiated Kitty's next contract.

22

The main thrust of Kitty Kelley's earliest moves in marshall-
ing scandal about Nancy Reagan was to nail down—with a
Nancy Davis twist—the same story she had repeatedly told
around the offices of *Today Is Sunday* magazine. It was a tale
she was never able to write in *Jackie Oh!* regarding Jacqueline
Onassis: that one of her children walked in on Jackie while she
was performing oral sex on a lover . . .

In Nancy Davis/Reagan's case, unlike Jackie O., Kitty found a
source to appropriate: *The Peter Lawford Story: Life With the
Kennedys, Monroe and the Rat Pack.*

In that book, Lawford's widow Patricia recorded anecdotes
she said Peter told her. Nancy Davis appears first on Page 23,
after a detailed account of Peter Lawford's sexual experiences
with a nanny who raised him in England. Those encounters,
says Patricia, prompted Peter to focus his attention in later years
on oral sex and multiple partners in the bedroom.

"When he reached Hollywood," Patricia writes, "his name
would be linked with the wilder actresses of the 1940s—Lana
Turner, Judy Garland, Nancy Davis, and numerous others."

Thirty pages later, it becomes apparent just how "wild" Nancy Davis purportedly was. According to Patricia Lawford, her
husband recounted incidents that occurred on trips he and

Robert Walker, another Hollywood star, had taken with the young starlet from Hollywood to Phoenix, Arizona, where her mother and father resided.

"Nancy would visit her parents, Dr. and Mrs. Loyal Davis, while Peter and Walker picked up girls at Arizona State University in Tempe, a Phoenix suburb. He claimed that she entertained them orally on those trips, apparently playing with whichever man was not driving at the moment.

"I have no idea if Peter was telling the truth, though I have to assume that he was because Peter was not one to gossip. When it came to both the good and bad qualities of people he had known over the years, he was always brutally frank and honest. Both Peter and Bob Walker are dead now [Walker died in 1951, Lawford in 1984], but in researching the book, the business with Walker was repeatedly mentioned by old time Hollywood friends of both men.

"Checking the fan magazines and publicity releases, Nancy Davis was known to have dated many men. However, by the time she was engaged to Ronald, the studios had even restored her virginity. An effort was made to give the impression that she had been working so hard on her career that she had had no time for men until Ronald Reagan came along. Care was also taken to avoid mentioning his divorce from Jane Wyman.

"The deeply-loving relationship between Ronald Reagan and Nancy Davis Reagan has never been questioned. But the Hollywood version of their lives before they fell in love differed greatly from the truth. Nancy Davis was rather wild, the delight of a number of men and the regular lover of the alcoholic actor Robert Walker, who died tragically in his early thirties. 'I remember when three or four of us walked into Bob Walker's house and saw a naked Nancy Davis standing there, looking shocked at having been caught like that. She grabbed a towel and ran into the bathroom,' said a longtime friend of Peter's, recalling an incident that remained in his mind after Nancy became the First Lady. She was single at the time and there was nothing wrong with the affair except for the embarrassment at its memory after her life changed radically. He explained that his son became friends with Ron Reagan Jr., and he always had the feeling that Nancy was afraid he would reveal the incident."

Patricia Lawford recalls her husband watching newscasts on TV at home after Reagan was elected President:

"He went over to the set, laughing and calling Mrs. Reagan a vulgar name. I was shocked and wanted to know what was bothering him. He laughed again and said that when she was single, Nancy Davis was known for giving the best head in Hollywood."

Kelley encountered uncommon resistance chasing scandal about the First Lady despite the fact that Mrs. Reagan, like the President himself, was in the last year of her reign—a lame duck.

"Just this morning," Kitty told writer Dermot Purgavie after she launched her latest literary venture, "I was talking to a guy who happened to know something about Nancy Reagan, and he referred me to somebody else. He said, 'Now you be sure to call him. It's going to wreck his whole week.' "

Hearing such talk at a lunch given by Washington hostess Jane Dawson for Betty Wright, wife of the then-embattled Speaker of the House Jim Wright (D-Texas), sent Sheila Anthony the wife of Rep. Beryl Anthony Jr. (D-Ark.), running from Dawson's elegant eighteen-room Connecticut Avenue town house in disgust in early April, 1988. It was obvious at the luncheon that Kitty had clout despite the aversion of many of Nancy's friends to speak out. For the mistress of ceremonies, who fashions herself as a modern-day Perle Mesta, Washington's legendary "Hostess With The Mostest," announced—even before the first hors d'oeuvre was dished out—that in order to eat, everyone had to fork over a juicy Nancy Reagan tidbit. Betty Wright's sister, Mary Connell, was one of the first to contribute an anecdote and that recital, later described as "tawdry", prompted Sheila Anthony's flight.

Jill Gore, a relative of one-time Presidential hopeful Senator Albert Gore (D-Tenn.), was more politic. She claimed she knew plenty about Nancy—but refused to tell any stories.

At the outset, Kitty sent a letter to the First Lady, handing her the same dish of sweet-talk she tried to feed Liz Taylor. She reminded Mrs. Reagan that she had met her at a White House photo session.

The request was turned down flatly by Nancy's Press Secretary, Elaine Crispin, who made it known publicly the First Lady would not cooperate with Kelley.

"We got dozens of requests every year from people trying to write books," Crispin said. "We have no time to accommodate them. Moreover, Mrs. Reagan intends to tell her own story. She'll write her autobiography, taken from her journals once she leaves the White House."

In one of the earliest interviews about the kind of book she would do on Nancy Reagan, Kitty told *USA Today* columnist Jeannie Williams that she was aiming to make the biography another "full-scale" work. Then she cut in with this line:

"Yes, I intend to ask Nancy Reagan to speak with me. I asked her five times about Frank Sinatra. I asked the President, too. He wrote me a letter saying he was busy with a summit. But I never heard from her. I guess she's busier than the President."

Kitty was correct on all counts. Yes, she had heard from the President—but not directly. One of Reagan's army of letter writers responded and told her no, so far as an interview on Sinatra went.

****

Kitty Kelley had found it easy to persuade some people to talk about Sinatra, even about Taylor and Onassis on account of old grudges. But as Kitty made her way around those who had dealings with Nancy, she found fewer willing to share secrets. It mattered to most not a snippet that the press had been critical of the First Lady for her astrological leanings, her domineering hold over the President, and for other reasons that portrayed her as a hen-pecker of the highest order.

The Reagans had many friends. Kelley stumbled over more than a few potholes in her travels to closets that might hold family skeletons. After a sequence of consecutive turndowns for interviews, Kitty reached such a state of exasperation that she announced to all who would listen, "Goddamn these people. I'm the biggest- selling author in America! They must talk with me!"

No sooner had Kitty signed her lush contract with S&S than along came former White House aide Donald Regan's tell-all book, *For The Record,* which revealed to the world, among other secrets, that Nancy Reagan was so deep into astrology that she'd hardly get out of bed unless the astrological signs were auspicious. Kerplunk went one of Kelley's selling points on the biography that brought one of the largest advances for a single book in the history of publishing.

Then a reader of *Parade* magazine, H.T. of Washington, D.C., wrote this question that appeared in Walter Scott's "Personality Parade" in the issue of July 24, 1988: "If Joan Quigley, the San Francisco socialite who provided Nancy Reagan with astrological forecasts, would write a kiss-and-tell book on her true relationship with the First Lady, what effect do you think it would have on the book Kitty Kelley plans to write on Nancy?" The answer ploughed more buckshot into the brash biographer: "It probably would detract from it and might even cause Kelley to postpone writing her book, although she says it won't. Moreover, Quigley's revelations in print surely would compel Mrs. Reagan to write about them in her autobiography, reportedly scheduled for publication by Random House in the fall of 1989."

Of no help either to Kitty was *On the Outside Looking In,* number one son Michael Reagan's autobiography. Afterward he expressed hope to *Washington Post* writer Donnie Radcliffe that three of his wishes would come true while his father was still President: "I'd like to go to a State Dinner, I'd like my kids to turn on the Christmas tree, I'd like to fly in Air Force One. But I'm not mad about it anymore." On April 1, 1988, father Ronald satisfied one of his son's desires when he took Michael home to California after a visit to the White House—aboard the vaunted plane.

Not nearly as reverent as Michael's book was the one written a wee bit earlier by his half-sister Patricia Ann Reagan, who calls herself Patti Davis. (She adopted her mother's maiden name

277

because she didn't want to ride on her father's coattails). She wrote a candidly autobiographical novel, *Home Front*, the chronicles of a rebellious teenage girl whose unfeeling father is President and whose ice-cold mother is a fashion plate.

Another annoyance for Kitty was the book by Maureen Reagan who, unlike adopted brother Michael, emerged from first wife Jane Wyman's womb. Here was yet another aspect of life in the Reagan household, long before Ron was into politics and still a struggling actor, often eclipsed by his wife's superior acting before the cameras. The book, *First Father, First Daughter*, is a compendium of the bad memories of a neglected child.

The next tell-all author who beat Kitty to print with stories about Nancy Reagan and her husband was Larry Speakes. The former White House Press Secretary turned out gossipy memoirs entitled *Speaking Out*.

Finally came Nancy Reagan's autobiography. Unlike Kitty Kelley's biography, the former First Lady's work is totally based on first hand information. She kept a diary of daily activities— her husband's and her own—from day one. Day one begins with her first encounter with Ron, their romance, their marriage, their years when he was Governor and she the First Lady of California—but is most heavily focused on the eight most important years she experienced with the President: life in the White House.

The book, *My Turn*, came out in late 1989 and became a short-lived best-seller. Nancy Reagan went on the TV-radio talk show circuit. She even trekked to Manhattan's antiquated Municipal Building and did a stint on New York City's WNYC radio station. Most of what she talked about was that:

* She never trusted Donald Regan and urged her husband to dump him long before the President did.

* Not until after the assassination attempt on her husband by John Hinckley did Nancy turn to astrology. And then only in the belief that if it didn't help it couldn't hurt.

* The guilty party in the disappearance from his closet of many of Ronald's clothes was she. She confessed to getting rid of

them whenever she found an item of wearing apparel that she felt didn't look good on the President.

****

"Kitty is in a deep sweat," Lucianne Goldberg told me. "It's not just [the other] books. It's a lot more. She's been hit with everything but the kitchen sink . . ."

First, former President Ronald Reagan himself had signed on to write two books. One was an annotated collection of his speeches, the other his memoirs. He was to craft both books himself, without the aid of a ghostwriter, as wife Nancy had for herself in the $2 million deal she struck with Random House. Reagan's contract was with Simon & Schuster—Kitty's own publisher—for a reported $5 million!

Second, almost at the very moment S&S announced that the deal with the President had been made, Kitty Kelley's literary agent, Lynn Nesbit, left International Creative Management to become a partner with Morton Janklow, a powerful authors' representative. That meant the new partnership would do the bidding for the world's heaviest-hitting wordsmiths. Janklow did his pitching for the likes of Barbara Taylor Bradford, Jackie Collins, Judith Krantz and Sidney Sheldon. In Nesbit's stable were such best-selling writers as Nora Ephron, Toni Morrison and Tom Wolfe.

But Kitty Kelley couldn't move with Nesbit because she had an exclusive contract with ICM.

ICM assigned Sam Cohn to handle Kitty—and she hated that. Cohn was a hard-nosed, highly respected agent—but his specialty wasn't authors. His clients were mostly actors. He let people know he didn't care for Kitty personally.

"How am I going to make out with my Nancy Reagan book when Ronald Reagan has the same editor!" Kitty Kelley protested after S&S announced that it had signed the President to do two books. "How can Michael Korda edit Reagan's manuscripts, and at the same time handle my biography of his wife . . . ?"

Lynn Nesbit's departure from ICM upset Kitty because, as

one ICM staffer put it, "she lost a shoulder she could cry on," but it created an alliance that was an even harder blow to take. For Morton Janklow was Ronald Reagan's literary agent—and by extension, so was Lynn Nesbit!

***

In the aftermath of these developments, the word around publishing circles was that Michael Korda faced a difficult task. On the other hand, a director of S&S remarked, "When you work in a whorehouse, you service each customer in turn."

The S&S executive who signed Kitty Kelley to the $3.5 million contract and sanctioned a Mercedes as a bonus was Joni Evans, the president of the trade books division. Joni left S&S to join Random House.

"I asked Kitty to come along with me to Random House," Evans admitted. "But she was reluctant because Random had signed Nancy Reagan to do her official memoirs. Kitty couldn't envision herself being edited by the same blue pencil as the one going over Nancy Reagan's manuscript."

So Kelley stayed with S&S and had this to say to *Los Angeles Times* staff writer Josh Getlin:

"Publishing sure makes for strange bedfellows. Strange and interesting bedfellows . . ."

Getlin journeyed to Manhattan, took an elevator to the 14th floor of 1230 Avenue of the Americas, and faced Michael Korda, the English-born nephew of famed film director Sir Alexander Korda and actress Merle Oberon. Then the reporter repeated that Kelley had complained about sharing the same editor as Ronald Reagan.

Korda "fiddles with his pink powder tie, swivels in a desk chair and stares out the granite canyons of midtown Manhattan," Getlin wrote. In Getlin's account, Korda smiled and gestured expansively with his hands, then said:

"I wouldn't have used her exact words perhaps, but yes, I guess that's true about publishing. That's certainly the situation I'm looking at here."

Getlin raises the central question: "How is Korda going to edit Kelley's decidedly unauthorized biography of Nancy Reagan while also editing the forthcoming memoirs of Ronald Reagan? How will he keep the peace?"

"Obviously," Korda later told the *Los Angeles Times*, "the situation requires on my part a certain tact and decent behavior. Because clearly, whatever Kitty would tell me about what she's doing I would have to be absolutely sure not to pass it on to the Reagans. And vice versa, whatever the Reagans might tell me I'd be sure not to pass on to Kitty Kelley.

"No publisher would be stupid enough to become the President's publisher for his memoirs and then go out and buy Kitty Kelley's book," Korda stated. "That would seem like gouging an esteemed public figure in the eye unnecessarily. But, on the other hand, if you already own Kitty Kelley and you go out and buy Ronald Reagan, then you can't be expected to not publish Kitty Kelley. I think everybody understands that."

****

Kitty Kelley phoned Michael Korda in the late fall of 1988 to assure him she was going to produce a "blockbuster" on Nancy Reagan despite the publication of so much of what she thought would be her "exclusive material."

Speaking in a tone described as "more conspiratorial than convincing," Kelley was quoted by an S&S source:

"I'm going to reveal that Nancy Davis is illegitimate . . ."

A long silence at the editor's end of the line.

"Are you with me, Michael . . . Michael, say something . . ."

"In what sense?" Korda is said to have finally asked, nonplussed.

"We all know that Dr. and Mrs. Davis have acknowledged, just as Nancy has, that she was adopted by them. But I am going to reveal that Mrs. Davis actually gave birth to Nancy to a down-and-out first husband who was a shiftless stumblebum—and, out of compassion and love for his wife, Dr. Davis channeled the infant into the family through the adoption route."

Did Michael Korda do cartwheels over this news? Did he scream from the tops of his lungs to be heard by Chairman Dick Snyder that Kitty Kelley had made the discovery of the century about Nancy Davis's origins? Just exactly what did he do?

According to the most-informed word that filtered out of the publishing company's executive offices, Korda took a deep breath and let out a long sigh that was described as sounding something like . . .

"Ohhhh . . . uh uh . . ."

23

"Two entries on Nancy Reagan's birth certificate are accurate—her sex and her color. Almost every other item has been invented. In truth, the certificate itself gave birth to two generations of lies . . ."

Thus opens Kitty Kelley's book set in type below a bootlegged birth certificate from New York City's Department of Health. Readers of *Nancy Reagan: The Unauthorized Biography* are informed that the original facts about the infant Anne Frances Robbins, later Nancy Davis, and today Nancy Reagan, were carefully rewritten:

"She revised her date of birth, concealed her birthplace, and cast aside her father.

"In her memoirs, she asserted she forgot the name of the hospital where she was born and added that 'it burned down years ago.' In fact, not only did Sloane Hospital in New York City not burn down, but according to its official history it did not have a fire."

Only four paragraphs into the book and Kitty Kelley has yet to provide a single accurate fact—other than to attest to the accuracy of Mrs. Reagan's sex and color. Nonetheless she proclaims that "almost every other item is invented." Not so.

The parents' names listed in the document are, in fact, correct. So is their address, given as 417 Amity Street, Flushing, L.I. Flushing is a section of Queens, one of New York's five boroughs. It is where Shea Stadium towers over the flat landscape of Flushing Meadows and where the New York Mets play their baseball games. Flushing is also where both the 1939-40 and 1964-65 World's Fairs were held. It's where Kitty Kelley did her ushering at General Electric's Progressland Exhibit.

Flushing is where the New York Police Department investigated the loss of several hundred dollars from the General Electric Progressland Exhibit locker rooms, where Kitty Kelley and other usherettes and employees changed clothes. Kitty was among a number of GE workers questioned about the disappearance of the money, but the detectives of the 110th Precinct in Elmhurst failed to apprehend the culprit.

Kitty flatly states that, contrary to what Nancy Reagan claimed, Sloane Hospital did not burn down and "according to its official history it did not have a fire."

Wrong. On January 5, 1928, the hospital, situated since its opening in 1886 on Manhattan's 59th Street and Amsterdam Avenue, closed its doors to further admissions and began discharging its 170 remaining patients as they completed their convalescences.

When the last of the patients were sent home, Sloane Hospital moved uptown, to 622 West 168th Street. There it changed its name to Sloane Hospital for Women and became affiliated with Columbia Presbyterian Medical Center. This is the medical facility affiliated with Columbia University.

The 32-year-old building left behind was then rehabilitated for conversion to a building for commercial occupancy.

Kelley's assault on Nancy Reagan began with the charge that Nancy's mother, Edith Luckett Robbins, deducted four years from her own age on the birth certificate, and made an adjustment on her husband's age as well.

"Her husband was twenty-seven, but she listed him as twenty-eight."

"Her father was a 'Princeton graduate from a well-to-do fami-

284

ly,' she asserted in her memoirs,' " Kelley writes. "In fact, he did not attend Princeton—or any other college. His family, from Pittsfield, Massachusetts, was not well-to-do. But even after disowning him, Nancy clung to those pretensions."

Here's how Mrs. Reagan "clung to those pretensions" in her own autobiography, *My Turn*, published by Random House in 1989:

"In 1917 she [Nancy's mother] married a man named Kenneth Robbins, a Princeton graduate from a well-to-do family *that had lost its money* [the emphasis is mine]. He wasn't very ambitious, and he worked as a car salesman in New Jersey."

To what pretense was the former First Lady clinging when she flatly stated that the family "had lost its money?" Kitty, carefully neglected to report that Nancy had admitted that her father's family had fallen on hard times. That was after the woolen mill owned by her grandfather in Pittsfield, Massachusetts, closed down.

True, the subject of Kelley's book didn't tell us in her first autobiography, *Nancy*, published in 1980 by William Morrow and Company, that her father was a Princeton graduate. This embellishment in the second of her memoirs suggests pretentiousness on the part of the former First Lady. But that trait is not alien to Kitty Kelley, whose own resumes have been chock full of false information.

Kitty continues: "When the brown-haired, brown-eyed Anne Frances was born, her parents were living *in a poor section of Flushing, Queens* [my emphasis], an outer borough of New York City. They were renting *one floor of a two-story frame house on Amity Street near the railroad tracks* [my emphasis again]."

No. 417 Amity Street is not "near the railroad tracks." It lies mid-block on a thoroughfare whose name was changed in 1921, even while the infant Anne Frances Robbins resided there with her parents. The new name was and still is Roosevelt Avenue, after President Theodore Roosevelt.

The house, according to the deed lodged in the Queens Branch of the City Registrar's Office, was built in 1901. The present owner, Luis Caso, an optician, bought the residence in

1981 when it was in a state of disrepair. Since he acquired the property, Caso has rehabilitated the three-story clapboard Victorian-designed dwelling and today it stands as one of this neighborhood's most attractive buildings. Its green clapboard aluminum siding, neat two-level front porches, and cinder-block barbecue pit in the back lend a rustic charm that totally eluded Kelley—who doubtless failed to visit the neighborhood while doing her "thorough research" on Nancy Reagan.

"The house is modest," said Franco Veraldi, a neighborhood denizen. "She [Kelley], lamentably, is not."

Historian Vincent Seyfried, who has written extensively about the borough, said that Kitty's description of the area as "a poor section of Queens" is a total distortion.

"It's malice to say that," said Seyfried, the vice president of the Queens Historical Society. "It was a good enough neighborhood [in 1921-22, when Nancy began her life there] that the first apartment house in Flushing was built nearby. It was a perfectly nice residential street like most of the best in Flushing at the time."

Had Kitty been accurate when writing about Nancy Reagan's birthplace, she would have reported that in the Twenties, the neighborhood was one of the choicest in Queens—with a population which included many actors and actresses from the Broadway stage and the numerous silent movie studios that dotted the borough's landscape, before Hollywood became the world's movie capital in the latter years of that decade.

Kelley takes issue with the entry in the box on Nancy's birth certificate which called for "mother's occupation."

"She is listed as a housewife," says Kitty. "But she was an actress, a declassé [the one and only time she uses the word] profession in those days."

Is it likely that Edith Luckett was ashamed to call herself an actress—or was she planning, as Nancy Reagan told us in both memoirs, to be a housewife and raise her daughter for the next two years before returning to the stage? Is it plausible that a Broadway actress would feel abashed about her line of work when "she played with the greats of her day," as Mrs. Reagan assured us in her memoirs? The array of talent Nancy's mother performed with included David Belasco, George M. Cohan, Alla Nazimova, Spencer Tracy, Walter Huston and Louis Calhern.

Twelve paragraphs spread over a mere three pages make up the first of this 24-chapter, 604-page book. But in that brief space, Kitty Kelley sets the tone for the tome.

To obtain a birth certificate from the Bureau of Vital Records in the New York City Department of Health, the law states that the applicant must either be the person for whose birth the certificate was issued or be a blood relative. And at least three pieces of valid identification must be presented before a photostatted copy of the document can be issued.

Anyone who fraudulently presents credentials to obtain a birth certificate is committing a crime and is liable to prosecution by the law. The penalty upon conviction of this charge, "offering a false instrument for filing," is a Class E Felony under New York State law.

When several books about Mrs. Reagan were published, one after another, they eroded Kelley's hottest "disclosures." Now, she could no longer be the first to tell the world Nancy was into astrology and advised her husband according to the position of the planets andstars. The infighting and the feuds between the President's wife and members of Reagan's administration were no longer secret either.

What was left for Kitty? Very little. But she could "make things up," something she admitted doing in the past.

24

He is a widely-known medical doctor and owner of a string of clinics in the Washington, D.C. area. He happens to be Jewish and had a long-running affair with Kitty—until one morning (the only time he had ever stayed with his concupiscent bedmate overnight) when he awakened and stared at her sleeping, makeup-free face. "I was startled," he told Susan Cooke, the ex-wife of Washington Redskins owner John Kent Cooke. "She looked very unappealing to me. I had to get out of there before she awakened. I dressed as fast as I could and flew into the wind. I never went back. Kitty kept calling me repeatedly. She wanted to continue the relationship. There was no way I was going to do that. She left a pair of earrings on my night table one time when I was having it with her at my place. 'Please, please, darling,' she kept saying, 'can't I just drop over to get my earrings?'

" 'No way' I told her. 'No way!'

"I took the earrings and mailed them to her. That's the last I've seen of Kitty Kelley."

Meanwhile Kitty's researchers Melissa D. Smalling and Pamela Warrick were at work.

Smalling represented herself as a reporter for *Washingtonian* magazine to Patti Davis, pretending to do an article interview about ex-First Daughter's 1989 novel *Deadfall*.

Even with her researchers, Kitty still doesn't seem to be able to get a handle on correct dates.

"Two months after the Reagans were married," she wrote, "nature nudged them into announcing the exceedingly obvious. The heir was apparent . . . Patricia Ann Reagan was born [five months later on] October 21, 1952."

Kitty gave Patti the wrong birth date. (She was born on October 22).

Nancy Davis and Ronald Reagan were married in the Little Brown Church in California's San Fernando Valley on March 4, 1952. That was after they'd announced their engagement on February 21, 1952, and Hollywood gossipist Louella Parsons correctly trumpeted that the wedding would be early the following month.

So how does Miss Kelley doctor the facts? She pulls a hocus-pocus with the time frame of Nancy's pregnancy by suggesting she gave birth seven months after she married Ron, and that she may have been carrying the baby for as much as two months before the wedding.

Kitty's attempt to manipulate the calendar is a practice she employs. Here are the facts:

* Nancy and Ronnie were married March 4, 1952.

* Daughter Patti, the first of their two children, was born October 22, 1952.

* The number of calendar days between those dates is exactly 230, or 33 weeks. A normal pregnancy should endure for nine months or 36 weeks. This contradicts Kitty's claim that Nancy was pregnant when she wed.

If Nancy Davis indeed had carried for a full term, the pregnancy would have begun on or about February 12, 1952—nine days prior to Louella Parsons' story, which broke the day before—(actually eight days prior to the day Nancy's pregnancy began) the start of a nine-month (36-week) gestation period which ended on October 22nd, the day she gave birth to Patti.

Nancy would not have known she was going to have a baby until she missed her menstrual cycle. The question is: How long after she missed her period did Nancy go to a gynecologist and decrease the world's rabbit population by one? And how soon after the doctor told her she was expecting did she jump on Ronnie and break the news to him—and, as Kitty Kelley claims, demand he marry her?

* In her autobiography, Mrs. Reagan writes that "Patti was born—go ahead and count—a bit precipitously but very joyfully, on October 22, 1952." How precipitous was the birth? Let's return to the earliest time Nancy Davis could have become pregnant—nine full months prior to the delivery, February 12th. However, the most significant question is how soon after conception had Nancy learned she was pregnant?

The bottom line: If Nancy conceived on February 12th, in all likelihood she would not have become aware of her pregnancy before the 20th of the month when Metro-Goldwyn-Mayer's publicity department put out the announcement Nancy Davis and Ronald Reagan were to marry. It's inconceivable that in those brief eight days between conception and time out for an examination by a gynecologist and the wait for test results to confirm the pregnancy, that Nancy could have known she was carrying a child when MGM trumpeted Nancy's and Ron's wedding plans.

Kelley twists and insinuates—but she doesn't have the skills to structure her fiction so it sounds believable. In turning Mrs. Reagan into the world's most unpliable bitch, Kelley commanded the ultimate salute from the April 22, 1991 edition of *Newsweek* magazine, which hit the stands a week after the Nancy Reagan book was published:

"Kelley has repeatedly described her critique of Nancy Reagan as 'balanced.' Obviously, that's a crock. For those who missed the massive publicity grind pumping up Kelley's *Nancy Reagan*, 'Mommy' (as the former President calls her) is depicted as cruel, cheap, temperamental, manipulative, vindictive, pushy, phony, insecure, callous, grasping and cold. Other than that, as Norman Schwarzkopf might say, she looks great. By the time all the trash has been collected, Kelley accomplishes the impossible.

She takes a woman who may indeed possess many of those character flaws and makes readers feel sorry for the way the evidence has been marshaled to abuse her."

When Nancy called her folks with the news that she was getting married, Kitty seems to have been listening on their phone lines. How else to quote this conversation?

" 'Of course,' said Edith. 'If [Ronald] is a nice guy and you like him, then I'm sure he's all right.'

" 'He is, you'll love him.'

" 'Find out what you want for a wedding present. It can't be extravagant, but I want you to have what you want,' said Edith.

"Shortly thereafter, Nancy called back. 'I'll tell you what we want,' she said. 'We want a camera that can take moving pictures and a screen that we can show them on, and that's all we want.'

" 'Sold,' said Edith, who soon ordered 350 engraved wedding announcements to send to all her friends."

Are we to believe the future Nancy Reagan, a Hollywood contract actress who virtually grew up in the theater, would ask for "a camera that can take moving pictures and a screen that we can show them on, and that's all we want?"

Wasn't she more likely to say, "Mother, can you give us a movie camera and a screen . . ."

Questions about accuracy also arise when Kelley discusses Michael Reagan. There are two versions of the way Michael was informed that he was adopted. One is Kitty's rendition:

" 'When Nancy got ahold of my bad report card, she verbally ripped into me, concluding with, "You're not living up to the Reagan name or image, and unless you start shaping up, it would be best for you to change your name and leave the house," she said.' "

[So far, very accurate. Taken right out of Michael's book, *On the Outside Looking In*. But Kelley rarely attributes to the books and articles she copies from.]

" 'Fine,' I said, 'why don't you just tell me the name I was born with so at least when I walk out the door I'll know what name to use.'

" 'Okay, Mr. Reagan, I'll do just that.' "

Still quite correct. That's the way Michael had it in the next phase of the story he told in his own book. Now Kitty conveniently goes into a third-person narrative to avoid direct quotes and to twist and reshape the truth:

"A week later, Nancy *confronted* [the emphasis is this author's to point out the confrontational verb used to skewer Mrs. Reagan] her stepson with the information that his given name was John L. Flaugher and that he was born *out of wedlock* [again my emphasis], his father an army sergeant who went overseas and never returned."

Here's how Michael Reagan treated that traumatic teenaged experience in his book:

"At that time Dad and Mom still used the same business manager. To this day I don't know how Nancy managed to get into my mother's file because, as far as I know, it was sealed.

"The following week when I came home from school, Nancy told me, 'I have the information you requested.' I thought she was joking. She proceeded to tell me my given name was John L. Flaugher, and she spelled out my surname. She said that I had been born at Queen of Angels Hospital. My father had been a sergeant in the Army who, while on leave, had had an affair with my mother. Then he went overseas, leaving her pregnant. He never returned. 'You are the offspring of that relationship,' Nancy said in a cold voice.

" 'Were my parents married?' I asked in a small voice.

" 'No,' she said.

"The other shoe had dropped.

"I told Nancy I wanted to talk to Dad when he came home.

" 'So do I,' she said."

To illustrate the way Kelley skimmed from Michael Reagan's autobiography and altered the text by omission, we next go to Nancy's own memories:

"Once, when Ronnie was away on a speaking trip, Mike asked if I could find out the name of his birth mother," Mrs. Reagan writes. "He was sixteen at the time, and I thought his request was a fair one which deserved an answer. In those days, Ronnie and I had the same business manager as Jane Wyman, so I called and asked him to find out.

"When I heard from him, I told Mike that the name of his biological mother was Irene Flaugher, and that he had been named John L. Flaugher at birth. His father had been a military man who went overseas, leaving his mother pregnant—and unmarried.

"I was told that Jane was not pleased that I had answered Michael's question. But he was obviously troubled by having been adopted, and I thought he had the right to know the truth about his own background . . ."

Mrs. Reagan then says she hoped the information would "give him some peace of mind." But it didn't. Michael was adversely affected when told his "biological parents hadn't been married" and "confirmed his worst fear—that he was illegitimate."

But in the end, all turned out well. Michael accepted the truth of his birth out of wedlock—but no way could you get that impression from Kitty Kelley's book.

Here is another clear example of the inaccuracy of Kitty Kelley's reporting, this time on Frank Sinatra.

Read what Kitty wrote about his gaming:

"During the graveyard shift [at Caesars Palace in Las Vegas] on September 6, 1970, an Internal Revenue Service secret agent working in the cashier's cage watched as one of Sinatra's entourage approached the window with a pile of black chips and walked away with $7,500 in cash. The agent had been watching Sinatra carefully for weeks because the singer was cashing in chips that had not been deducted from his salary and were not paid for by his winnings. To make matters worse, he was bragging that when he performed at Caesar's [sic] and then sat down to gamble, he attracted so much big money that the casino profited enough so that his markers didn't need to be repaid.

"Sinatra kept cashing in his chips throughout the night until the IRS agent finally summoned the manager Sanford Waterman who confronted Frank and demanded $10,000 in cash.

"That's when the trouble started, and Frank called Waterman

a kike and Sandy called him a son-of-a-bitch guinea," said the IRS undercover agent. "They went back and forth like that in front of a big crowd of people, including three security guards, until Sandy whipped out his pistol, and popped it between Sinatra's eyeballs. . . . Sinatra laughed and called him a crazy Hebe. He said he'd never work at Caesar's again and walked out."

As it happens, Kelley's report concerns people she didn't know and a subject on which she is totally ignorant. Here are ten examples of inaccuracy and contrast this with a first-hand report of what actually happened:

1. In those days identity wasn't required and a cashier wouldn't know that someone was a member of Sinatra's entourage. The baccarat pit at Caesar's Palace isn't visible from the cashier cage.

2. Sinatra never played with black ($100) chips. He played only with white ($500) chips. Nor was he "cashing in his chips throughout the night." When he had chips to cash, usually his daughter Tina, his pal Jilly Rizzo, or one of his gofers went to the cage for him. Sinatra *never* stood in line to cash chips.

3. No notice would be taken of $7,500. Nor would most players walk up to a cage with 75 chips—a number large enough to be clumsy. Dealers are trained to exchange large quantities of chips for chips of greater value. Thus someone with 75 black chips would exchange them for seven yellows ($1,000 chips) and a $500 white.

4. The statement that "the singer was cashing in chips that had not been deducted from his salary and were not paid for by his winnings" is total nonsense. What would an employee in the cashier cage know about Sinatra's salary? Why would chips be deducted from it? Saying the chips "were not paid for by his winnings" is meaningless gobbledegook. If he had more chips than he'd signed markers for, they *were* his winnings.

5. The incident took place at around 10 p.m. The "graveyard shift" starts at midnight. Kelley has not only lost the thread of the story but even her total sense of time!

6. Top performers who "shill" play to attract crowds and the

understanding is that their action is make-believe. Sinatra would sometimes do this but certainly the most important performer in the history of Las Vegas didn't have to "brag" about a custom that had existed and that he had done for decades.

7. Sinatra, as the following account will show, owed several hundred thousand dollars. Why would Sanford Waterman "demand $10,000"? (Sinatra was betting $8,000 on each hand.)

8. Waterman is dead but his widow and several eyewitnesses confirm that neither man used any real racial epithets during the exchange. Kitty, who has an obsession about Sinatra, put the anti-Jewish words into his mouth in yet another attempt to make him look bad.

9. Waterman didn't "whip out his pistol." He went to his room to get it.

10. Sinatra didn't "walk out" as you will read in the eyewitness account.

The following is taken verbatim from Lyle Stuart's *Casino Gambling For the Winner*—the largest selling hardcover book on casino gambling ever published. Incidentally, Sinatra didn't like this account but admitted that it's the way it happened—as do all parties involved.

"Frank Sinatra . . . was no hero to baccarat dealers. He was noisy and rude. He made demands that he knew couldn't be met. He insulted casino employees.

"He had an $8,000-a-hand limit but kept insisting that he wanted $16,000. He would often hold up the game, hand after hand, insisting on the $16,000. Instructions were very firm. Sinatra was not to be dealt cards unless he committed himself.

" 'Mr. Sinatra, are you shilling or going for the money?'

"He balked at answering. Too often he had played and then gotten up and said he was 'only fooling' or 'just being a shill for you'—and refused to make good his losses.

"No commitment, no cards.

"Over the course of a few weeks, Sinatra and Beverly Hills real estate broker Danny Schwartz had won nearly a million dollars from Caesars Palace. They'd collected every penny.

"Now, Sinatra, doing a solo, was losing it back rapidly. But instead of cash he was peppering the cage with markers.

"On the night of drama, instructions were to cut off his credit when he owed $400,000. He still had a handful of white ($500) chips with him but kept insisting on another $25,000.

"The croupier called the casino manager, Sandy Waterman. Sandy, usually cool and wise, should have sent security men to the troubled baccarat pit. Instead, he hurried over himself.

" 'Frank,' he explained, 'you owe us four-hundred big ones. If you want more you've got to pay off something. The boys want their money.'

"Sinatra stood up. He flung his white chips into Sandy Waterman's face, at the same time smacking him on the forehead with the palm of his hand.

"Waterman turned and ran to his room. Within minutes he returned with a loaded pistol in his hand. He pointed it at the singer.

" 'Listen you! If you ever lay a hand on me again I'll put a bullet through your head!" Sanford Waterman had lost his cool.

"Sinatra hadn't lost his. 'Aw come on,' he said with a disparaging gesture, 'that gun stuff went out with Humphrey Bogart!'

"Disconcerted by Sinatra's nonchalant response, Waterman's arm lowered just enough for one of Sinatra's gofers to strike it. The gun fell to the floor. Waterman knew he was in trouble. He turned and ran to the cage, with Sinatra and his wolf pack in hot pursuit.

"Sinatra's left arm was in a sling, the result of some surgery on his veins.

"The cashier door opened. Waterman tried to close it behind his bad arm. Blood spurted upward. Everyone stood appalled. The drama was over as Sinatra hurried to his third floor suite and a gofer went for the house doctor."

25

Columnist Liz Smith published an item that TV and radio celebrity talk-show host Larry King was courting national best-selling author Kitty Kelley. Her source was a newspaper society page photo of King with his arm around Kelley when the two attended a book party for Patrick Buchanan, a former aide to President Reagan and an intellectual touchstone for the extreme right.

The item had come to her in an unmarked envelope containing the photo and the comment, "Hot ticket romance!"

Larry King responded with an angry phone call. He assured Smith he had no romance going with Kitty Kelley, whom he likened to a Washington groupie. He demanded a retraction and he got it.

A week later, the one-line letter was submitted to the CIA's forensic expert Dr. David A. Crown by Gerri Hirshey of the *Washington Post* who borrowed it from Smith. He concluded that the same machine that typed the message and envelope to Liz Smith was used to type two of the anonymous letters sent to Hirshey while she was doing her research for her series on Kitty Kelley. More, he reported that "all matched the type samples . . . of Kitty Kelley's business correspondence . . . one being on her embossed stationery, signed by Kitty Kelley."

The anonymous "tip" to Liz Smith followed another incident that angered Larry King. King reported that at the Buchanan book party, "Kitty got chummy and asked if I wanted to have fun one night. I knew she had this groupie reputation so I said 'sure.'

"She told me to call her and leave a sexy message on her machine," King said. "I figured maybe this was part of her kinkiness, so I did. I laid it on heavily by describing in anatomical detail certain things I would do to and with her. It was a gag and intended as such. Imagine my surprise when I learned that she was playing that tape for friends."

After King got over his initial shock, he called Kelley to protest. "I told her she wasn't going to blackmail me." He paused and shook his head. "She's very strange. She must have something wrong with her."

King added, "For the record—I've *never* dated her and I *never* would!"

Star magazine reporter Joanna Patyna was assigned to interview Kitty Kelley for her then-forthcoming biography of Elizabeth Taylor. She flew down to Washington from New York. Kelley admitted Patyna into her Georgetown mansion but seemed unwilling to respond to questions.

"I've got some errands to run in the neighborhood," she said brusquely, "Come along with me."

"We walked to a dry cleaning store nearby where Kitty picked up some garments. She wasn't in a good mood. Every time Patyna asked a question about Taylor, Kitty would evade answering and, instead, go into a harangue.

"She kept this up at a street corner where we just stood. She sounded like a soap box orator. Finally I said, 'Listen! I've had enough of your bullshit. You agreed to be interviewed and now you're just wasting my time. If you don't cut the crap and stop your ranting, I'm taking the next plane out of here!'

"Instantly Kitty did a hundred-and-eighty-degree turn. She calmed down, took me to her house, talked her bleached-blond head off about Liz Taylor and was sweet and pleasant. During the interview she bought me a soda.

"I came away from that interview realizing she could be charming one minute and obnoxious the next. I don't dislike her but I certainly wouldn't have her as a friend."

"I'm telling you some things that are very personal to me," Teddy Vaughn said. "I'm gay and I had a lover. My lover and I split. And so Diana McLellan organized a 'Teddy Going Away Lunch' . . ."

Teddy Vaughn was speaking. He's the Washington gossip columnist who had to augment Kitty's gossip material for *Today Is Sunday* because her output was lacking in quantity and quality.

"Kitty was at my party and decided I'd be a good source of gossip for her since I knew practically everyone in town. Among those I knew extraordinarily well—because I was living with him at the time—was Jamie Auchincloss, Jackie Onassis's half-brother."

At the time, Kitty was collecting material for her *Jackie Oh!* book.

Vaughn continued, "She knew the situation posed a terrific entree for her, so she cultivated a close friendship with me. She struck paydirt when she learned that Jamie and I gave parties at our place every Tuesday. She invited herself to them and became a regular.

"She became very cozy with Jamie and began to pump him for material about Jackie. She also went around town telling people she was a close friend of Jamie's."

At that point a strange turn occurred.

"Kitty asked me to meet her at Sarsfield's," Vaughn said. "That's the bar near Watergate. We had dinner and then she said, 'Tell me something, Teddy,' she began, 'Is Jamie gay?' She knew he was gay but she wanted me to corroborate it for legal purposes. I refused. I said, 'I have no idea.'

"Then she tried a different approach. 'You don't have to say so

301

directly . . .' She knew Jamie was fascinated by very young boys. We're talking twelve or thirteen. She also knew he had an extensive amount of kiddie porn. She asked if I'd go there with her and take out the porn and leave it where she could find it.

"I refused that one too. I told her that anyone's bedroom activities have nothing to do with me unless I happen to be in that bedroom.

"As for the material on Jackie that I gave her, she ignored all the favorable material because she wanted only derogatory things."

After *Jackie Oh!* was published, Vaughn complained that Kitty "cold-shouldered" him. She didn't give him credit or even mention him in the book.

Vaughn reports: "It was that way until she started to do her book on Elizabeth Taylor. Then she practically crawled to me on her hands and knees because she wanted me to get her some dirt about Taylor."

Vaughn had met Elizabeth Taylor in Manhattan when he was ballet critic for the *Soho News.* "After that I ran into her several times at other such affairs," he said. "I was a face she knew. So when I moved to Washington and attended a function at the Iranian Embassy I was dancing with Liza Minnelli, and we almost fell into the arms of Elizabeth who'd had too much to drink.

"My God, Teddy, what are you doing in Washington?" she asked.

"I live here now," I answered.

"You poor thing," Elizabeth quipped.

Vaughn continued: "She was dancing a lot with Baryshnikov. But I believe it was at that dance that she first met John Warner who became her sixth husband."

"Much later I was a frequent guest at Atoka [Warner's country estate in Virginia] where Elizabeth and I would go horseback riding together or take long walks. She told me a lot about what was going on between her and John [Warner] and she even confided in me that the breakup was coming.

"Kitty knew I was seeing Elizabeth and she clung to me like a leech. She would ask constantly, 'How are they getting along?' and she would ask about their sex lives—and anything else she could think of.

"Sure, I knew a little about their sex lives, but I don't betray friends.

"Kitty was consistent. She gave me the same zero credit in her Taylor book. I was frozen out again. That is, until she was assigned her Sinatra book. Then she begged me for an introduction to Peter Malatesta. He was Bob Hope's nephew and owned the Pisces Restaurant. Peter knew the skinny on Sinatra and Kitty knew he would be a marvelous source.

"Eventually she apparently did get to him and he did talk. He liked to boast. He was proud of the fact that if Sinatra would say impulsively, 'Let's go to Monte Carlo,' Peter would be included in the group. What little fresh material there was in *His Way* probably came from Peter. Kitty gave him lots of credit in her book. He didn't have long to enjoy it. He died of AIDS a few years later.

"Peter had been a Special Assistant to Vice President Spiro Agnew. It was Peter who introduced Agnew to Sinatra. Then the Veep and the Voice developed a close friendship."

We'll call them Mary and Penny. They asked me not to use their maiden or married names.

They met Kitty when she arrived in Washington. They shared a small flat on a tight budget. Most of the trio's limited income went for rent, food and clothes. Food was the subject of their disagreement.

The tiny kitchen had a Kelvinator refrigerator. In it the roommates stored their perishable food. Each bought those things that suited her taste. Then the rations began to disappear.

Mary and Penny often complained about the vanishing food but Kitty said nothing. Finally the two turned on her and accused her.

Kitty burst into tears. "Okay, so I ate a little of your food," she sobbed. "Is that so terrible? My lousy mother used to padlock the refrigerator in our home and I stole food whenever I was hungry . . ."

The explanation didn't cover "The Case of the Missing Designer Trousseau."

Penny, who was soon to marry, had taken out one of her dresses and hung it in her closet. The rest of the bridal wardrobe remained in the gift-wrapped boxes that were given to her at her shower on the closet floor. The garment that hung in the closet was a one-of-a-kind chiffon dress with a modified bouffant hem. She'd worn it only twice to parties and she figured it was certainly good for dozens of additional wearings.

She never got to wear it a third time.

"My dress is gone!" she screamed after going to the closet and not finding it. Even the fancy hanger it hung on had vanished.

Another scream. "My God! All the boxes with my trousseau—what happened to them!"

Penny asked Kitty and Mary if they had any clue as to the missing wardrobe's whereabouts. Neither could offer any explanation for the disappearance.

Months passed. Kitty moved out of the three-way rental to once again join Mike Edgely.

Then she went to work at the *Washington Post* as a research assistant. This allowed her to afford a vacation at a Virginia playground. When she returned, she gave a small party whose guests included Penny and Mary.

Kitty proudly passed around the Polaroid photos taken on her vacation.

One picture almost floored both Penny and Mary. There, in a coquettish pose, stood Kitty.

She was wearing Penny's one-of-a-kind designer dress.

26

In none of her previous books did Kitty Kelley come across as a "borrower" as clearly as she does in the narrative bearing on private White House "lunches."

Kitty struck gold when celebrity author Frances Spatz Leighton published a comprehensive biography on the First Lady, *The Search For The Real Nancy Reagan.*

To cover her tracks, Kitty cunningly avoided listing Miss Leighton's book in her Author's Notes for chapter 16. That despite the fact that she had no other source from which to appropriate Leighton's sketch of Nancy and Frank having *a very private lunch* (without quotations), which she warps into *a very private "lunch,"* and then unconscionably leaps into the realm of unsupported anecdotes by labelling their White House get-togethers as an "affair."

However alien honesty is to Kitty Kelley's nature, she does make a belated effort to give *The Search For the Real Nancy Reagan* grudging recognition by including it among the more than one-hundred books listed in her bibliography.

****

The moment has come again to expose Kitty's duplicitous disfigurement of facts. This time let's go to the split page:

LEIGHTON'S
NANCY & FRANKIE

"To Nancy the phone was a lifeline, daytime and night-time. To Ronnie it was a nuisance. He hated to talk on it after a day in the Oval Office. And he would much rather have someone come up and tell him something in person than through a contraption attached to wire.

"But you could still be lonely if all you did was talk on the phone—there was no substitute for seeing people, now and then.

"Sometimes Frank Sinatra slipped in and out of the White House just to have a very private luncheon with Nancy—only the two of them.

'The family household help knew that if they were going to disturb the First Lady on these occasions, it had better be because the White House was on fire.'

"Nancy viewed Francis Albert as very special and they seemed content with each other's company. Nancy even made sure on formal occasions to have Sinatra sit next to her, which did not

KELLEY'S
NANCY & FRANKIE

"The close relationship between the singer and the First Lady had concerned people close to the President for some time.

" 'It was those private "lunches" in the family quarters that were the most troublesome,' said one presidential assistant, shaking his head. 'Sinatra's name was never on the First Lady's schedule, and he was always brought in the back way, but I still worried about the press picking it up.'

" 'We always knew better than to interrupt those private "lunches," ' said a member of Mrs. Reagan's White House staff. The staff and quarters were off limits to everyone during that time. You could feel the air charge when he was around her. She played the music low, all his songs, of course, which she played in her bedroom day and night. She scheduled their private lunches in the solarium and fussed over the menu and the flowers . . . Few people knew when he was up there. She usually

306

endear her to Frank's wife, Barbara, who did not, in an even exchange, get to sit next to the President."

would arrange those "lunches" when the President was out of town, and they'd last from about 12:30 to 3:30 or 4:00 p.m. Sinatra came to the gate and Muffie Brandon (White House social secretary) would escort him up there. Then she would get lost immediately. All calls were put on hold. We were under strict instructions not to disturb. No matter what. When the First Lady was with Frank Sinatra, she was not to be disturbed. For anything. And that included a call from the President himself.

Nearly 400 years ago, the Athenian orator Aschines bequeathed to the world this classic definition of *character*:

"He who acts wickedly in private life, can never be expected to show himself noble in public conduct."

Some additional words on the nuts and bolts of Kitty's writing:

FICTION—The studio's [MGM-UA's] legal files contain an interoffice memo sent to the head office on January 31, 1971, asking about the possibility of renewing her (Nancy Davis's) contract. "I think we'll drop the option," writes Al Corfino, a production executive. "Don't worry about it."

FACT—As detailed earlier, MGM-UA legal files were sold to Turner Broadcasting in March, 1985, after Kelley'd been given access to them in her "research" for the bios on Elizabeth Taylor and Frank Sinatra. Kitty didn't begin work on the Nancy Reagan book until 1987. And we know she couldn't access those files any longer since Turner Communication president Roger Mayer told us: ". . . if she [Kitty Kelley] were to ask, we would not grant [permission]." Another lie!

FICTION—First Lady Barbara Bush once gave Nancy Reagan (when she was still in the White House) a sprayed white wreath for Christmas, only to find the President's wife had mailed it to someone else.

FACT—"I did not give her a wreath for Christmas," retorts Mrs. Bush, who calls Kelley's book nothing but "trash and fiction," then offers a final comment on the phony wreath tale: "If you're going to make up a story, you can certainly make up a better one than that."

FICTION—Kitty or her researchers interviewed Jimmy Stewart and his wife Gloria, Robert Stack, Patti Davis, Michael Reagan, Ron Reagan, Maureen Reagan, Sinatra lawyer Milton (Mickey) Rudin, syndicated columnist R. Emmett Tyrrell Jr., journalist Fred Barnes, historian Kenny Lynn, and nearly 1000 other persons.

FACT—None of the above spoke with the biographical larcenist nor to her "researchers" for contributions to Kelley's book. What hasn't been nailed down as absolute fact and has still to be determined is how many other people said no to interviews.

FICTION—Shirley Watkins, who is quoted extensively about "exclusive" White House "secrets" and goings-on, is identified by Kelley as "one of Mrs. Reagan's secretaries," and in one instance she's quoted as saying, "I had to answer a lot of the calls that came in from people saying he [Sinatra] was a crook and a member of the Mafia . . ."

FACT—Shirley Watkins was not a secretary to the First Lady and couldn't be privy to White House scuttlebutt or anything else. She was a computer technician with access to no area of the mansion other than the cramped work space she was assigned.

FICTION—On Pages 422–23, Kitty describes a scene in Michigan after the First Lady found "her jewelry box was missing," Kelley has an unnamed "aide" relating the story in order to hammer home the point made in the previous paragraph, that Mrs. Reagan's demands were "so intrusive . . . that

she had people running in all directions to do her bidding."
Meanwhile, Kelley has President Reagan (this is while Air Force
One is in the air) indifferent to "the friction she [Nancy] was
causing" and hiding his face behind a newspaper. Finally she
has political consultant Stuart Spencer join the three-ring circus
Kitty is fabricating for her readers: " 'Yo, Ron,' said Spencer,
rattling the newspaper. 'This is serious. You've got to get your
wife off this plane before everyone goes for the parachutes.'
Finally the President peeked out. 'You do it,' he said, putting
the newspaper in front of his face again.

FACT–Truly a three-ring circus, fabricated by Kitty Kelley
who's never been near Air Force One.

So were Frank Sinatra's visits to the White House clandestine
and were the "luncheons" with Nancy likewise covert because,
as Kitty misinforms her readers, they were "private"?

Mrs. Reagan's personal White House schedule confirms that
"private" does not connote lustful conduct, as Kelley wants us to
believe.

In fact, *Pvt. appt.*—not *"Private"* as Kitty misshapes these
perfectly harmless words—is the term appearing no fewer than
twenty-four times in the First Lady's personal White House
schedule for the month of October, 1985, which is reproduced
in Kitty's book. The schedule is actually a calendar of events
logged by her appointments secretary for Mrs. Reagan, to receive friends, relatives, officials of organizations representing,
for example, fund-raising and social activities, and wives and
families of visiting dignitaries, and heads of state. Names are not
ever listed!

So much for this fiction of love in the afternoon.

27

The marketing of Kitty Kelley's Nancy Reagan biography was one of the smartest campaigns in the history of book publishing. The Simon & Schuster publicity department conducted a symphony designed to make the book a national "happening" no matter what the material was between its covers.

Top professionals worked on Kitty's face; her makeup and her style of dress. More important, she was carefully coached on how to smile (no matter how upsetting the questions) and how to parry questions with questions. She was ready.

The book's publishers made the operation seem like some clandestine revolutionary campaign. Copies of the finished manuscript were supposedly kept "top secret." Kitty sent one to Garry Trudeau who, by arrangement, included material from the book in his *Doonesbury* cartoon-strip.

Kitty-day was about to happen. By announcing that its contents were a "secret" the book was given enormous cache. Book critics are usually sent copies of a book four to eight weeks in advance of its publication so they have time to write reviews to coincide with publication day. By not sending reviewers their copies in advance, S&S was hoping for large sales before anyone could examine the book's content or criticize it.

One day before the book's national release to the bookshops,

S&S scored an unprecedented coup. *The New York Times*, having managed to secure access to the book, published a long piece that amounted to a virtual unpaid publicity blurb for it on the front page of its Sunday edition. No matter that the story, written by one Maureen Dowd, had the flavor of a gossip column in that it repeated the book's rumors and insinuations as though they were fact. One example is the description of the lawsuit which Frank Sinatra brought to stop Kelley from saying she was his official biographer and had his approval. The *Times* picked up the much-repeated erroneous assertion that he sued to prevent publication of the book about him.

The story contained the open-mouthed acceptance of the suggestion that Sinatra had an affair with Nancy Reagan and even had sex with her in the White House. Not a single drop of skepticism. Not even puzzlement that Sinatra, who had been married to three Hollywood beauties and could have his pick of the most beautiful women in the world would have gone two steps out of his way with a tryst with an aging, moderately attractive woman—risking his own marriage to the far-more-beautiful Barbara Marx.

Dowd referred to Kitty Kelley on the front page of the *Times* as having "developed a reputation as a giant killer." No specifics on which giants she'd killed. Certainly Frank Sinatra was still in his prime. Elizabeth Taylor was riding a new crest of popularity. Jackie Onassis wasn't showing any scars.

Dowd referred to Nancy Reagan changing her resume, but made no mention of the oft-exposed facts about Kitty's own false resumes.

It was a shameful moment for *The New York Times*.

Not since President John Kennedy said that he enjoyed reading the James Bond books had any volume received a send-off to equal the *Times* story. How could this book be trash if the staid gray lady of West 43rd Street considered it page one news?

Criticism of the *Times*'s editorial judgment was lost in the rush of people to buy the book. But the criticism was heavy, particularly among top-level journalists.

R. Emmett Tyrrell Jr., in his syndicated column, described

the book's contents as "scabrous" and wondered aloud why the *Times* saw fit to front-page it. He dismissed the fact that Nancy was a president's wife, because Jackie Onassis had also been a president's wife. "No," he wrote, "I'm afraid that the only reason this ponderous compendium of ordure received notice on the front page of the nation's newspaper of record is that the Old Order cannot get Ronald Reagan out of its mind. And so a *Times* reporter was assigned to speed-read the 600-page book and report on its fanciful revelations . . ."

Added Tyrrell: "Within a column inch, the reporter speaks of the Reagans' 'desperate' campaign to improve their image and of the Reagan White House 'desperately' soft-peddling Nancy's vanities. There is indeed desperation here, but it issues from those who remain so overwrought by the Reagan presidency that they will debauch the front page of one of the world's most respected newspapers.

"Think of it. The *Times* reporters have been covering the Reagans for over a decade. Not one of its reporters has been able to uncover the Reagans acting like the Palm Beach Kennedys. Not one has been able to show Nancy running national security policy. Apparently the *Times* editors who put Kelley's gossip on their front page believe she is a greater reporter than any of the dozen who covered Washington for the *Times* during the Reagan era."

Finally, Tyrrell wrote: "Kelley lists scores of public figures who she says took 'time to answer questions and share their stories.' One name on the list is mine. I refused to see her. Other names on the list are Fred Barnes and the historian Kenneth Lynn. They refused her too. And none of us accepted an offer to have sex with her. Pass it on."

Don Hewitt, originator and executive producer of TV's *60 Minutes* spoke for many when he said at a New York Public Library function: "The *Times* should hide its face in shame. What it has told us in effect is that this book is a book so important we must all buy and read it."

And buy it they did. On April 8th, the first day of publication, many bookshops reported record sales. The first printing of

650,000 looked to be a sellout, so S&S hurried back to press with several hundred thousand additional copies.

Newsweek and *Time* devoted cover stories to the book. *Crossfire, Nightline* and even the seriously-inclined *MacNeil-Lehrer News Hour* devoted time to a roundtable discussion on the book's cultural importance.

Kitty appeared on every program that would have her. Her attractive smile was ever present, almost as if it were pasted on. Her well-rehearsed answers to questions became stock. "I don't tell you what Nancy and Frank did at those lunches. I just take you to the bedroom door." And the theme, "She ran the country. She was really the president."

A gullible public relished every piece of salacious innuendo. Skepticism was put aside. Credulity was buried by the publicity blitz.

At her publication party, hundreds of guests were confined to a hot room while Kitty stayed locked behind closed doors. When she finally made her entrance, someone remarked, "Here comes the Queen!" and there were snickers. Society columnist and fellow author Doris Lilly walked up to Kitty: "Kitty, I'm Doris Lilly. We've never met but I've spoken with you many times on the phone." Kitty stared at her unresponsively.

Lilly later commented: "I had the feeling she was either drunk or on drugs of some kind. She seemed so out of it."

The TV and radio blitz continued. At first, all was sweetness and light. Nobody had hard questions. No one questioned even the most foolish assertions in the book. The fact is that few people had yet read it. The 'happening' wasn't just the book, it was Kitty herself.

"Kitty Kelley" became household words. Cartoons featured her. Comics made reference to her in their acts. Commentators reached out to mention her. Lyricist Fred Ebb inserted an amusing Kitty Kelley reference in one of the Ebb and John Kander songs being performed in the pair's hit Manhattan show, *And the World Goes 'Round.*

The book leaped to the #1 spot on the *New York Times* best-seller list, pushing the Hollywood gossip tome, *You'll Never Eat Lunch in This Town Again* by Julia Phillips into the second spot. Few people had read the book and only a smattering of reviews had appeared in the press.

All was sunshine and sales in Kitty's world. But every silver lining has a cloud and there were storm shadows on the horizon.

28

The backlash came. At first it was a hum and a small amount of static. Then it became a hurricane.

There were irritating questions like: "How do you feel about the biography being written about you?"

"I don't think there is one," came Kelley's reply.

Or: "Would you comment on the book being written about you?"

"I don't care to talk about that," Kitty Kelley said.

When questioners persisted on the subject of her biography, Kelley would dismiss them with banter: "I wonder who'll play me in the movie?" she'd respond.

After days of constant interviews and racing from studio to studio, an edge crept into her voice. The fixed smile was often replaced by fleeting grim looks.

Mike Capuzzo, writing for the *Philadelphia Inquirer* observed, "As she sat in her suite . . . her mask of composure faded quickly. Dressed ironically in the sort of Chanel-style ensemble favored by Nancy Reagan (except Kitty wore green while Nancy preferred red), Kitty seemed tightly wound, defensive, nervous, as if she were on a Diet Coke caffeine high . . . [she was] already sick of being trashed. And this comes on only Day Two of a 32-city press tour . . ."

The *Washington Post* described her Nancy Reagan book as

317

"the revenge of former friends and associates who feel that they have been badly treated, plus some hazily substantiated gossip, and free-floating bits of innuendo. Odds of it winning a Pulitzer for biography are slim."

Kitty responded by saying the *Washington Post* comment came because Nancy Reagan is a good friend of *Washington Post* publisher Katharine Graham.

More hurtful was a full column by ex-friend Liz Smith which dismissed the book as "dull". Said Liz Smith: "I dozed through most of it . . ." This was the book's first national review. And when it appeared, Broadway wags dubbed it "sour grapes." Then they read some of the book and were surprised to agree that it *was* dull! Liz Smith *was* on target!

The word had not yet gotten out on how much of its content was dishonest.

Liz Smith wrote: "Look, if Frank Sinatra and Nancy Reagan ever got beyond exchanging confidences, swapping Hollywood gossip and reminiscing about the good old days, then it surely must be the most remarkable coupling since Leda and the Swan."

Kitty had, once again, put together a book from a mishmash of borrowed material from previously published books and articles. To this she'd added a generous portion of innuendo and inaccuracy.

Hard questions began to surface. She didn't want to face them.

The turning point of her tour came when Kitty was scheduled to appear on the important no-holds-barred morning show in Philadelphia, *AM-Philadelphia*. There she would face newsmen from the *Philadelphia Inquirer*. At this point, paranoia seemed to govern her actions. She insisted that the S&S publicity people question the station to see if the newsmen had spoken directly to her former publisher, Lyle Stuart. (She was aware that Stuart's son-in-law, Mark Jaffe, was an *Inquirer* reporter.)

The station's representative replied, "I honestly don't know who the reporters have talked with but I do know that they're well prepared."

One hour before air time, Kitty canceled her appearance.

When she heard that NBC's *Live at Five* planned to have her spar with Ronald Reagan impersonator Jim Morris, she canceled that appearance.

New York Channel 5 reporter Penny Crone broke the news that President Reagan's White House security detail chief branded as totally false the story that Frank Sinatra had spent hours with Nancy Reagan in her "private quarters."

Kitty didn't respond. By then, she'd canceled scheduled appearance in the cities that remained on her tour. A typical response to this came from Jim Ryan on the Fox network's *Good Day, New York* show. He announced to his audience that he was furious because Kelley canceled only minutes before she was to appear on his program. He called her "unprofessional" and echoed the Liz Smith critique that the book was dull.

Pat Piper, producer of Larry King's national radio show was amused by the excuse given for the cancellations. "They say that to continue the author tour would be redundant. Do I believe that? Absolutely not. I've never heard of anyone canceling a tour because of too much publicity."

A few days later Kitty agreed to do satellite interviews for local TV shows in several cities. On the second of these, a member of the studio audience stood up to ask if George Carpozi had tried to interview her. She replied, "Of course not!"

This despite the dozen or so calls to her from me, plus three letters to her, as well as several to her attorneys, a letter to her agent, etc. Her denial amused C. David Heymann. Heymann whose *A Woman Named Jackie* outsold Kitty's *Jackie Oh!* by six to one was now at work on a biography of Elizabeth Taylor— another Kitty Kelley victim. "She gets so much of it wrong," Heymann told friends facetiously, "that I almost feel compelled to write a serious biography on every one of her subjects just to cancel out the fiction she produces."

Heymann made a phone call to Kitty. Of course it was answered by her machine. "Kitty," he said, "this is Clem Heymann. I understand that George Carpozi has been trying in the worst way to interview you and you've been saying you haven't received any such request. So I'm acting as arbiter. Carpozi wants to interview you. Let me know when this can be arranged."

Heymann taped the entire exchange including Kitty's recorded message. Kelley didn't respond.

Meanwhile, the cancellation of her 20-city tour created even more publicity.

The first official explanation was that she was exhausted. Then came the excuse that she'd been physically threatened on her home answering machine. (The Georgetown Police Department said they'd not received any complaint from her about this.) When challenged on this, she changed her story again to, "I can't talk about it because it involves security." And when questioned further, she said, "I dismissed the threat. I don't take it seriously." When asked by a reporter if he could listen to the threat on her phone answering machine tape she said, "I erased it."

Shades of Richard Nixon!

Another embarrassment was a Kitty Kelley profile in *Mirabella* magazine by Susan Lee. The cover said: "Kitty Kelley In The Soup."

The article began: ". . . Kelley is rich. She commands millions of dollars for [her] books. But Kitty Kelley has a problem. There are tons of people who don't like her. Tons . . ."

Lee quotes former *New York Times*-man Warren Weaver as saying, "She's a candy-box blond whose appearance seems to be totally at odds with her personality." Adds Lee, "Right on target. When I met with her, Kelley looked utterly disarming; a small, plumpish woman with big sunglasses pushed back on a bright blond do, in her signature Adolfo suit. She also *seemed* disarming. She leaned toward me, one black pump dangling seductively from her toes. Then I asked her a question she didn't like . . . her spine straightened and her kittenish expression became total priss."

Lee commented: "As a writer, Kelley doesn't have much flash. Her focus on the dailiness of her subjects' lives means she delivers a lot of weather reports in which rain is 'driving' and days 'dawn clear and bright.' Her prose features a world where rumors 'fly,' tragedies 'take their toll,' men are 'proud and domineering,' abuse comes in 'torrents' and pretenses are 'kept up.'

"[Her books are] politely put, amateurish. They read like cut-and-paste efforts."

"Cut-and-paste efforts"? How could that be for a book for which the author claims she conducted "more than 1,000 interviews"?

Nearly one hundred persons have stepped forward to proclaim publicly that although Kitty claims to have interviewed them, they never at any time spoke with her.

A typical example: Kitty claimed two interviews with astrologer to the White House, Joan Quigley. Said Quigley: "She called me from New York and asked if I'd give her an interview. I said 'no' and hung up. Then she called to say she was in San Francisco and asked if I would meet with her? I said 'no' and hung up. These two 'no's' were the total extent of my conversation with her."

Among those key people who denied ever having conversation or contact with her were Michael Reagan, actress Ann Doran, White House aide Ed Rollins, etc., etc.

Several people quoted in the book complained that they'd been misquoted. For example, Doris Lilly said that Kitty quotes her as talking about Ronald Reagan being drunk. "He was *never* drunk in my presence," Lilly corrected. "And I never said we had an intimate relationship. I didn't talk about sex. That's not my generation."

Selene Walters was described as a virginal innocent upon whom Reagan forced himself and committed date rape. Said Walters after the book appeared, "Date rape? God no. That's Kelley's phrase." Walters was not the virginal innocent: she'd already been married and divorced twice when Reagan dated her. Confronted with this information on a TV show, Kitty shrugged her shoulders.

The most talked-about "information" in the tome, that of a sex tryst between Sinatra and Nancy Reagan brought the most

321

wrath from people in a position to know. Sheila Tate, Nancy Reagan's former press secretary called the entire report trash. Sinatra met the entire senior staff of the White House. Then he and Nancy had lunch but were back in the Oval office within an hour. All guests were escorted to the residence elevator. Kelley loosely calls that 'being brought in the back.' Nor was it unusual for calls to be held during a meeting or when a guest was visiting. That was done as a common courtesy.

Former presidential assistant Joseph Canzeri said, "I'm not saying that they couldn't have been alone together for a short time. But if Kitty Kelley says they were jumping up and down on top of one another, that would be a lie. There are too many people upstairs at the White House. There's the Secret Service right outside the door."

Comedian Jackie Mason added a line to the routine he was performing in his Broadway show: "I can't do comedy tonight. I'm depressed. I just discovered Nancy Reagan has slept with everybody but me."

29

The jokes, the barbs and the needles were everywhere. Jim Mullens writing in *Entertainment Weekly* asked, "Is it me or does Kitty Kelley look a lot like Miss Piggy?"

Mark Simone on New York's WNEW-radio reported: "Kitty Kelley interviewed more than a thousand people for her book, and two of them had actually once met the Reagans!"

There was the satire, as the letter published in the *Washington Post* written by Edmund Morris, who is writing Ronald Reagan's authorized biography: "Readers shocked by Kitty Kelley's recent revelations of private tete-a-tetes upstairs in the White House don't know the half of it.

"As Ronald Reagan's authorized biographer, I can now report that every Thursday noon for eight years, Mr. Reagan and George Bush retired to a small chamber adjoining the Oval office for intimate 'lunches' or 'luncheons'. Staff were under strict orders not to disturb the couple as long as they stayed there . . . And here's the really kinky detail—on at least one occasion the two men were joined by a photographer . . . I think the above flagrant facts speak for themselves."

And there were the dirty jokes. This one rapidly made the rounds of the nation's capital. Kitty, who spends her time examining garbage pails and getting into places where she wasn't invited and doesn't belong, somehow made her way into a conference with President Bush and his top aides. She stood quietly in the background as the President announced: "I'm tired of people thinking of me as a wimp. I'm not a wimp and I'm going to prove it right here and now."

He opened a box to let out a snapping turtle. Then he unzipped his fly and took out his penis. The turtle snapped and caught the penis. It hung on for five minutes while the President, obviously in pain, stared at his watch. Finally he took a pencil and jabbed the turtle in the eye. The turtle let go and Bush put his penis back into his pants and zipped up his fly.

"There!" he said in triumph. "Do any of you here have the nerve to do that?"

Kitty spoke up. "I'll try it, Mr. President," she volunteered, "if you promise not to poke my eye with a pencil."

And so it went. Even consumer advocate Ralph Nader—no fan of the Reagans—had unkind things to say about both the book and its publisher. He accused Simon & Schuster of lacking "conviction" about the contents of the book. He expressed the belief that S&S knew "deep inside its corporate soul" that the book was fiction.

M.W. Harris of New Hope, Pennsylvania, wrote to the *Philadelphia Inquirer*: "Instead of helping the sale of Kitty Kelley's book on Nancy Reagan, I plan to donate $25 to my favorite charity. I would like to have others join me."

Harris added: "If you must read it, borrow it from your local library."

There was a certain irony in the bad review of the book that appeared in *New Republic*, for its author was Maureen Dowd, the same lady who wrote the front-page story for *The New York Times*. Almost as if she were atoning for her sin, she wrote: "Kitty Kelley's achievement is extraordinary. She has provided a reason for sympathy for Nancy Reagan . . . Kelley is a mean and greedy writer, so drunk on sensationalism that she lacks compassion and understanding . . . [She] is rancid with revenge . . ."

A majority of the reviews were similarly angry and down-putting. But the *coup de grace* came from Andrew Ferguson. Ferguson, an editorial writer for the Scripps-Howard News Service reviewed the book for *The Wall Street Journal*.

He began his review with: "Yeah, yeah, yeah: As a biographer, Kitty Kelley has the ethics of a sewer rat, the literary gifts of a Penthouse Forum correspondent, and the historical judgment of Cindy Adams . . .

"Only a total genius could have shaped the marketing strategy for *Nancy Reagan: The Unauthorized Biography*, with each move designed to lend her work a substance it otherwise lacks.

". . . Kitty boasted that lawyers had vetted the book, as if a lawsuit from a public figure like Nancy Reagan were even a remote possibility. (Editor's note: Not only does the person who sues have to prove the information false but they must also prove that it was written with malicious intent. This is virtually impossible to do.)

". . . There's something odd about excoriating sleazy greed after being paid $4 million to retail unverifiable allegations about private lives."

Among the few favorable comments was one in *The Nation* which editorialized that "We can all sleep more easily now that gross hypocrisy has been exposed and moralism revealed as turpitude . . . In a real sense the Reagans are getting the comeuppance they deserve."

On the opposite side of the political forum, George F. Will wrote in his column: "Kitty Kelley, who fattens like a leech on the lives of famous people, is a retailer of falsehoods." Will goes on to quote Barbara Bush as she pounced on a Kelley falsehood and denounced the book as "trash and fiction" and "scummy."

Will advises those readers "whose lives are evidently so arid they can only be irrigated by lurid gossip" to "get a life!"

New York magazine told its readers that "Kelley's book is swill."

Syndicated columnist Richard Cohen concluded, "It's probably fair to say that many journalists were appalled by Ronald

Reagan's intellectual laziness and considered both him and his wife raging hypocrites on social issues. That might explain why some of the media, bested in a PR sense by the Reagan White House staff and daunted by his popularity, have so uncritically accepted Kelley's allegations."

Cohen concluded: "But anyone who thinks Kitty Kelley has damaged the reputation of the Reagans has it wrong. It's the press that's been soiled by this affair."

Newsweek observed: "Because Kelley knew this book would get serious attention, she tried to create the impression of serious research . . . At the front of the book she thanks scores of people, including some who never talked to her, spoke only to decline to be interviewed or explicitly (and futilely) asked that their cooperation not be acknowledged."

The 603-page book reached the shops on April 8.

By May 8, sales had dropped. The book remained #1 on *The New York Times* list but its dominant role had been diminished. And the book had ceased to be newsworthy.

When Kitty was writing her Sinatra book, her phone answering machine played Frank Sinatra singing *I Could Write A Book.* After her Sinatra biography was published, it played *My Way* by Sinatra. After the Nancy Reagan biography hit the bookshops her machine played Sinatra singing *Nancy With The Laughing Face.* One of the writers of the latter song was the late Phil Silvers. The comic once appeared in a Broadway musical which featured a song, *Make Someone Happy.* An observer suggested that Kitty might do well to ponder a line from the lyric of this one: "Fame, when you win it, comes and goes in a minute."

Sinatra told a sold-out concert audience in Phoenix: "I hope the next time she crosses a street four blind guys come along driving cars."

He added: "If Kelley were a man, someone would be whacking her out every 15 minutes."

The New York Times reviewed the book on May 5, 1991, in its Book Review. The review was written by journalist-critic Joe Queenan. It began: "There is an old saying that once you have shot, hanged, stabbed, drawn and quartered the person you are writing about, you do not also have to drown him. Or her. Obviously, no one told this to Kitty Kelley."

"Should this book be taken seriously?" Queenan asks. "Perhaps, but only by people who can shine flashlights directly through one ear and have light come out the other." He adds: "Ms. Kelley is an entertaining hatchet person whose mutilation techniques could put Jack the Ripper to shame, but as a historian and social critic, she's about as savvy as Geraldo Rivera. Consider her barmy observation about the 1960s: 'The era of sex, drugs and rock 'n' roll became the most turbulent decade of the twentieth century . . .' Gosh, Kitty, in the competition for most turbulent decade of the twentieth century, a lot of us would still have to give the nod to the 1940s, what with Adolf Hitler and Heinrich Himmler and Joseph Mengele and the boys killing off tens of millions of people and whatnot. And there *did* also seem to have been a bit of stir back in 1914. And, oh yeah, there *was* the Great Depression. But never mind."

And on May 5th, although the Nancy Reagan biography remained at the #1 spot on the *Times* best-seller list, it had already dropped to second place on the list compiled by Long Island's *Newsday*.

After she short-circuited her American tour, Kitty flew to London aboard the Concorde for a 7-day promotion campaign on behalf of the British publication of her book by Bantam Press. She held court at the posh Dorchester Hotel in Suite 506.

"The woman reminds me of an old-fashioned Hollywood movie star," commented Johnny Behlan after he photographed the author for a feature in the prestigious London *Sunday Telegraph*. "She acts as though she were royalty."

The articles that appeared in the British press were anything but flattering. Bantam's Mark Barty-King attributed this to "envy" by the women who wrote the articles.

Chrissy Iley, writing for the London *Daily Mail* said, "I dub her the emotional terrorist, the intellectual bandit . . . a small fluffy thing, snowy hair over-treated and over-teased around the pussycat features. I notice she seems balder on one side than the other . . ."

There were angry editorials. One in the London *Daily Express* proclaimed: REAGAN IS STILL A HERO DESPITE KITTY'S CLAWS.

The reviews were no kinder across the Atlantic than they'd been in the U.S.A. Godfrey Hodgson, writing in *The Independent*, said: "Kelley . . . builds a picture of Nancy Reagan as a woman who was tasteless, unkind, snobbish and would do virtually anything for money and success. What she does not perhaps realize is that she paints a very similar portrait of herself."

Brian Masters wrote in the *Sunday Telegraph*: "She never intended to write a biography. She does not know what a biography is. One despairs that such an empty exercise should pass for a major publishing event."

Robert Rhodes James is a Member of the British Parliament. He is also an author and is currently at work on a biography of the late Lord Boothby. James remarked, "The political biography is an English art form. It is a balanced portrait. The Americans don't have a tradition of writing biographies. The Nancy Reagan book is not history, it's not biography, it's muckraking. If there were a similar book on, say, Mrs. Thatcher, the libel damages may be astronomical."

All the negative feature stories and the bad reviews only sparked interest and within a short time a first printing of 50,000 copies was followed by two additional printings of 25,000 each.

On May 11th, Kitty Kelley made the front page of *The New York Times* for the second time. This time an article bearing the byline of Larry Rohter.

Under the headline "Nancy Reagan: Mending a Frayed Image" Rohter wrote, "The First Lady has resurfaced, acting as if nothing untoward has happened to her or her image . . ."

"As Ms. Kelley's reporting methods and some of her most sensational allegations have been called into question in news reports following the publication of the book, these friends say, a wave of sympathy has been generated on Mrs. Reagan's behalf."

"There was definitely a backlash," according to Mrs. Reagan's former press secretary, Sheila Tate. "I could actually feel the story turn and I've seldom been in a position where I could say that. The one characteristic you can always count on in the American people is that when they perceive something as unfair, they react to it. That's what happened here."

The article mentioned that support for Mrs. Reagan against the Kelley book had come from such far-apart personalities as George F. Will and talk show host Joan Rivers.

"This book is just damn trash and I'm sick of it," Joan Rivers said at the start of her program. She held up a copy of the Kelley biography before tossing it into a wastebasket.

People magazine reported that "readers had little good to say about Kitty Kelley, her motives or her book. Many were pleased to note that a tell-all book about Kelley will soon be released."

Letters published included one by Gloria Grinta of Vienna, Ohio who wrote: "If Kitty Kelley was so sure Nancy Reagan and Frank Sinatra had an affair in the '70s, why was it not mentioned in her book on Sinatra, written in the '80s? I feel Kitty's 'litter' should be buried with all her other books—six feet deep."

A woman named Virginia Ketcham wrote from Wasilla, Alaska: "A book coming out about Kitty Kelley? Wonderful! There's an old saying: 'What goes around, comes around.' Let's see how she likes being on the other side of the poison pen."

Hunter Thompson, writing in *Rolling Stone*, declared that "Kelley's book . . . was good for a few laughs but not many. And there is meaning in it, for sure, but not much. It is an ugly mean little package that made me feel cheap for just reading it or even holding the thing in my hands."

Thompson added: "The book is a shit rain of old gossip and sleazy little stories that we read a long time ago and never quite believed . . . for good or evil."

In the long pull, none of it matters. The people involved may have suffered some emotional distress. But they can console themselves in the fact that Kelley has been exposed internationally as a teller of inaccurate tales, manufactured scandal, and malicious mounds of made-up muck.

And they can remember this bit of wisdom: Truth is often struck down by irresponsible writers and reporters but she always manages to get up from her sick-bed to triumph over her assailants.

30

My publisher, Lyle Stuart, once pointed out that he never uses the expression "well-known" when referring to people. "A person may be widely-known," he commented, "but few of us are known well. Each of us is a unique mystery, never to be unraveled."

I thought of that when evaluating the personality of Kitty Kelley. And I thought about the allegations of kleptomania.

The notion of taking things without permission is known as kleptomania, and is defined by the dictionary as "an uncontrollable tendency to steal things . . ."

Is Kitty Kelley a kleptomaniac? I don't know: I'm not a psychiatrist. Psychiatry says that people often steal things because they feel deprived of love. The movie queen of the 30's and 40's, Hedy Lamarr did it. So did former Miss America Bess Myerson.

Does internationally famous Kitty Kelley feel unloved? Does this account for her bitterness and her vicious hatchet jobs on people more talented than she is . . . people who are loved by many . . ?

The theme of missing items kept cropping up again and again in my research. A book publisher and his wife missed two items after Kitty visited their apartment. A writer allowed Kitty to use his home for several weeks. When he reclaimed it, the house was in neater order than it had been when he'd left it. Except that a collection of rare wine labels was missing.

I've mentioned incidents of Kitty Kelley stealing food. Then there is the case of the missing dress that showed up on her body weeks after it disappeared.

Shortly before the writing of this book was completed, I began to receive wide publicity. Mention of this project appeared in all the major national magazines and newspapers.

My publisher put a lid on pre-publication publicity and turned down requests for appearances on such expose shows as *Hard Copy* and *Entertainment Tonight*. In all, he totalled more than forty requests for interviews and/or personal appearances within a 10-day period.

Then came the phone call I'd been waiting for. Throughout my research for this book the kleptomaniac theme surfaced again and again and again. I'd dismissed it for lack of confirmation. This phone call brought the confirmation.

"I'm Barbara Askins," the caller introduced herself. "I was Kitty Kelley's sorority sister at the University of Arizona. I'm phoning because I want to find out whether you've learned *all* the things about her you should know . . ."

If the heavens opened wide and a booming voice had roared at me from above, "I'm coming down to answer your prayers, George," I couldn't have felt more fulfilled than when the welcome voice of Barbara Askins pulsed over Ma Bell's fiber optic longline from Seattle in the State of Washington to my home in Melville, New York.

"What is it you can tell me about Kitty Kelley that I don't already know?" I asked.

"Do you know about her activities in Delta Gamma Sorority?"

"Yes . . ."

"About the thefts . . . ?

I proceeded to tell Barbara Askins about my investigations into the many reports of thefts that occurred on the University of Arizona campus during the three years Kitty Kelley was there as an undergraduate. But prior informants could only intimate

Kitty was the culprit—they could offer no convincing evidence. The campus security forces had declined to discuss the case with me.

The Tucson police, the District Attorney's office, and courts in that city were more forthcoming. They searched records of thefts on the campus. But no document on file turned up the name of Katherine Ann Kelley, as she was listed in the registrar's office when she enrolled as a freshman for the Fall semester of 1953. She'd never been charged or arrested.

Q. Barbara, what can you tell me about the thefts?

A. Kitty Kelley stole my merry widow.

Q. Your what?

A. Today it's called a bustier.

Q. What's that?

A. It's an item of lingerie women wear, usually under a gown with a deep cleavage. It keeps the breasts firmly contained in the push-up cups of the bustier, which hugs the body down to the waist.

Q. So Kelley stole your bustier?

A. Yes, to wear it herself. Or so she thought.

Q. What happened?

A. She couldn't wear it. Her bust was too big for the bustier.

Q. Did she return it?

A. No. I'll tell you what she did. Kitty took it into a sorority sister's room next door, tried it on, and when it didn't fit she ripped out the spongy padding in the cups. But even after she had torn that out, she still had to make more room for a proper fit on her oversized bust. That's when she put a scissor to the garment, snip, snip, snipping around the cups, probably hoping she could make them accommodate her big breasts. Apparently she didn't succeed.

Q. How do you know?

A. Because the girl next door told me she found my merry widow on her closet floor, under a pile of clothes bound for the laundry.

Q. Go on, please.

A. It was totally destroyed by Kitty's efforts to make it fit.

333

Barbara was convinced Kitty Kelley was the culprit who appropriated the merry widow for herself. Yet . . .

"Like so many of my sorority sisters in the dorm who had things missing from their rooms, I couldn't prove what I suspected—that Kitty had taken not only my merry widow but other valuables of mine."

The thefts continued. Then . . .

"A day came when one of the girls spotted several plastic bottles in Kitty's room," continued Barbara Askins. "The bottles were of the type found in make-up kits that go into travel carrying cases—clear, small plastic vials that contain just small amounts of liquid shampoo, toilet water, and perfume from a woman's toilette that are taken on a trip."

Q. What did this discovery prove?

A. That Kitty was going into her sorority sisters' rooms and, instead of stealing their perfume bottles outright, she was emptying their contents into the plastic containers.

Q. How do you know that?

A. Because one day a Delta Gamma girl went into Kitty's room and saw the vials on her dresser. All but one had been sealed with beeswax. The girl unfastened the cap from the unsealed container and sniffed its contents. She instantly recognized the fragrance as a perfume one of our sorority sisters was wearing. She put the cover back on, went to the girl's room, and asked where her perfume was.

" 'On the dresser,' the girl replied.

"The visitor went to the dresser, picked up the bottle, and said, 'This is empty.'

" 'What!' the other girl screamed. 'I just bought it a few days ago! I've scarcely used it.'

" 'Well there's no perfume in the bottle anymore . . .' "

It was then that the two ladies concluded Kitty was the thief in the Delta Gamma Sorority House. Her Delta Gamma sisters now began keeping a sharp eye on Kelley.

No one caught her in the act. The thefts continued without letup. Both genuine and costume jewelry disappeared. Various amounts of cash vanished. Dresses, coats, lingerie, shoes, stockings, and other wearables were mysteriously lost by their owners.

The thefts weren't limited to the sorority house. Losses were also experienced in Yuma Hall, as I reported earlier. Yuma was Kitty Kelley's official university dormitory. The sorority house was a privileged residence where Delta Gammans could stay over after they were pledged and their first-semester grades were satisfactory.

Finally on a late spring day in 1962, about a dozen sorority sisters, angry at being ripped off by a sneak thief, closed ranks. They approached Kitty's Pledge Mother Barbara Svob, by then a senior. They voiced their mutual suspicions that the girl who came under her wing as a freshman in 1959 was a kleptomaniac.

"I gave my immediate attention to the complaint," said the former Barbara Svob, now Mrs. Barbara Sherman, living in Los Altos, California.

This Barbara, like the other Barbara who was "merry-widowed" or "bustiered" by Kitty, had in the recent past been devastated when she found her leather-bound volume of the *Complete Works of William Shakespeare* missing from her room in the sorority house. Barbara knew the time had come to do something about the larcenies.

"We went to the security police and reported what we suspected," said Barbara. "Things happened quickly after that . . ."

The university's security chief David Paxton rounded up a handful of his men and visited the Delta Gamma Sorority House and Yuma Hall. Entering rooms while the coeds were out, the security force dusted valuables, such as rings, bracelets, wristwatches and pendants with an invisible powder.

[Since Paxton died in 1990 while living in retirement after more than twenty-five years as University of Arizona security chief, I turned to the Nassau County Police Department for a description of this "invisible powder." Detective Thomas Kubic of the Scientific Investigative Unit explained:

"In all likelihood the powder used at the university was one

335

produced under the trade name of several manufacturers, but which is always alluded to by its generic name, 'Sneak Thief Powder.' It's an almost foolproof tool in the fight against sticky-fingered thieves. Once the crook touches a valuable that's been dusted with this powder, it's curtains. For the instant the thief's hands are put under the UV (ultra-violet) light, the glow the hands give off spells T-H-I-E-F . . ."]

"Very few of us knew what Paxton had done [dusted 'Sneak Thief Powder' on Delta Gamma girls' possessions.]," the former Barbara Svob went on. "The idea was to wait until some girl reported a theft—and then the chief'd lower the boom."

The boom was lowered almost at once. It surprised no one that the stakeout was short-lived. The frequency with which the thefts were being committed in the two buildings precluded any likelihood that the wait would be anything but a short one.

Let's hear of the way "Lady Five Fingers" (as Kitty was later dubbed by the victims of her forays) fared when she took the litmus test Paxton had prepared to trap the campus culprit.

"Just as soon as one of the girls reported jewelry taken from her room, a call went out to all sorority sisters to assemble in the main hall . . ."

Speaking here is the former Sue Nelson, now Mrs. Sue Jean of Tucson, who was in Kitty Kelley's 1959 Gamma Delta pledge class.

"The campus police took the girls, one by one, into a room and sat them at a table," Mrs. Jean explained. "They were asked to place their hands on a desk, under an ultra-violet-ray lamp. Then the room's fluorescent lights were dimmed. Anyone whose hands had come into contact with any article dusted with powder would glow in the dark under the lamp." It would be like a magic show . . .

The parade of coeds began uneventfully. The young women quietly passed through the "glow little glow-worm" room one by one. Then along came Kitty Kelley. Kitty broke the darkness of the room with a telltale luminescence that tattooed her forever in the eyes of her 1963 graduating class, who after that referred to her as "The Golden Fleecer."

*Immediately, Kitty Kelley was placed under house arrest.

*As her sorority sisters lustily booed and cat-called, she was escorted by the campus police in disgrace to her Yuma Hall dormitory room.

*With Chief Paxton and his campus cops scrutinizing her, Kitty emptied her bureau drawers, one by one, then her closet. All the articles went on the bed.

*Then the victims—said to have been twenty-eight co-eds in all who'd been stiffed by "Lady Five Fingers"—were brought to her room and asked to look over the pile of articles on the bed—and could anyone identify anything that belonged to her?

They could. And they did.

"It was like Christmas at Easter," said Barbara Sherman, the former Barbara Svob, Kitty's Pledge Mother. "I was one of the first to shout, 'Hey, that's my book!' "

Sure enough, *The Complete Works of Shakespeare* reposed on Kitty's bed. Also on the coverlet were wristwatches, rings, pendants, broaches, bracelets, and other "hardgoods" snitched from her sorority sisters. Not to overlook "softwear" like monogrammed panties, slips, knit hosiery, bras, skirts, and blouses. Kelley had all the loot stashed in her room.

No one knows what happened to the stuff authorities believe she palmed in her freshman year of 1959-60 and sophomore year of 1960-61. To assume Kitty Kelley's slate was clean during her first two years in school would be like presuming Kitty's early years on campus were likewise virginal. Perhaps they were, but listen to the heavy odds against that possibility:

"Kitty liked parties. She liked the guys. And the guys all liked her—mainly because of that big chest . . ."

This report comes from Kelley's fellow Delta Gamma pledge Sue Jean, nee Nelson, of Tucson.

"They loved to take her to parties and get her three sheets to the wind. And when she was inebriated, oh boy, did they have their fun with her."

I asked Sue whether the pounds Kitty had put on during her junior semester, the year that came to a scandal-stained standstill in the spring of '62 for Kelley, could have, by some remote chance, been attributed to a pregnancy.

"I'm not the one to ask," Sue Jean giggled. "Why don't you ask Kitty—or the politicians she slept with in Washington?"

"Who told you she slept with politicians?" I asked, not in surprise but out of curiosity. That she had sex with politicians was no secret to me. I had proof-positive that she had. Nor was I unaware that she had affairs with journalists, lawyers, businessmen, and doctors, among other professionals. The only males I wasn't able to establish had made it to Kitty's bed were butchers, bakers, and candlestick makers.

In fact, I have it first hand from London's *News Of The World*, a Sunday tabloid with the world's largest newspaper circulation of 6 million, that Kitty Kelley was having it on in London with "two very unctuous twerps" when she toured the United Kingdom to promote her Frank Sinatra book.

"Two of my reporters made that discovery while she was holed up in a house in London," I was told by editor Paul Conyers. "She struck my men as a pretty mangy bimbo. I really have no idea why they got that impression, but perhaps this bit of intelligence will help you in your pursuit of the hidden side of Kitty Kelley."

Conyers then asked, "George, have you found any skeletons in her closet so far?"

"More than are buried in all the cemeteries in America," I replied.

****

Sue Jean told me she had heard about Kitty's mattress romps with politicians "from Barb."

She was referring to Barbara Askins. But Mrs. Askins wasn't about to tell.

"I know a lot of things about Kitty Kelley . . . but I'm protecting my sources," Barbara protested.

Before we report the outcome of Kitty's house arrest as a campus crook extraordinaire, let's hear some last words on other aspects of Kelley thievery—of the off-campus variety.

"One Christmas, one of her sorority sisters took Kitty home with her to California," recalled Barbara Askins. "When they returned to the university, the girl—she was from a very wealthy family—received a call from her parents. They told her items of great value were missing from the house. Suspicion pointed to Kitty but nothing could be proved.

I also spoke with Carol West of Spokane, another Delta Gamma who was at Arizona with Kitty. Carol, who today is married to Patrick West, a stockbroker, was registered at the university by her maiden name, Carol McCrary.

The Wests lost a son to cancer some years ago and joined the pioneering movement that led to establishment of the Ronald McDonald House, the outreach program which provides care and comfort for children afflicted with the disease.

"I am in a position that compels me not to comment," Mrs. West told me, after a long hesitation, when I reached her at home by phone.

"Are you afraid of Kitty Kelley?" I asked Mrs. West.

"I'm not afraid of her at all," the answer came quietly. "But living in the town where she's from makes me not want to comment . . ."

****

After she'd been caught red-handed as a campus crook, Chief Paxton and the University of Arizona regents wasted no time laying the groundwork to boot her out of the school.

She was told she would be turned over to the Tucson Police Department, arrested, fingerprinted, mugged, and booked on charges of theft. She then would be incarcerated in the city lockup until her appearance for arraignment in the Pima County Superior Court, where a judge would impose bail for her release and turn the case over to the District Attorney. The DA would seek a grand jury indictment on fifty or more counts of theft and possession of stolen goods (one count for each piece of loot recovered in her dormitory room). Then she'd go to trial.

Kitty was also told that, having been caught red-handed with the booty, it went almost without saying that she'd be convicted—even if her father were to retain one of the country's top criminal lawyers, such as an F. Lee Bailey or a Melvin Belli, to defend her.

She was, they told her in unequivocal terms, "dead meat."

A terrified Kitty Kelley, "shaking and sobbing hysterically, pleading to be forgiven, crying repeatedly that she was sorry, promising never to steal again, and begging for just one more chance," was offered only one option to escape the ignominy that faced her. She was told that if she left the campus right then and there and promised never to return, charges would not be lodged against her. If she refused, she'd face due process—and in the end, be confronted with the prospect of a prison sentence as well as outright expulsion from the university.

She departed.

****

One mystery remains: how did the ex-University of Arizona junior spend the next eight months before arriving at the University of Washington to finish her senior year as an English major, with journalism as a minor?

Back at Arizona, she majored only in English. Her records, I was finally able to learn from official sources at the university who did not want to be identified, fail to show a minor, in journalism or in any other course.

Disgraced by the scandal, Kitty's parents apparently refused to let her return home. They sent her off to live with her maternal grandparents, the Martins, in Seattle. There she suffered a breakdown and was confined to a wheelchair for part of the time. There is still no way of finding out whether she gave birth to a baby or whether the weight she shed between her departure from the University of Arizona and arrival at the University of Washington was the result of a dieting regimen.

Only one last word remains to be spoken before we close out this chapter of Kitty Kelley's life that catapulted *Glow Little Glow-Worm* into one of the most popular songs on the University of Arizona campus and, at the same time, introduced into usage the sobriquets "The Golden Fleecer" and "Lady Five Fingers."

That final word is left with us by Barbara Svob Sherman whose voice over the AT&T longlines came loud and clear from Los Altos to Long Island:

"I don't even have any idea of why Kitty Kelley wanted my *Complete Works of Shakespeare*. She never struck me as the type of person who read Shakespeare . . ."

Acknowledgements

No book is ever written without lots of help from others. This one was a particularly tough project because the subject of this biography refused to meet with me or answer any questions, although I wrote to her and to her agents and to her attorneys.

This made my task more formidable.

I began by reading everything that had ever been written about Kitty Kelley. The *Star* magazine's Washington Bureau Chief Norma Langley was marvelous in obtaining this material.

My own research took me to the libraries of the *New York Post* and the New York *Daily News*. At the former I was aided by head librarian Merill Sherr and his associates, Jack Begg, Bea Greene, David Hacker, Mary McGeary and Jay Rodriguez. At the *News* I owe particular thanks to Fagie Rosenthal.

Marvelous research material was provided me by Library Coordinator Susan W. Mulvihill at the *Spokesman-Review*, the newspaper published in Kitty Kelley's hometown of Spokane.

On New York's Long Island, Chief Research Librarian Erna Newman and Assistant Research Librarian Thomas Barnes at the Half Hollow Hills Library in Dix Hills conducted extensive searches of reference books and periodicals, and also provided me with microfilms of newspapers and magazines that were beneficial in gaining a better understanding and developing a clearer portrait of the many persons involved in the four unauthorized biographies Miss Kelley has written.

I was assisted greatly in my research and fact-finding missions by publishers, editors, writers, and reporters from many areas of the United States. Those to whom I am most indebted for their advice, guidance, and help—given directly or through mediaries or assistants, or, as in some instances, through their own published works that provided the author with indispensible information that he could not otherwise have obtained: Cindy Adams, syndicated columnist and feature writer of the *New York Post*; syndicated Washington columnist Jack Anderson and associates; Stuart Applebaum, vice president of Bantam Books; Larry Ashmead, executive editor of HarperCollins (formerly Harper & Row); James Bacon, columnist for the *Los Angeles Herald-Examiner*; Smith Bagley, former publisher of *Today is Sunday* magazine; Dick Belsky, news editor of *Star* magazine; Bruce Bennett, of the *Minneapolis Star-Tribune*; Ross Benson, columnist of the *London Express*; English journalist Malcolm Boyes; American feature writer-author Dennis Brian; Philip Bunton, editorial director of *Globe Communications*; Jerry Capeci, organized crime expert and columnist for the *New York Daily News*; Ken Chandler, editor of the *Boston Herald*; Garry Clifford, Washington bureau chief of *People* magazine; Patricia L. Coates, of the University of Arizona Library's Special Collection Section; Richard Cohen, of the *Washington Post*; Editor Paul Conyers of London's *News of the World*; Elaine Crispin, secretary to former First Lady Nancy Reagan; author and official Kennedy family historian John Davis; Paul Dinas, senior editor of Zebra Books; Jeanne Dixon, astrologer of *Star* magazine; Paul Donnelley, features editor of *Penthouse* magazine in the United Kingdom; Steve Dunleavy, of Fox Television's *A Current Affair*; Betty Liu Ebron, editor of the *New York Daily News* "Apple Sauce" page; Henry Eckert, formerly with the library of the *New York Times*; author and screen writer Nora Ephron; Joanna Patyna Elm, features editor of *TV Guide*; Steve Emerine, Associate Director of Public Information, University of Arizona; actress Mia Farrow; Peter Fear-

on, editor of CBS-TV's *Inside Edition*; syndicated gossip columnist Karen Feld; Mary Fiore, editor of *Good Housekeeping*
magazine; Don Flynn, of the *New York Daily News*; Betty
Burke Galella, former editor of *This Is Sunday* magazine; Barry
Golson, editor of *Playboy* magazine; reporter-writer Earl Golz,
of the *Star* magazine; Shirley Grubb, executive assistant to the
publisher of *Today Is Sunday* magazine; syndicated columnist
and author Pete Hamill; Joan Hanauer, show business writer for
United Press International; Phil Geyelin, former editorial page
editor of the *Washington Post*; author, feature writer and book
critic Barbara Grizutti Harrison; *Washington Times* "Charlotte's
Web" columnist Charlotte Hays; Murray Hedgecock, London
Bureau Chief of *News Limited of Australia*; author C. David
Heymann; Gerri Hirshey, free-lance writer and former reporter
for the *Washington Post*; James Hoge, editor of the *New York
Daily News*; Warren Hoge, assistant managing editor of the *New
York Times*; Barbara Howar; Juliette Hurd, London correspondent of *News Limited of Australia*; Marc A. Jaffe, imprint editor,
Houghton Mifflin Co.; Janice Johnson, Knight-Ridder News-
papers "Washington Peopletalk" columnist; Richard Johnson,
columnist for the *New York Daily News*; Richard Kaplan, editor
of *Star* magazine; New York political reporter Mimi Kazon;
Pamela Keough, feature writer for *Dossier* magazine; CNN-TV
and Mutual Network talk show host Larry King; Michael Korda,
editor-in-chief of Simon & Schuster; Lor-Ann Land, motion
pictures secretary; Richard Lay, U.S. Correspondent for United
Kingdom newspapers; author-playwright Lawrence (Larry)
Leamer; Stephen LeGrice, managing editor of *Star* magazine;
author Frances Spatz Leighton; syndicated columnist Max
Lerner; John A. Limpert, editor of *Washingtonian* magazine;
Kelvin MacKenzie, editor of the *London Sun*; *Washington Post*
executive Donna Crouch Mackie; author Norman Mailer; Scott
Malone, author and Public Broadcast Service producer; Step-
hanie Mansfield, feature writer of the *Washington Post*; Holly-
wood free-lance writer Jack Martin; Sam Marx, former Metro-
Goldwyn-Mayer executive; *Washingtonian* magazine columnist
Rudy Maxa; Stan Mays, syndication manager and New York

bureau chief of the *London Express Newspapers*; Peter McKay, Washington correspondent of the *London Daily Mail*; *Washingtonian* magazine columnist Diana McLellan; Marianne Means, White House correspondent for the Hearst Newspapers; Judy Michaelson, feature writer of the *Los Angeles Times*; Pat Miller, editor-in-chief of *New Woman* magazine; feature writer-author Dan Moldea; Owen Moritz, of the *New York Daily News* "Apple Sauce" page; Jerry Nachman, editor of the *New York Post*; Chris Oliver, reporter-writer of the *New York Post*; Dick Oliver, of Fox's WNYW-TV's *Good Day New York* show; the late John Pascal, columnist of *Newsday* (on Long Island) and Broadway playwright; Eugene Patterson, former managing editor of the *Washington Post*; reporter Mike Pearl, of the *New York Post*; Nicholas Pileggi, author of *Wise Guy* and other books; Tom Poster, editor of the *New York Daily News* "People" page; English writer and American-based magazine correspondent Dermot Purgavie; Dorothy Rabinowitz, Op Ed Page columnist of the *New York Post*; Ian Rae, station director of Fox TV's WNYW in New York; the late Thomas A. Renner, organized crime expert-writer for *Newsday* on Long Island; Phil Roura, editor of the *New York Daily News* "People" page; *Newsday* syndicated gossip columnist Liz Smith and her assistants St. Clair Pugh and Dennis Ferrara; author-writer Barbara Raskin; Bill Ridley, executive editor of *Star* magazine; Joe Robinowitz, editor-in-chief of *TV Guide*; John Scow, book critic of the *New York Times*; James Seymore, managing editor of *People* magazine; Vernon Scott, Hollywood columnist of *United Press International*; Nancy Siracusa, of New Jersey's *Hudson Dispatch*; reporter Marvin Smilon, of the *New York Post*; author-book critic Robert Slatzer; *Baltimore Sun* feature writer Alice Steinback; Fred Stolz, editor of Washington's *Dossier* magazine; Carole Stuart, associate publisher of the Carol Publishing Group; *Denver Post* feature writer Allison Teal; English author and feature writer Michael Thornton; "Bud" Tobay, former president of Delacorte Press; Teddy Vaughn, gossip columnist for *Today Is Sunday* magazine; Barbara Walters, of ABC-TV; Mike Wallace, of CBS-TV's *60-Minutes*; Paul Wieck, Washington correspondent for New Mexico newspapers; Jeannie Williams, gossip columnist of *USA Today*; George C. Wilson, Pentagon correspondent for the *Washington Post*; Peter Winterble, former reporter for the *Philadelphia Inquirer*; Roger Wood, publication director of *Star* magazine; Jonathan Yardley, book critic of the *Washington Post*; Walter Zacharias, publisher of Zebra Books; and the late Maurice Zolotow.

****

I also want to thank and express wholehearted appreciation to my sources who contributed information that has made it possible to complete *Poison Pen* without the cooperation of the subject. I interviewed most of my sources either in person or on the telephone; my researchers also spoke with the sources listed here when I was unable to conduct the interviews or investigations myself.

My thanks to: Barbara Askins, Kitty Kelley's Delta Gamma sorority sister at the University of Arizona; Jamie Auchincloss, Jacqueline Kennedy Onassis's half-brother; Janet Auchincloss, Jamie and Jackie's mother; Robert G. (Bobby) Baker, former Secretary to the U.S. Senate Democratic Majority; William Baucon, ambulance driver who took First Lady Jacqueline Kennedy to give birth to her son John F. Kennedy Jr.; Ed Becker, chairman and CEO of the security firm Ed Becker & Associates; U.S. Senator Joe Biden (D.-Del.); process server Irving Botwinick, president of New York-based Serving By Irving; Dana A. Brown, Privacy Acts Officer in the Freedom of Information Department of the U.S. Secret Service; Diane Brown, of the Metro-Goldwyn-Mayer legal department; Madelein Brown, former aide in President Lyndon B. Johnson's Administration; Gary Clifford, Washington Bureau Chief and national correspondent for *People* magazine; literary-theatrical agent Sam Cohen, of International Creative Management; Suzanne Elizabeth Martin Cooke, ex-wife of Washington Redskins owner John Kent Cooke; Charlie Conner, assistant to President Lyndon B. Johnson; Dr. David A. Crown, former CIA forensic expert of questioned documents; Arnaud deBorchgrave, editor-in-chief of

347

the *Washington Times*; Anthony DeStefano, art director of Manor Books Inc.; actor Brad Dexter, and his agency Dan Fana Productions; show business attorney John Diamond; staff members of U.S. Representative Norman D. (Dizzy) Dicks (D.-Wash.); Janet Donovan, Washington, D.C. publicist-party planner and Kitty Kelley's former best friend; Kitty Kelley's former husband Michael Edgley; Joni Evans, of Turtle Bay Books; Judy Imoor Campbell Exner; Dr. John Wesley Field, of Lake Tahoe, California; singer Eddie Fisher; literary agents Joan and Joe Foley; Speaker of the House Thomas A. Foley and his wife Heather; John Forbess, attorney with Forbess & Roth in Century City, California; U.S. Representative Barney Frank (D.-Mass.); staff in the Freedom of Information Office at the Federal Bureau of Investigation in Washington, D.C.; Ron Galella, celebrated paparazzi photographer; Marcia Gallucci, Miss Kelley's one-time best friend in Spokane; retired New York Police Department Detective Jack Gannon; actress Ava Gardner; literary agent Lucianne Goldberg; Mark Goodin, communications director of the Republican National Committee; feature writer Josh Getlin, of the *Los Angeles Times*; Charles Gray, Miss Gardner's friend and neighbor in London; Donald D. Green, a stockbroker and former campaign official in the 1968 Democratic Presidential Primary campaign of Senator Eugene McCarthy; Judge Oliver Gresch, of the U.S. District Court in Washington, D.C.; the office and hotel staff of New York City's Hampshire House; Theodore Hausman, a friend of Miss Kelley; Morgan Hudgins, of the Jeff Morgan Company; sources close to George Jacobs, Frank Sinatra's former valet; Sue Nelson Jean, Kitty Kelley's Delta Gamma sorority sister at the University of Arizona; Beth Johnson, private secretary to President Reagan's White House aide Lynn Nofziger; Wesley Joyce and his wife Judy, the owners of the Lion's Head Pub in New York's Greenwich Village; literary agent Morton Janklow; Kitty Kelley (for information she supplied before she stopped talking to me in 1986); attorney William V. Kelley, Miss Kelley's father and partner in the law firm of Witherspoon, Kelley, Davenport & Toole in Spokane, Washington; Richard Krinsley, executive vice

president and publisher, Scholastic, Inc.; Detective Thomas
Kubic of the Nassau County Police Department Scientific Investigation Unit; Patricia Seaton Lawford, widow of actor Peter
Lawford; literary agent Irving (Swifty) Lazar; attorney Christina
Lenz, of Bonne, Jones, Bridges, Mueller, O'Keefe & Hunt;
Peter Malatesta, former Vice President Spiro Agnew's friend
and charter member of Frank Sinatra's Rat Pack; Dr. Douglas
Marcus, of South Oaks Psychiatric Hospital on Long Island;
actress Kelley Martin, Miss Kelley's sister; Mary . . . and Penny
. . . who don't want their real names revealed; Roger Mayer,
president of Ted Turner Communications Corporation; sources
who requested anonymity in former U.S. Senator Eugene J.
McCarthy's law offices; Henry McQueeney, president and publisher of Manor Books Inc.; Laura Morales, former aide to
retired U.S. Senator William Proxmire; literary agent Lynn
Nesbit, of International Creative Management (now a partner
with Morton Janklow); associates of the Nevada Gaming Control
Board; Richard Newcomb, president of Creators Syndicate;
attorney Herbert Nusbaum, Metro-Goldwyn-Mayer/United Ar-
tists legal counsel; literary agent David Obst; Sister Paulus, of
the Roman Catholic Sisters of St. Colette in Jefferson City,
Wisconsin; former U.S. Senator Charles Percy (D.-Ill.); columnist Donnie Radcliff, of the *Washington Post*; Barbara Reynolds,
appointments secretary to U.S. Representative Carlos Moor-
head (R.-Calif.); actress Debbie Reynolds; Frank Sinatra's publicist Susan Reynolds, vice president of Burson-Marsteller; bartender Mike Reardon at the Lion's Head; Pete Rozelle, former
commissioner of the National Football League; attorney Milton
A. (Mickey) Rudin, of the law firm of Rudin, Richman and
Appel in Los Angeles; retired Lieutenant Frank Salerno, of the
New York City Police Department's Criminal Investigation Bureau; actress Elizabeth Taylor's publicist Chen Sam; Ted Schwartz, who attended the University of Arizona with Miss Kelley;
Barbara Svob Sherman, Kitty Kelley's Delta Gamma sorority
pledge mother at the University of Arizona; Joseph W. Shimon,
retired Inspector of the Washington, D.C. Police Department;
literary agent Don Short, of London's Solo Agency; Frank Sin-

atra Jr., Ol' Blue Eyes' son; Nancy Sinatra, Frank's first wife; Nancy Sinatra Jr., his daughter; Richard C. Snyder, chairman and CEO of Simon & Schuster; Joseph Swaney, of the Metro-Goldwyn-Mayer publicity department; former U.S. Senator George Smathers, best friend of President John F. Kennedy; Fred Tamburo, former member of *The Hoboken Four* singing group; Elizabeth Taylor; Judge Harriet R. Taylor, of the Superior Court in the District of Columbia; Jean Toomey, former speechwriter for Senator McCarthy; Murray Traub, chairman of the board of Manor Books Inc.; members and staff of the Tucson (Ariz.) Police Department and the Superior Court Record Office; actress Lana Turner; Pamela Turnure, former press secretary of First Lady Jacqueline Kennedy; Don Uffinger, Virginia police officer and now head of Uffinger & Associates private investigators; attorneys Robert C. Vanderer and William W. Vaughn, of O'Melveny & Meyers in Los Angeles; Dr. John A. Walsh, the obstetrician who delivered JFK Jr.; U.S. Senator John Warner, ex-husband of Elizabeth Taylor; attorney David N. Webster, of Washington, D.C.; Carol McCrary West, Kitty Kelley's Delta Gamma sorority sister at the University of Arizona; writer Michael Whelan, president of the Washington (D.C.) Independent Writers; London literary agent Dina Wiener; former Speaker of the House Jim Wright of Texas; and attorney Benjamin L. Zelenko, of Landis, Cullen, Rauh & Zelenko in Washington, D.C.

Thanks too to Walter Baran, Janel Bladow, Leon Freilich, Emil Halupka, Brian Haugh, Rita Ross, Bob Smith, Jock Veitch, and Phil Wilkinson.

I owe special thanks to Reed Sparling, who read every word of this manuscript. From the beginning he helped sculpt this book by editing, imposing grammar, punctuation, and correct spelling. In the three years the book was in production, Reed kept me honest.

Nor can I forget Christopher Bowen, the chief librarian at *Star* who was also my colleague for many years before at the *New York Post*. Chris dug deeply to come up with any and all fragments of information about Kitty Kelley and the scores of

characters populating her world. Without his great good services this book would not have been possible.

The marvelous people at Barricade Books were immensely
helpful. First there are Arnold Bruce Levy and Dan Simon who
helped make some of what I wrote more readable. Add to these
Larry Alson and Jon Gilbert. I must also take my hat off to Allen
G. Schwartz, one of America's top litigators, for his careful
reading of this text. And finally, to Lyle Stuart who encouraged
me to be as thorough and accurate as possible and whose
courage enabled publication of this book where other publishing
houses chickened out!

Appendix:

QUESTIONS FOR KITTY KELLEY

During my three-year investigation into the life of Kitty Kelley, I drew up questions I would have asked her if a face-to-face interview had been granted. On December 7, 1988 I sent these by Certified Mail to her Georgetown home at 3037 Dumbarton Avenue. The envelope was returned by the U.S. Postal Service with the notation that the addressee refused to accept delivery.

Copies of the questions were then sent to Miss Kelley's then-agent Lynn Nesbit, as well as to her lawyers in Washington, D.C., and in Los Angeles with a request to forward the sixteen pages of queries to their client. I have been told by reliable sources that Miss Kelley received all three of those mailings. She has yet to respond. These are the questions I posed:

1. Why didn't you complete your undergraduate studies at the University of Arizona? I have yearbooks for 1961 and 1962 with your picture as a member of Delta Gamma Sorority. I have gotten in touch with your sorority sisters to see what information they could provide on the curious eight-month gap in your life in 1962. I urge you to tell me your side of the story because I want this biography to be eminently fair. In your response to

this question, could you also tell me whether or not you boarded for any part of those eight months in a home for unwed mothers?

2. Does the saying in Spanish at the beginning of "Elizabeth Taylor: The Last Star" (A Nino de su osita rubia sempre) [translated to "A child from his little female bear blonde and fair—ever at all times"]

3. Did you actually burst into tears when your then-agent Lucianne Goldberg, asked you what those words meant?

4. Was William Kelley's and Adele Martin's engagement and rapid marriage such a surprise to the folks in the community as the *Spokane Chronicle* said it was—and why a rush-rush wedding?

5. Many Spokanites I've spoken with report that your mother was an alcoholic. Can you tell me, if you know, why she drank?

6. As the oldest child you cared for your five sisters and brother. I would like some details about how you looked after them—and was that because your mother was always spaced out?

7. You said in an interview that as a small girl you slipped into your mother's high heels and traipsed out to the street in your diapers. Is this true? If so, can you tell me why you did that?

8. Can you also explain why, at age nine, you again took your mother's high heels, put on a dainty dress, and went as a welcoming committee of one to make Virginia Hall—slain mobster Bugsy Siegel's "Mafia Rose"—feel at home in your neighborhood after she moved in with her husband?

9. I've gathered a great deal of information about your days at Holy Names School, about your cheerleading for Gonzaga High, your selection as the Lilac Princess, and that Tom Shine was your boyfriend. I'd like to speak with you about all this so I can report that early period in your life with total accuracy, as well as with all the "color" that only the person who lived those experiences can provide.

10. I interviewed your classmates at the University of Washington to learn about your undergraduate days there. How would you characterize that period of your life?

11. Please tell about the period in Spokane when you were a

teacher. I'd like to know the name of the school where you taught and something about your experience in the classroom. And did you say this: "That didn't last long because I was teaching in what they call a culturally deprived area, a ghetto. I decided I wasn't ready for that yet?"

12. Following your trail from Spokane, I pick up on you at the 1964-65 New York World's Fair. There are some interesting anecdotes in the *Chronicle* about your experience as a hostess at the General Electric Progressland exposition. Can you tell me a bit about your encounters with Julie Andrews, Margaret Truman, and Jacqueline Kennedy?

13. Can you tell me whether it was there at the World's Fair that you met Mike Edgley? If so, please explain what he was doing there and circumstances under which you met.

14. I have been told that Mike was a bartender at the Lion's Head tavern in Manhattan. Is that a fact? I was also informed that he was a heavy drinker—one source described him as "an alcoholic bartender" and purports that you "straightened him out" by steering him into Alcoholics Anonymous. And that after he "dried out", he went on the circuit lecturing for AA. Is any of this true? In either case, I just want the facts, ma'am, so I can tell it just like it was.

15. While you were at the World's Fair, did you encounter a young scrivener named Liz Smith, newly arrived from Texas? At the time, Liz was gathering society gossip anonymously for Igor Cassini, who ghosted the "Cholly Knickerbocker" column for Hearst's *New York Journal-American*. Some of the old-timers on the J-A tell me they believe you fed Liz tidbits about the rich and famous whom you escorted through the GE exhibit. True or false?

16. Before you wrote *Jackie Oh!* you did a paperback for Pocket Books called *The Glamour Spas*. In an interview you gave OJ Parsons in the *Chronicle*, you say that you received a $10,000 advance to do that book. Yet I have information from several sources that the advance was $1500. Which amount is correct?

17. Several of the spas that you visited are still disturbed by

what you wrote about them. I'm told they extended you every courtesy—all on the cuff. And then you went out and "shafted" them. Is this part of your nature—to bite the hand that feeds you?

18. Is there any truth to the report that you sold the idea to write *The Glamour Spas* for Pocket Books as a way to shed your own accumulation of flab?

19. There are reports bearing on your honesty. For example the Howar Papers Affair. My information is that Barbara Howar was having a "garage sale" and the manuscript of her soon-to-be-published memoir, *Laughing All The Way*, was in Barbara Howar's third-floor study. The facts show that although you were not permitted access to the third floor during the garage sale, you got your hands on the manuscript somehow, then sold it to the *Washingtonian* magazine. After Miss Howar protested and threatened legal action, the magazine didn't print the story. What I would like to know is whether you did indeed pilfer the manuscript? If not, how *did* you get it and why did you peddle it to the magazine for a price? You've been quoted since the incident as saying that you bought the manuscript from an elderly woman at the garage sale for two dollars. Do you swear that's the way it happened?

20. Another question of pilferage arises—bearing on the whereabouts of valuable wine labels that were being pressed between the pages of books in the Beverly Hills home of our mutual friend, journalist Jack Martin. You and Stanley Tretick, it is my understanding, rented the house for a four-month period in 1985 while you were doing research in California for your Frank Sinatra book. Jack tells me that you left the house in better shape that what it was when he turned it over to you. But he's deeply disturbed about this disappearance of his valuable wine labels. He says that you are the last person in the world he would suspect of taking them—yet he doesn't know what to make of it. Can you shed any light on this mystery? Also, do you have any idea what might have happened to a set of Tiffany cufflinks that Jack says was in the house when he left it and was not around any longer after he returned?

21. When you submitted your biographical data to Lyle Stuart for the jacket cover on the *Jackie Oh!* book, you listed among your credentials that you had been an editorial writer for the *Washington Post*. According to the *Post*, you had been employed as an editorial researcher and secretary. Can you explain why you described yourself as an editorial writer when, in fact, you were not?

22. Lyle Stuart says he had to go to considerable expense to reprint the book jackets for *Jackie Oh!* not alone for the correction he had to make about your true status with the *Post*, but also because you had listed yourself as "Press Secretary" for Senator Eugene McCarthy during his unsuccessful campaign for the 1968 Democratic Presidential nomination. Stuart learned from the Senator that you were not his Press Secretary but "a letter-stuffer of sorts . . ." How do you respond to this allegation?

23. I must also ask you about the profile of yourself that you gave to Washington businessman Smith Bagley who claims that you falsified your resume. Is that true?

24. Bagley also says that you rifled through his wastepaper baskets and obtained personal items about him that you supplied to the *Washington Star*—and that he laid a trap and caught you. Can you respond to this charge?

25. Is the story true that while you were doing research for your Elizabeth Taylor biography, you sent your husband Mike Edgley to sift through garbage from the house in Virginia that Miss Taylor shared with her then-husband Senator John Warner?

26. In your book about Frank Sinatra, you say in your "Author's Chapter Notes" that you interviewed Peter Lawford on November 5 and 6, 1984, and January 5, 1985. Did you know that on the November dates Peter Lawford lay on his deathbed after a portion of his stomach was removed in surgery? Or that Peter Lawford died on Christmas Eve 1984—and was no longer available for interviews on the January date you cite?

27. Pending in the Superior Court of California for the County of Los Angeles is a suit for damages claiming libel filed by

Frank Sinatra's former valet, George Jacobs, who says the nearly two-thousand words in the book that you attribute to him in
interviews you claim he gave you, are not his words—that he
never spoke to you. Can you give me your side of this story?

28. Steve Dunleavy and Malcolm Boyes interviewed Peter
Lawford intensively and extensively over a period of years from
1976 through 1982. Both writers tell me they were astounded to
find in *His Way* profanity attributed to him. Both Dunleavy and
Boyes insist Lawford would not mouth such phrases as : ". . .
he's pissed. Really pissed off" or "Do you want your legs broken,
you fucking asshole?" Boyes, for example, told me Lawford was
"too refined and too well-bred to utter such words in a conversation with a woman—even if she was Kitty Kelley." Speaking
from long years of experience as writers and experts on
Lawford's life and times, Dunleavy and Boyes suggest that you
simply put those words in Peter's mouth because you knew he
couldn't protest from the urn in which his ashes reposed. How
shall I handle this chapter in my book on you?

29. Can you tell me who actually wrote the novel *Reunion*
which your then-publisher rejected as unpublishable? Is it true
that it was written by your husband—and you used it as an
"option buster"?

30. In your book on Elizabeth Taylor, you quote Roddy
McDowell at great length, leaving the unmistakable impression
that you interviewed him. But then you were zapped by his
lawyer, Howard Lowe, and were compelled to delete material
his client strongly disputed and to make substantial changes in
the text when the book was published in softcover. You've done
this with scores of other people whom you never interviewed
but give the impression that you did. What compulsion drives
you to put words in people's mouths that they didn't say?

31. When you were at the *Washington Post* as researcher,
you were caught in a bind that led to your forced resignation
from the job. The scenario I have been given is that you took
extensive notes at meetings publisher Katherine Graham had
with her editorial people, that an editor discovered what you

were doing, asked you to submit to him the notebooks in which you recorded that dialogue, and you failed to do so—saying that you had destroyed them. Inasmuch as you've been quoted as saying that you have "enough" on Miss Graham to do a number on her, I don't think I have to ask why you took those copious notes at the meetings. But what I would like to know is—did you really destroy the notebooks or do you still have them?

32. When *Washington Post* reporter Gerri Hirshey was gathering background on you for her three-part series, "Kitty Oh!: The Unauthorized Biography of Kitty Kelley," you were phoned, sent certified mail, brought a hand-delivered letter, and your lawyer was approached with requests to interview you. Yet you steadfastly refused to talk with the reporter—except to say, "Tell your editor I'm not sanguine towards it." After uncovering the secrets of celebrities such as Onassis, Taylor and Sinatra, why wouldn't you talk when Miss Hirshey tried to ask questions about your life?

33. "I understand she [Nancy Reagan] has very stupidly written to a lot of people warning them not to talk to me. Why would she write all those letters saying, 'Don't talk'? What does that tell a biographer?" This was your complaint about the President's wife after you let it be known she was the subject of your next poison-pen biography. Is spreading that kind of rumor just a tool of your technique? Can you name just one person in the whole world who received such a note from the First Lady—and show us that message?

34. Do you have or did you ever have an "arthritic Underwood" typewriter that former CIA forensic expert Dr. David A. Crown identifies as the machine used for the profusion of correspondence that cascaded on Gerri Hirshey and which ultimately grew into such a pile that she labeled it "Kitty Litter"? Do you send those notes—or do you direct someone else to do so?

While I would like to tape my questions and your answers, I would happily settle for your responses to these questions in writing.

If I do not hear from you—or from your agent or lawyers, to whom I've sent copies of these questions—I shall nevertheless proceed to produce your biography.

Yours truly,

George Carpozi Jr.

INDEX

361

Poison Pen

367